CRISIS INTERVENTION

Theory and methodology

CRISIS INTERVENTION
Theory and methodology

DONNA C. AGUILERA, R.N., Ph.D., F.A.A.N.

Professor, Mental Health Nursing,
California State University at
Los Angeles

and

JANICE M. MESSICK, R.N., M.S., F.A.A.N.

Chief, Clinical Evaluation Section,
Program Evaluation Service,
Brentwood Veterans Administration Hospital,
Los Angeles

THIRD EDITION

The C. V. Mosby Company

Saint Louis   1978

THIRD EDITION

Copyright © 1978 by The C. V. Mosby Company

Previous editions copyrighted 1970, 1974

Printed in the United States of America

The C. V. Mosby Company
11830 Westline Industrial Drive, St. Louis, Missouri 63141

Library of Congress Cataloging in Publication Data

Aguilera, Donna C
 Crisis intervention.

 Includes bibliographies and index.
 1. Crisis intervention (Psychiatry).   I. Messick,
Janice M., joint author.   II. Title.
RC480.6.A38 1978   616.8′91   77-22527
ISBN 0-8016-0094-4

C/VH/VH 9 8 7 6 5 4 3 2

To

All from whom we have learned

and

all who will yet forever teach us

FOREWORD

It will soon be two decades since I wrote *Mental Health Manpower Trends* for the Joint Commission on Mental Illness and Health. It was a book that surveyed the nation's professional resources in the mental health field and found them sadly wanting. As part of the Commission I chaired the Task Force on Manpower. Since then I have come to reject the terms "mental illness" and "manpower" as being prejudicial and inappropriate. Terms such as mental disturbance, mental disorder, or emotional disturbance seem to me to be ideologically more neutral, less supportive of the illness model. *Human resources* certainly is to be preferred to the more sexist term *manpower*. And *intervention* is better than *treatment*.

Anyway, in that survey I concluded that our nation did not have, and for the foreseeable future would not have, enough professionals in the conventional mental health fields to reach all the people who want, or are judged to require, intervention. Experience since then bears out the accuracy of this prediction. For example, despite a fourfold increase in the total membership of the American Psychiatric Association during the past 25 years, fewer psychiatrists are available now than then to the poor in the tax-supported institutions.

The mental health professions largely have concentrated their attention on the delivery of individual psychotherapy to persons who are predominantly affluent, white, Protestant, and female. In William Ryan's dramatic survey of mental health service delivery in Boston *(Distress in the City)*, he found the typical psychiatric patient to be a white, middle-class, college-educated female between the ages of 30 and 40. Most of these "patients" were concentrated in a very small number of census tracts. Ryan found, too, that general practitioners, clergymen, and social agencies such as community centers were providing more intervention to the disturbed children and adults of Boston than were the traditional mental professions, despite the fact that Boston is Psychiatryland.

There are further problems with conventional mental health services. For one, many traditional clinics have a waiting list that delays the start of intervention for periods up to 6 months or a year. People in crisis situations want help now, not 6 months from now. This is particularly true of poor people with problems. They cannot send their kids to camp or take a trip to Europe while they wait for help.

Another sacred cow that needs to be hamburgerized is the belief of conventional agencies that meaningful intervention can be accomplished only by highly trained professional people possessing hard-to-get credentials that are based on extensive theoretical knowledge and often indoctrination into some particular school of therapy. Carl Rogers has recently blasted the whole credentials system for therapists. I agree with him and believe that the research evidence supports the fact that some persons with little formal training are often as effective, or even more effective, in human intervention with disturbed people than are the experts.

Crisis intervention by a variety of people makes so much sense in so many ways. It sweeps aside the artificially created psychiatric and related personnel shortages by providing good, meaningful, and time-limited training to persons outside the traditional mental health professions. It provides support and help to people when it is needed, not months later to those lucky enough to survive a waiting list. It provides prompt access to help and so eliminates the dropping out that occurs in conventional systems between the move to seek help and the time it is available.

The authors have shown great skill and sensitivity in the preparation of this volume. Their blend of theory, history, and practical methods of crisis resolution should make the volume useful in a variety of training programs. It will be useful to both professionals and nonprofessionals. Its message should be heard and understood by legislators as well.

George W. Albee, Ph.D.
University of Vermont

PREFACE

We developed this textbook because we recognized the need for a comprehensive overview as well as an introduction and guide to crisis intervention from its historical development to its present utilization. Although the techniques and skills of a therapist must be learned and practiced under professional supervision, we believe that an awareness of the basic theory and principles of crisis intervention will be of value to all who are involved in the helping professions. It should be of particular value as a guideline to those in the mental health field who are in constant proximity to persons in stressful situations who seek help because they are unable to cope with them alone.

Since it was not our intent in the prior editions of this textbook to imply that crisis intervention was limited only to one profession, we have revised and added selected sections in response to our readers' requests.

Chapter 1 deals with the historical development of crisis intervention methodology. Its intent is to create awareness of the broad base of knowledge incorporated into present practice, the fundamental procedures of brief psychotherapy, its implementation in community psychiatry, and an overview of the current trends in utilization of manpower resources in community mental health centers.

Chapter 2 explores the differences between the psychotherapeutic techniques of psychoanalysis and psychoanalytic psychotherapy and between brief psychotherapy and crisis intervention methodology in the major areas of their goals, foci, activities of the therapists, indications for treatment, and the average lengths of treatment.

Chapter 3 presents an overview of therapeutic groups and group therapy to show the bases from which crisis groups evolve. Two studies on crisis groups are presented to show their implementation, advantages, and disadvantages, and a case study is included to demonstrate the use of crisis intervention techniques in a group therapy session.

Chapter 4 presents some of the sociocultural factors that can act as barriers in the psychotherapeutic process. The purpose of this chapter is to discuss certain key areas that are usually considered to be problems and to make the reader aware of the nature of these difficulties.

Chapter 5 focuses on the problem-solving process and introduces the reader to basic terminology used in this method of treatment. We have devised a paradigm of intervention for the purpose of clarifying the sequential steps of crisis development and crisis resolution and have included a brief case study to illustrate its application as a guide to case studies in subsequent chapters.

Chapter 6 deals with stressful events that could precipitate a crisis in individuals regardless of socioeconomic or sociocultural status, such as prematurity, status and role change, rape, physical illness, divorce, suicide, and death and the grief process. Hypothetical case studies based on factual experience are presented to illustrate the techniques used by therapists in crisis resolution. Theoretical material preceding each case study is presented as an overview relevant to the crisis situation.

Chapter 7 is devoted to those changes that occur during concomitant biological and social role transitions, such as birth, puberty, young adulthood, marriage, illness or death of a family member, the climacteric, and old age. Maturational crises have been described as normal processes of growth and development and differ from situational crises in that they usually evolve over an extended period of time and frequently require more characterological changes of the individual. Case studies are included with appropriate theoretical material.

Chapter 8 is a new chapter that focuses on the chronic psychiatric patient in the community and how crisis intervention methodology and techniques can be utilized to maintain such an individual in his community. A case study is presented to illustrate its applicability.

We are indebted to many people who have been of direct and indirect assistance in writing this book. Specifically we wish to thank several persons for their roles in bringing the manuscript to fruition. We want to acknowledge our gratitude to Dr. G. F. Jacobson, Dr. W. E. Morley, and the Research Committee of the Los Angeles Psychiatric Service – Benjamin Rush Centers for their encouragement and advice. Our sincere thanks go to Dr. Evelyn Crumpton, Brentwood Veterans Administration Hospital, who served as our liaison with the Brentwood Research Committee, to Mrs. Betty Connolly, Medical Librarian, Sepulveda Veterans Administration Hospital, who assisted in our research of the literature, and to Steven Farrow for the cover idea. We are especially grateful to Mrs. Jean Hansen, without whose valuable and expert assistance the manuscript could not have been prepared in its final form. To our families, who were our kindest critics and strongest supporters, we owe a very special kind of debt.

D. C. A.

J. M. M.

CONTENTS

4   Sociocultural factors affecting therapeutic intervention, 46

5   Problem-solving approach to crisis intervention, 62

6   Situational crises, 73

7 Maturational crises, 132

8 Crisis intervention with the chronic psychiatric patient, 173

1 □ Historical development of crisis intervention methodology

The Chinese characters that represent the word "crisis" mean both danger and opportunity. Crisis is a *danger* because it threatens to overwhelm the individual or his family, and it may result in suicide or a psychotic break. It is also an *opportunity* because during times of crisis individuals are more receptive to therapeutic influence. Prompt and skillful intervention may not only prevent the development of a serious long-term disability but may also allow new coping patterns to emerge that can help the individual function at a higher level of equilibrium than before the crisis.

A person in crisis is at a turning point. He faces a problem that he cannot readily solve by using the coping mechanisms that have worked for him before. As a result, his tension and anxiety increase, and he becomes less able to find a solution. A person in this situation feels helpless — he is caught in a state of great emotional upset and feels unable to take action *on his own* to solve his problem.

Crisis intervention can offer the immediate help that a person in crisis needs in order to reestablish equilibrium. This is an inexpensive, short-term therapy that focuses on solving the immediate problem. Increasing awareness of sociocultural factors that could precipitate crisis situations has led to the rapid evolution of crisis intervention methodology. Therefore, these factors will be discussed first in order to understand their social and cultural implications better.

Everywhere today we hear talk of the changes in our lives that have been made by "urbanization" and "technology." A closer study of these changes will add to our understanding of what they have meant to families and to individuals.

Before the revolution in technology and industrialization, most people lived on farms or in small rural communities. They were chiefly self-employed, either on

1

their farms or in small, associated businesses. When sons and daughters married, they were likely to remain near their parents, working in the same occupations, and, in this way, trades and occupations were a link between generations. Families therefore tended to be large, and because family members lived and worked together and relied chiefly on each other for social interaction, they developed strong loyalties and a sense of responsibility for one another.

Contemporary urban life, however, does not encourage or allow this kind of sheltered, close-knit family relationship. People who live in cities are likely to be employed by a company and paid a wage. They work with business associates and live with neighbors rather than with their immediate family. Because of housing conditions and the necessity of living on a wage, families in cities usually consist of parents and unmarried children.

These differences between rural and urban life have important repercussions with regard to individual security and stability. The large, extended rural family offered a large and relatively constant group of associates. Family size and the varying strength of blood ties meant that there was always someone to talk to, even about a problem involving two family members. But urban life is highly mobile. There is often a rapid turnover in business associates and neighbors, and there is no certainty that these relative strangers will share the same values, beliefs, and interests. All these factors make it difficult for people to develop real trust and interdependence outside the small immediate family. In addition, urban life requires that people meet each other only superficially, in specific roles and in limited relationships rather than as total personalities.

All of these factors taken together mean that people in cities are more isolated than ever before from the emotional support provided by the family and close and familiar peers. As a result, there are no role models to follow—the demands of urban life are constantly changing, and coping behavior that was appropriate and successful several years before may be hopelessly ineffective today.

This creates a favorable environment for the development of crises. As defined by Caplan (1961:18), crisis may occur when the individual faces a problem that he cannot solve. There is a rise in inner tension and signs of anxiety and inability to function in extended periods of emotional upset.

HISTORICAL DEVELOPMENT

The crisis approach to therapeutic intervention has been developed only within the past few decades and is based on a broad range of theories of human behavior, including those of Freud, Hartmann, Rado, Erickson, Lindemann, and Caplan. Its current acceptance as a recognized form of treatment cannot be directly related to any single theory of behavior; all have contributed to some degree.

Our intent in presenting an overview of historical development is to create awareness of the broad base of knowledge incorporated into present practice.

Although not all theories of human behavior are necessarily dependent on Freudian concepts, and only a selected few are presented here, we chose to begin with the psychoanalytic theories of Freud because these are a major basis for further investigation of normal and abnormal human behavior. The fundamental procedures of brief psychotherapy are derived from hypotheses based on studies of the reasons for normal as well as abnormal human behavior.

Sigmund Freud was the first to demonstrate and apply the principle of causality as it relates to psychic determinism (Bellak and Small, 1965:6). Simply put, this principle states that every act of human behavior has its cause, or source, in the history and experience of the individual. It follows that causality is operative, whether or not the individual is aware of the reason for his behavior. Psychic determinism is the theoretical foundation of psychotherapy and psychoanalysis. The technique of free association, dream interpretation, and the assignment of meaning to symbols are all based on the assumption that causal connections operate unconsciously.

A particularly important outcome of Freud's deterministic position was his construction of a developmental or "genetic" psychology (Ford and Urban, 1963: 117). Present behavior is understandable in terms of the life history or experience of the individual, and the crucial foundations for all future behavior are laid down in infancy and early childhood. The most significant determinants of present behavior are the "residues" of past experiences (learned responses), particularly those developed during the earliest years to reduce biological tensions.

Freud assumed that a reservoir of energy that exists in the individual initiates all behavior. Events function as guiding influences, but they do not initiate behavior; they only serve to help mold it in certain directions.

Since the end of the nineteenth century, the concept of determinism, as well as the scientific bases from which Freud formulated his ideas, have undergone many changes.

Although the ego-analytic theorists have tended to subscribe to much in the Freudian position, there are several respects in which they differ. These seem to be extensions of Freudian theory rather than direct contradictions. As a group, they conclude that Freud has neglected the direct study of normal or healthy behavior.

Heinz Hartmann was an early ego analyst who was profoundly versed in Freud's theoretical contributions (Loewenstein, 1966:475). He postulated that the psychoanalytic theories of Freud could prove valid for normal as well as pathological behavior. Hartmann began with the study of ego functions and distinguished between two groups: those that develop from conflict, and the others, "conflict free," such as memory, thinking, and language, which he labeled "primary autonomous functions of the ego." He considered these important in the adaptation of the individual to his environment. Hartmann emphasized that man's adaptation in early childhood as well as his ability to maintain his adaptation to his environment in later life had to be considered. His conception of the ego as an organ of adaptation required further study of the concept of reality. He also described man searching for an environment as another form of adaptation—the fitting together of the individual and his society. He believed that although the behavior of the individual is strongly influenced by his culture, a part of the personality remains relatively free of this influence.

Sandor Rado developed the concept of adaptational psychodynamics, providing a new approach to the unconscious as well as new goals and techniques of therapy (Salzman, 1962:124-125). Rado saw human behavior as being based on the dynamic principle of motivation and adaptation. An organism achieves adaptation through interaction with its culture. Behavior is viewed in terms of its effect on the welfare of the individual, not just in terms of cause and effect. The organism's patterns of interaction improve through adaptation, with the goal being the increase of possibilities for survival. Freud's classical psychoanalytic technique emphasized the developmental past and the uncovering of unconscious memories, and little if any importance was attached to the reality of the present. Rado's adaptational psychotherapy, however, emphasizes the immediate present without neglecting the influence of the developmental past. Primary concern is with failures in adaptation "today," what caused them, and what the patient must do to learn to overcome them. Interpretations always begin and end with the present; preoccupation with the past is discouraged. As quickly as insight is achieved, it is used as a beginning to encourage the patient to enter into his present, real-life situation repeatedly. Through practice the patient automatizes new patterns of healthy behavior. According to Rado, it is this automatization factor that is ultimately the curative process, not insight. He does not believe that it takes place passively in the doctor's office but actively in the reality of daily living (Ovesy and Jameson, 1956:165-178).

Erik H. Erikson further developed the theories of ego psychology, which complement those of Freud, Hartmann, and Rado, by focusing on the epigenesis of the ego and on the theory of reality relationships (Rappaport, 1959:14). Epigenetic development is characterized by an orderly sequence of development at particular stages, each depending on the other for successful completion. Erikson perceived eight stages of psychosocial development, spanning the entire life cycle of man and involving specific developmental tasks that must be solved in each phase. The solution that is achieved in each previous phase is applied in subsequent phases. Erikson's theory is important in that it offers an explanation of the individual's social development as a result of his encounters with his social environment. Another significant feature is his elaboration on the normal rather than the pathological development of man's social interactions. He dealt in particular with the problems of adolescence and saw this period in life as a "normative crisis," that is, a normal maturational phase of increased conflicts, with apparent fluctuations in ego strength (Pumpian-Mindlin, 1966:475). Erikson integrated the biological, cultural, and self-deterministic points of view in his eight stages of man's development and broadened the scope of traditional psychotherapy with his theoretical formulations concerning identity and identity crises. His theories have provided a basis for the work of others who further developed the concept of maturational crises and began serious consideration of situational crises and man's adaptation to his current environmental dilemma.

Lindemann's (1956) initial concern was in developing approaches that might contribute to the maintenance of good mental health and the prevention of emotional disorganization on a community-wide level. He chose to study bereavement reactions in his search for social events or situations that predictably would be followed by emotional disturbances in a considerable portion of the population. In his study of bereavement reactions among the survivors of those killed in the Coconut Grove nightclub fire, he described both brief and abnormally prolonged reactions occurring in different individuals as a result of a loss of a significant person in their lives.

In his experiences in working with grief reactions, Lindemann concluded that it might be profitable for investigation and useful for the development of preventive efforts if a conceptual frame of reference were to be constructed around the concept of an emotional crisis, as exemplified by bereavement reactions. Certain inevitable events in the course of the life cycle of every individual can be described as hazardous situations, for example, bereavement, the birth of a child, and marriage. He postulated that in each of these situations emotional strain would be generated, stress would be experienced, and a series of adaptive mechanisms would occur that could lead either to mastery of the new situation or to failure with more or less lasting impairment to function. Although such situations create stress for all people who are exposed to them, they become crises for those individuals who by personality, previous experience, or other factors in the present situation are especially vulnerable to this stress and whose emotional resources are taxed beyond their usual adaptive resources.

Lindemann's theoretical frame of reference led to the development of crisis intervention techniques, and in 1946 he and Caplan established a community-wide program of mental health in the Harvard area, called the Wellesley Project.

According to Caplan (1961:34-37), the most important aspects of mental health are the state of the ego, the stage of its maturity, and the quality of its structure. Assessment of its state is based on three main areas: (1) the capacity of the person to withstand stress and anxiety and to maintain ego equilibrium, (2) the degree of reality recognized and faced in solving problems, and (3) the repertoire of effective coping mechanisms employable by the person in maintaining a balance in his biopsychosocial field.

Caplan believes that all the elements that compose the total emotional milieu of the person must be assessed in an approach to preventive mental health. The material, physical, and social demands of reality, as well as the needs, instincts, and impulses of the individual, must all be considered as important behavioral determinants.

As a result of his work in Israel (1948) and his later experiences in Massachusetts with Lindemann and with the Community Mental Health Program at Harvard University, he evolved the concept of the importance of *crisis* periods in individual and group development (Caplan, 1951).

Crisis is defined as occurring "when a person faces an obstacle to important life goals that is, for a time, insurmountable through the utilization of customary methods of problem solving. A period of disorganization ensues, a period of upset, during which many abortive attempts at solution are made" (Caplan, 1961:18).

In essence, the individual is viewed as living in a state of emotional equilibrium, with his goal always to return to or to maintain that state. When customary problem-solving techniques cannot be used to meet the daily problems of living, the balance or equilibrium is upset. The individual must either solve the problem or adapt to nonsolution. In either case a new state of equilibrium will develop, sometimes better and sometimes worse insofar as positive mental health is concerned. There is a rise in inner tension, there are signs of anxiety, and there is disorganization of function, resulting in a protracted period of emotional upset. This he refers to as "crisis." The outcome is governed by the kind of interaction that takes place during that period between the individual and the key figures in his emotional milieu.

EVOLUTION OF COMMUNITY PSYCHIATRY

Community psychiatry is, even now, emerging as a new field. New concepts and new biopsychosocial problems arise continually in rapidly changing cultures so that it is a broad, fluid field. A difference is now perceived between long-term, psychoanalytic therapy of the individual and short-term, reality-oriented psychotherapy as practiced in community psychiatry.

In the middle 1960's the term crisis intervention was not yet included in psychiatric dictionaries. In 1970 the fourth edition of Hinsie and Campbell's *Psychiatric Dictionary* listed crisis intervention as one of several modes of community psychiatry: "In the crisis-intervention model, the focus is on transitional-situational demands for novel adaptational responses. Because minimal intervention at such times tends to,achieve maximal and optimal effects, such a model is more readily applicable to population groups than the medical model" (Hinsie and Campbell, 1970:606).

According to Bellak (1964), community psychiatry evolved from multiple disciplines and is intrinsically bound to the development of psychoanalytic theory. The social and behavioral sciences that advanced during the first half of this century were predicated on psychodynamic hypotheses. At the same time, concepts of public health and epidemiology were advancing in community health programs.

After World War II the general public's increasing awareness and acceptance of the high incidence of psychiatric problems created changes in attitudes and demands for community action.

The discovery and utilization of psychotropic drugs were important steps forward. This resulted in opportunities for open wards and rehabilitation of the hospitalized patient in his home milieu.

It would be incorrect to assume that all of these factors merged spontaneously, creating a successful, structured cure for psychiatric illness. Rather, this was a slow process of trial and error. Widely different programs, each striving to meet problems involving different cultures, interests, knowledge, and skills, communicated and related to other programs similarly initiated. Disciplines once separated in goals became cognizant of their interdependence in attaining mutually recognized goals. New, allied disciplines developed; roles changed and expanded. There was a diffusion of tasks, and lines between disciplines became more flexible.

The origin of day hospitals for the care of psychiatric patients grew out of a shortage of hospital beds (Ross, 1964:190), which forced premature discharges of patients to their homes, rather than as a treatment innovation. The first reported day hospital was associated with the First Psychiatric Hospital in Moscow in 1933. As Dzhagarov (1937) states: "The need to continue treatment and for special observation in a setting similar to that of a hospital suggested a practical solution in the form of admission to the preventive section of the hospital. In a short time a transformation took place, the day hospital was created, proving to be adequately prepared to meet the new needs." In referring to this day hospital in Moscow, Kramer, as quoted by Ross (1964:190) says: "While this day center is little known and probably had little effect on later developments in the Western world, it is accurate to say that this was the first organized Day Hospital for individuals with severe mental illness."

In the late 1930's Bierer (1964:221-247) began the Marlborough Experiment in England. Patients, as members of a "therapeutic social club," lived outside the hospital and were treated at day hospitals or part-time facilities. According to Bierer, the primary goal of the program was to change the patient's concept of his role from that of a passive object of treatment to one of an active participant-collaborator. At the same time, the psychiatrist and his staff had to reconceptualize the patient as a human being accessible to reason, emphasizing his assets rather than concentrating on his psychopathology and conflicts. The reality of here and now was the focus of attention.

These innovations in attitude gave rise to the concept of "therapeutic community." The patient became a partner and collaborator with the staff and was granted equal rights, opportunities, and facilities. The medical staff and their assistants functioned as advisors.

The patient group assumed responsibility for the behavior of its members, as well as planning for activities, planning their futures, and offering support to each other. Group and social methods that encouraged the constant interaction of the members were used.

Other complementary projects developed in the Marlborough Program were the Day Hospital, the Night Hospital, the Aftercare Rehabilitation Center, the Self-Governed Community Hostel, Neurotics Nomine, and the Weekend Hospital.

Linn (1964:138) describes Cameron's first day hospital in Montreal (1946), in which he and others were responsible for defining and giving formal structure to the program as a treatment innovation.

With this frame of reference it was only natural that the general hospital should add to the various roles in which it serves the community — that of becoming a focal point of preventive medicine and public health functions in psychiatry.

In 1958 a "Trouble Shooting Clinic" was initiated by Bellak (1960) as part of City Hospital of Elmhurst, New York, a general hospital with 1,000 beds. The clinic was designed to offer first aid to emotional problems and was not limited to urgent crises. It combined two aspects of service: major emergencies as well as minor problems involving guidance, legal problems, and marital relations on a walk-in basis around the clock.

After the passage of the California Community Mental Health Act (1958) the California Department of Mental Hygiene established the first state agency in the country (1961) to undertake the training of specialists in community psychiatry.

It was recognized that clinics were needed to accommodate those individuals in the community who were unfamiliar with established forms of psychiatric treatment. A cause for these individuals' exclusion from treatment conceivable could have been due to divergency in social-cultural background, lack of communication, and lack of recognition of the need for services by both the population and the existing agencies.

In January, 1962, the Benjamin Rush Center for Problems of Living, a division of the Los Angeles Psychiatric Service, was opened as a no-waiting, unrestricted intake, walk-in crisis intervention center.

In 1967 crisis intervention replaced emergency detention at the San Francisco General Hospital. On each of the psychiatric units interdisciplinary teams were established whose primary goals were to reestablish independent functioning of the clients as soon as possible. In a follow-up study in 1972, Decker and Stubblebine (1972) concluded that the crisis-intervention program achieved the anticipated reduction in psychiatric inpatient treatment.

In the early 1970's the Bronx Mental Health Center (Morales, 1971) (Centro de Hygiene Mental del Bronx) was created for crisis intervention for the low socioeconomic Spanish-speaking people and was staffed by Spanish-speaking psychiatrists.

At about the same time, brief crisis-intervention services were being offered by suburban churches in Montreal, Canada (Lecker, 1971), on an experimental basis. The goal of the program was to reach families undergoing a variety of stress through a roving walk-in clinic. The clinics served to facilitate delivery of these services to a latent population at risk, not reached by other means and at a point early in the evolution of a life crisis.

The first hot line was started at Children's Hospital in Los Angeles in 1968. Hot lines and youth crisis centers have been created in recognition of the failure of traditional approaches to make contacts among adolescents. Twenty-four-hour crisis telephones, free counseling with a minimum of red tape, walk-in contacts, crash pads, and young people serving as volunteer staff in such services are becoming increasingly attractive to the youth who are emerging as the locus of a counterculture.

Trends such as these are being repeated around the country as community mental health programs recognize the value of providing services in primary and secondary prevention unique to the needs of their particular clients. Increasing recognition is also being given to the need to provide more services for those clients whose needs are for continuing support in rehabilitation after resolution of the immediate crisis.

According to Reissman (1970), a major concern for confronting community mental health centers is no longer that of discerning just what services are appropriate to the needs of their potential clients. It is not even that of recruiting clients for the services provided. The centers are now being faced with the problem of obtaining an adequate supply of human resources to meet the demands for their services. Professionals and nonprofessionals alike are being recruited and trained to fill the gap between supply and demand for their services. This has led to the deprofessionalization of many mental health functions previously considered to be solely within the scope of the professional's skills. Role boundaries have undergone increasing diffusion as the needs of the individual client and his community become the determining factors in establishing the appropriateness of services.

It is not our purpose at this time to define the levels of educational preparation and experience of the various disciplines now practicing crisis intervention. Our intent is, however, to provide an overview of the current trends being reported in the utilization of available human resources.

PARAPROFESSIONALS

Increasing numbers of paraprofessionals are now being provided with additional education and training to function as consultants or "therapists" in mental health centers. Rusk (1972) reports an increased trend toward the use of paraprofessionals in functions once considered to be only within the domain of the highly skilled professional. Leaders in community mental health are keenly aware of the many dangers inherent in random, unplanned deprofessionalization of major mental health functions. Increasing concern is being voiced about the lack of definitive criteria established for the different levels of educational preparation and experience required of those who conduct the various "therapies."

As new roles and careers are being created, some are being formed within well-structured, formal educational and training programs. Others, however, have tended to evolve gradually and informally, often in response to specific needs of innovative programs.

Interest in developing more innovative uses for the relatively untrained nonprofessional worker has led to a wide variety of training programs being offered in community colleges around the country. Currently there are wide differences in admission criteria and program content. Wilson and associates (1971) have reviewed programs throughout the country. They report that much has been written on the recruitment, education, and placement of the paraprofessional workers, but little has been written on their acceptance by the consumers. They also suggest that the development of new careers in mental health may not be the complete answer to the highly complex problems raised by the shortage in skilled manpower.

A prototype of the model for new careers in mental health was established by Lincoln Hospital Mental Health Services in New York City. According to Collins (1971) in a report on this program, indigenous people were trained to serve as mental health aides in neighborhood service centers. Rather than functioning as an ancillary extension of the professional, these individuals served as liaison between the social and experiential gap separating the middle-class professionals and the lower-class clients.

Christmas and associates (1970) expressed concern that the inappropriate use of the paraprofessional in community programs could lead to perpetuating the past patterns of providing second-class services for the poor and minorities. This reflects a predominant theme of concern currently being expressed that the same patterns of care reported by Hollingshead and Redlich (1958) might be perpetuated in the new community programs.

All emphasize that the functions for which each paraprofessional staff member is utilized must not be determined by the scope of his preparation alone. They must also be determined by the amount of professional supervision and consultation that will be made available to him. The public is becoming increasingly sophisticated in its understanding of its human rights to equal care and treatment. It may not accept less much longer.

NON–MENTAL HEALTH PROFESSIONALS

Another resource for manpower being recruited into liaison activities with community programs is the non–mental health professionals. These are the professional individuals who serve as the official caretakers within their communities.

Common to all is their traditional role of helping people who are in trouble. Included in this group are the medical professionals, teachers, lawyers, clergy, policemen, firemen, social and welfare workers, and so on. In the course of their daily work activities these highly skilled individuals can be found functioning in what could be called the front lines of preventive mental health care. They are frequently in contact with both individuals and groups who are in potential crisis situations because of a loss or the threat of a loss in their lives. Most often these professional community caretakers become the initial contact made by a person in crisis.

The contributions that this group can make to positive mental health education and practices have not gone unrecognized. Many new programs have been developed to include them as active participants on the treatment teams. How little or how much each can do is highly dependent on the availability and willingness of the mental health professionals to provide them with training and consultation services.

NONPROFESSIONAL VOLUNTEERS

Nonprofessional volunteers are another source of manpower being recruited by mental health centers. Schindler-Rainman (1971) predicted that by 1975 approximately 70% of all work roles would be in people-helping fields. Individuals would have much more leisure time and would probably make themselves available as volunteers. Not only could they be utilized in the traditional volunteer roles, but they could also seek training to develop skills to meet their human needs to be creative, to help others, to be recognized, to learn new skills, and to become meaningful members of the treatment teams.

Crisis hot lines, initially established by professionals and community leaders, rely heavily upon the nonprofessional volunteer for their 24-hour–day, 7-day–week services. According to Clark and Jaffe (1972), these hot lines seem to have originated in both the traditional and counterculture models of crisis intervention. Nonprofessionals were carefully selected, intensively trained, and closely supervised in these original psychiatric emergency centers.

Torop and Torop (1972), in their report on the use of volunteers in a crisis hot line program, call attention to the potential dangers for clients when unskilled volunteers are not provided with consistent and skillful professional supervision. In particular they point out the need to recognize and intervene when a volunteer may be responding to his own personal intuition and bias.

Later developments in crisis intervention history were the organization of free clinics and similar community help centers. These are predominantly staffed by volunteers from the counterculture communities to whom they provide services.

TEAM APPROACH TO CRISIS

A recent development has been the increasing use of the team approach to crisis intervention. Crisis team members are selected on the basis of their expertise to meet the specific needs of each patient in crisis. Members will vary with the structure and requirements of the individual mental health centers, as well as with the geographic and socioeconomic needs of the community. The unique skills of each member are utilized from the time of initial contact until the crisis is resolved and follow-up support is no longer felt to be necessary.

Team membership is open ended, expanding and contracting within highly flexible boundaries. Leadership of each team depends upon who has the skills and expertise most appropriate to help the individual resolve his crisis. This is not to say, however, that ultimate professional responsibility is removed from the physician. Rather, there is a greater scope in delegation of authority to make decisions in treatment planning.

Informal and, at times, unrecognized members of the community mental health team are the nonprofessional community caretakers. These individuals in the course of their usual daily activities have many contacts with fellow members of the community or are sought out for help and advice. They act as a source of information and are an integral part of the communication channels within the social systems of the community. In their formal roles, such as cab drivers, bartenders, grocers, barbers, beauticians, and neighbors, they provide a sympathetic ear and situational support to those in trouble and looking for help. If informed and aware of the purpose and services provided by the center, they can be a reliable and direct referral source for those in need of crisis intervention.

The non – mental health professional caretaker's function is a more formal role relationship with members of the community. These caretakers receive their communications within the system from a nonprofessional caretaker or directly from the individual who needs help. They could be incorporated into the community mental health team as consultants or as persons who make direct referrals to the center for treatment.

Selected nonprofessional volunteers could be used in liaison within the community as interpreters with foreign language population groups and as sources of referral. With appropriate training in crisis-intervention techniques they could be utilized as "therapists" under the supervision of mental health professionals at some centers.

Paraprofessionals function as members of the team in accord with their basic training and educational preparation. In their roles at the center they could focus on initial assessments and observations of behavioral changes in the clients. If a client were retained for 24 to 72 hours on a crisis ward, members of this group could be prepared to participate in various adjunctive therapies under professional guidance and supervision. Their realm of functioning would be within the immediate environs of the center.

The mental health professionals could function on the crisis team much as they function on any mental health team. The psychiatrist, psychologist, psychiatric nurse, and psychiatric social worker could conduct individual, family, or group therapy as needed by the clients. The diversity of local demands and problems underscores ability and accomplishment of individual team members more than professional background alone. Generalization, frequently required on the part of the staff, may be one factor accounting for the less strict division of roles and responsibilities among the professional in a community mental health center.

The administrator's task would be to create a climate in which each team member is free enough and challenged enough to actively participate in the care needed by the clients seeking help to resolve their crises.

REFERENCES

Bellak, L.: A general hospital as a focus of community psychiatry, J.A.M.A. **174:**2214, 1960.

Bellak, L., editor: Handbook of community psychiatry and community mental health, New York, 1964, Grune & Stratten, Inc.

Bellak, L., and Small, L.: Emergency psychotherapy and brief psychotherapy, New York, 1965, Grune & Stratten, Inc.

Bierer, J.: The Marlborough experiment. In Bellak, L., editor: Handbook of community psychiatry and community mental health, New York, 1964, Grune & Stratten, Inc.

Caplan, G.: A public health approach to child psychiatry, Ment. Health **35:**235, 1951.

Caplan, G.: An approach to community mental health, New York, 1961, Grune & Stratton, Inc.

Caplan, G.: Principles of preventive psychiatry, New York, 1964, Basic Books, Inc., Publishers.

Christmas, J. J., Wallace, H., and Edwards, J.: New careers and new mental health services; fantasy or future? Am. J. Psychiatry **126:**1480, April 1970.

Clark, T., and Jaffe, D. T.: Change within youth crisis centers, Am. J. Orthopsychiatry **42:**675, July 1972.

Collins, J. A.: The paraprofessional. I. Manpower issues in the mental health field, Hosp. Community Psychiatry **22:**362, Dec. 1971.

Collins, J. A., and Cavanaugh, M.: The paraprofessional. II. Brief mental health training for the community health worker, Hosp. Community Psychiatry **22:**367, Dec. 1971.

Decker, J. B., and Stubblebine, J. M.: Crisis intervention and prevention of psychiatric disability; a follow-up study, Am. J. Psychiatry **129:**101, Dec. 1972.

Dzhagarov, M. A.: Experience in organizing a day hospital for mental patients, Neurapathol-ogia Psikhiatria **6:**147, 1937. (Translated by G. Wachbrit.)

Eastman, K., Coates, D., and Allodi, F.: The concepts of crisis; an expository review, Can. Psychiatr. Assoc. J. **15:**463, 1970.

Ford, D., and Urban, H.: Systems of psychotherapy, New York, 1963, John Wiley & Sons, Inc.

Golan, N.: When is a client in crisis? Soc. Casework **50:**389, July 1969.

Hinsie, L. E., and Campbell, R. J.: Psychiatric dictionary, ed. 4, New York, 1970, Oxford University Press, Inc.

Hollingshead, A. B., and Redlich, F. C.: Social class and mental illness, New York, 1958, John Wiley & Sons, Inc.

Janis, L.: Psychological stress, New York, 1958, John Wiley & Sons, Inc.

Lecker, S., and others: Brief intervention; a pilot walk-in clinic in suburban churches, Can. Psychiatr. Assoc. J. 16(2):141, 1971.

Lindemann, E.: The meaning of crisis in individual and family, Teachers Coll. Rec. **57:**310, 1956.

Linn, L.: Psychiatric program in a general hospital. In Bellak, L., editor: Handbook of community psychiatry and community mental health, New York, Grune & Stratton, Inc., 1964.

Loewenstein, R. M.: Psychology of the ego. In Alexander, F., Eisenstein, S., and Grotjahn, M., editors: Psychoanalytic pioneers, New York, 1966, Basic Books, Inc., Publishers.

Morales, H. M.: Bronx Mental Health Center, N.Y. State Division Bronx Bull. **13**(8):6, 1971.

Ovesy, L., and Jameson, J.: Adaptational techniques of psychodynamic therapy. In Rado, S., and Daniels, G., editors: Changing concepts of psychoanalytic medicine, New York, 1956, Grune & Stratton, Inc.

Pumpian-Mindlin, E.: Contributions to the theory and practice of psychoanalysis and psychotherapy. In Alexander, F., Eisenstein,

S., and Grotjahn, M., editors: Psychoanalytic pioneers, New York, 1966, Basic Books, Inc., Publishers.

Rapoport, L.: The state of crisis; some theoretical considerations, Soc. Service Rev. **36**:211, June 1962.

Rappaport, D.: A historical survey of phychoanalytic ego psychology. In Klein, G. S., editor: Psychological issues, New York, 1959, International Universities Press.

Reiff, R.: Mental health manpower and community change, Am. Psychologist **21**:540, 1966.

Reissman, C. K.: The supply-demand dilemma in community mental health centers, Am. J. Orthopsychiatry **40**:858, Oct. 1970.

Ross, M.: Extramural treatment techniques. In Bellak, L., editor: Handbook of community psychiatry and community mental health, New York, 1964, Grune & Stratton, Inc.

Rusk, T.: Future changes in mental health care, Hosp. Community Psychiatry **22**:7, Jan. 1972.

Salzman, L.: Developments in psychoanalysis, New York, 1962, Grune & Stratton, Inc.

Schindler-Rainman, E.: Are volunteers here to stay? Ment. Hyg. **55**:511, Oct. 1971.

Sifneos, P. E.: A concept of emotional crisis, Ment. Hyg. **44**:169, 1960.

Torop, P., and Torop, K.: Hotlines and youth culture values, Am. J. Psychiatry **129**:106, Dec. 1972.

Tyhurst, J. A.: Role of transition states — including disasters — in mental illness, Symposium on Preventive and Social Psychiatry sponsored by Walter Reed Army Institute of Research, Walter Reed Medical Center, and National Research Council, April 15-17, Washington, D.C., 1957, U.S. Government Printing Office.

United States House of Representatives: A bill to provide for the assistance in the construction and initial operation of community mental health centers and for other purposes, No. 3688, Eighty-eighth Congress, first session, 1963.

VanAntwerp, M.: Primary prevention; a challenge to mental health associations, Ment. Hyg. **54**:453, July 1970.

Wilson, S. E., Courtney, C. G., Ota, K. Y., and Radauskas, B.: Evaluating mental health associates, Hosp. Community Psychiatry **22**:371, Dec. 1971.

ADDITIONAL READINGS

Arnhoff, F. N.: Manpower needs, resources and innovation. In Barten, H. H., and Bellak, L.,
editors: Progress in community mental health, vol. 2, New York, 1972, Grune & Stratton, Inc., pp. 35-61.

Bard, M.: The role of law enforcement in the helping system, Community Mental Health J. **7**(2):151, 1971.

Barten, H. H., and Bellak, L., editors: Progress in community mental health, vol. 2, New York, 1972, Grune & Stratton, Inc.

Barthal, H. S.: Resistances to community psychiatry, Psychiatr. Q. **45**(3):333, 1971.

Bartolucci, G., and Drayer, C. S.: An overview of crisis intervention in the emergency rooms of general hospitals, Am. J. Psychiatry **130**(9): 953, 1973.

Beigel, A.: The treatment team: paramedicals in the emergency mental health services, Med. Insight **4**(12):30, 1972.

Board, M.: The role of law enforcement in the helping systems, Community Ment. Health J. **7**(2):151, 1971.

Brandon, S.: Crisis theory and possibilities of therapeutic intervention, Br. J. Psychiatry **117**: 541, Dec. 1970.

Bruder, E. E.: The clergyman's contribution to community mental health, Hosp. Community Psychiatry **22**:207, July 1971.

Caplan, G.: Practical steps for the family physician, J.A.M.A. **170**:1497, 1506, 1959.

Cassell, W. A., and others: Comparing costs of hospital and community care, Hosp. Community Psychiatry **23**:197, July 1972.

Chandler, H. M.: Family crisis intervention; point and counterpoint in the psychosocial revolution, J. Natl. Med. Assoc. **64**:211, May, 1972.

Cobb, C. W.: Community mental health services and the lower socioeconomic classes; a summary of research literature on outpatient treatment (1963-1969), Am. J. Orthopsychiatry **42**: 404, April, 1972.

de Smit, N. W.: The crisis center in community psychiatry; an Amsterdam experiment. In Masserman, J. H., editor: Current psychiatric therapies, vol. 2, New York, 1971, Grune & Stratton, Inc.

de Smit, N. W.: Crisis intervention and crisis centers; their possible relevance for community psychiatry and mental health care, Psychiatr. Neurol. Neurochir. **75**:299, 1973.

Elias, P.: The state of crisis; implications for practice, Hong Kong J. Soc. Work **8**(2):17, 1974.

Ewalt, J. R., and Farnsworth, D. L.: Psychiatry

and religion. In Ewalt, J. R., and Farnsworth, D. L., editors: Textbook of psychiatry, New York, 1963, McGraw-Hill Book Co.

Farberow, N.: The crisis of chronic, Am. Psychol. 28(5):388, 1973.

Finestone, S., and Sobey, F.: Nonprofessional personnel in mental health programs, publication No. 5028, Chevy Chase, Md., 1969, National clearinghouse for Mental Health Information.

Flomenhaft, K., and others: After the crisis, Ment. Hyg. 55:473, Oct. 1971.

Freudenberger, H. J.: Crisis intervention, individual and group counseling, and the psychology of the counseling staff in a free clinic, J. Soc. Issues 30(1):77, 1974.

Greaves, G.: Crisis Intervention in a time of personal crises, Voices; the Art and Science of Psychotherapy 8(1):61, 1972.

Huessy, H. R.: Rural models. In Barten, H. H., and Bellak, L., editors: Progress in community mental health, vol. 2, New York, 1972, Grune & Stratton, Inc., pp. 199-220.

Kelly, J. G.: The mental health agent in the community. In Bindman, A. J., and Speigel, A. D., editors: Perspectives in community ·mental health, Chicago, 1969, Aldine Publishing Co., pp. 620-634.

Lau, H., and Cooper, S.: A night in crisis, Psychiatry, Journal of the Study of Interpersonal Process 36(1):23, 1973.

Mackenzie, M., and others: Family crisis unit, Lancet 1:642, March 1972.

McClellan, M. S.: Crisis groups in special care areas, Nurs. Clin. North Am. 7:363, June 1972.

Menolascino, F. J., and Acerra, P.: Annotated literature reference guide in community psychiatry, Omaha, 1974, Nebraska Psychiatric Institute.

Messick, J. M.: Crisis intervention concepts; implications for nursing practices, J. Psychiatr. Nurs. Ment. Health Services 10(5):3, 1972.

Moorehead, M. A.: Evaluating quality of care of the neighborhood health center program of O.E.O., Med. Care 8:118, 1970.

Naylor H.: New trends in volunteer services for the mentally handicapped, Hosp. Community Psychiatry 22:109, April 1971.

Polak, P.: Techniques of social system intervention, Curr. Psychiatr. Ther. 12:185, 1972.

Pretzel, P. W.: The volunteer clinical worker at the suicide prevention center, Bull. Suicidology 6:29, 1970.

Raffel, S.: Report of a successful community venture in the establishment of a crisis center. In Miller, L., editor: Fourth International Congress of Social Psychiatry, abstract of papers, Jerusalem, 1972, Ahva Cooperative.

Rubenstein, D.: Rehospitalization versus family crisis intervention, Am. J. Psychiatry 129:715, Dec. 1972.

Schneider, B.: Preparing general practitioners for community mental health work, Hosp. Community Psychiatry 22:346, Nov. 1971.

Schwartz, D. A.: Community mental health in 1972; an assessment. In Barten, H. H., and Bellak, L., editors: Progress in community mental health, vol. 2, New York, 1972, Grune & Stratton, Inc.

Schwartz, S. L.: A review of crisis intervention programs, Psychiatr. Q. 45:498, 1971.

Terashima, S.: Community psychiatry; basic theories of community psychiatry, In Kaketa, K., editor, Social psychiatry, Tokyo, 1970, Igaku Shoin Ltd.

Vail, D. J.: Community capabilities in crisis intervention, Br. J. Soc. Psychiatry Community Health 6(2):108, 1972.

Wellisch, D. K., and Gay, G. R.: The walking wounded; emergency psychiatric intervention in a heroin addict population, Drug Forum 1:137, Jan. 1972.

Wolberg, Lewis R.: Psychiatric technics in crisis therapy, N.Y. State J. Med. 72(13):1266, 1972.

2 □ Differentiation between psychotherapeutic techniques

Psychotherapy as a form of treatment has had many definitions, some conflicting and others concurring. Areas of divergence are generally those of methodology, therapeutic goals, length of therapy, and indications for treatment. All apparently agree that psychotherapy is a set of procedures for changing behaviors based primarily on the establishment of a relationship between two (or more) people.

PSYCHOANALYSIS AND PSYCHOANALYTIC PSYCHOTHERAPY

The original theories of Sigmund Freud, the founder of psychoanalysis, passed through several phases as he subjected changing hypotheses to the tests of experience and observation, all directed toward the goal of making the unconscious available to the conscious.

In collaboration with Breuer, Freud first developed the psychotherapeutic technique of "cathartic hypnosis." Recognizing that ego control of the unconscious was released under the influence of hypnosis, Freud used hypnotism to induce the patient to answer direct questions in an effort to uncover the unconscious causes of his symptomatology and to allow free expression of pent-up feelings.

Freud observed, however, that to obtain therapeutic results the procedure had to be repeated. He recognized that material brought to consciousness during hypnosis returned to the unconscious as the awakening patient regained control over his emotions. The therapeutic task of making the conscious patient recall and face repressed emotions in order to gain insight and increased ego strength was only transiently achieved by this technique.

Freud then experimented with what he referred to as "waking suggestion." Laying his hand on the patient's forehead, he would strongly suggest that the pa-

16

tient could recall the past if he tried. He soon learned that a person could not be forced to recall repressed, conflictual emotional events through this approach.

He next devised an indirect method of freeing unconsciously repressed material for confrontation by the conscious. Using the process of "free association," the patient was expected to verbalize whatever thoughts came into his mind, freely associating events from his whole life span of experiences, feelings, fantasies, and dreams without concern for logic or continuity. Freud concentrated on gaining an intellectual understanding of the patient's psychogenic past. He insisted on the "basic rule" that the patient tell the therapist everything that came into his mind during each interview. Nothing, no matter how inconsequential the patient might think it was, could be withheld from the analyst. In this process of a search for repressed memories he found that repressed emotions were gradually discharged as they emerged, although not as dramatically as in cathartic hypnosis.

One of the most important discoveries by Freud is considered to be "transference phenomena." He deemed transference to be a valuable therapeutic tool in overcoming the patient's defenses in resisting the release of unconscious, repressed emotional experiences. He thought of transference as an emotional reaction of the patient to the therapist in which the patient would relive his conflicts and emotions as they emerged from the past, from his unconscious. He would transfer to the therapist emotions that he felt toward authority figures in his childhood.

Freud referred to this reliving of the neurotic past in a present relationship with the therapist as transference neurosis. The principal factor in this process was that the patient expressed his aggressions against the therapist without any fears of the reprisal or censure that he may have been subjected to by the authority figure in his childhood. Through the therapist's nonjudgmental acceptance the patient was encouraged to face new material released from his own unconscious with reduced fear and anxiety. As these new experiences were assimilated into the conscious ego, coping skills increased. This in turn facilitated further release of repressed material. Alexander (1956:41) refers to this process as a "corrective emotional experience."

Psychoanalysis is concerned with theory as well as techniques. Alexander and French (1946:5) also state that the traditional approach in psychoanalytic therapy has been nondirective. The therapist is a passive observer who would follow the lead of the patient's verbal expressions as they unfolded before him. Tarachow (1963) indicates that psychoanalytic therapy is for those whose personalities and ego strengths are relatively intact, despite neurotic symptoms or mild to moderately severe characterological disturbances due to unconscious conflicts.

Stone (1951) lists eight factors in the situation and technique of psychoanalysis from which technical variations have derived: "(1) Practically exclusive reliance during the hour on the patient's free associations for communication; (2)

regularity of the time, frequency and duration of appointments and a clearly defined financial agreement; (3) three to five appointments a week (originally six), with daily appointments the dominant tendency; (4) recumbent position, in most instances with some impediment against seeing the analyst directly; (5) confinement of the analyst's activity essentially to interpretation or other purely informative interventions such as reality testing, or an occasional question; (6) the analyst's emotional passivity and neutrality (benevolent objectivity), specifically abstention from gratifying the analysand's transference wishes; (7) abstention from advice or any other direct intervention or participation in the patient's daily life; (8) no immediate emphasis on curing symptoms, the procedure being guided largely by the patient's free associations from day to day. In a sense the analyst regards the whole scope of the patient's psychic life as his field of observation."

In psychoanalytic psychotherapy the therapist is more active than in psychoanalysis. He interacts more with the patient and does not interpret the transference attitudes as completely as in analysis. His most helpful attitude is one of calmness, continued interest, and sympathetic, understanding helpfulness. This differs from the neutral attitude of the analyst in psychoanalysis. Contention is that this calm, helpful, interested attitude of the therapist in psychotherapy provides support for the patient in dealing with his tensions, sustains his contact with reality, and provides gratifications and rewards in the therapeutic relationship. These, in turn, provide incentives for the patient to continue to deal with emerging unconscious material.

Freud (1924) expressed the opinion that any digression from classical psychoanalysis that still recognizes the two basic facts of transference and resistance and takes them as the starting point of its work may call itself psychoanalysis, even though it arrives at results other than his own.

Alexander (1956:53-55) has noted that in procedures that deviate from the classical psychoanalysis of Freud, one or another of the basic phenomena is emphasized from the standpoint of therapeutic significance and is often being dealt with in isolation from others. For example, Rank centered on life situation, believing that insight into infantile history had no therapeutic significance. Feranczi placed emphasis on the emotional experience in transference (abreaction factor). Reich concentrated on the analysis of the resistances in order to allow, by their removal, the discharge of highly charged emotional experiences. He emphasized the importance of hidden forms of resistance and the understanding of the patient's behavior apart from his verbal communication.

Psychoanalytic psychotherapy procedures have customarily been divided into two functional categories based on methodology; these are frequently referred to as supportive (suppressive) and uncovering (exploratory or expressive) procedures.

According to Alexander (1956:155), the aim of the uncovering procedure is to intensify the ego's ability to handle repressed emotional conflict situations that are unconscious. Through the use of transference the patient relives his early interpersonal conflicts in relation to the therapist. Supportive and uncovering procedures overlap, but it is not difficult to differentiate between them. Primarily, supportive methods of treatment are indicated when functional impairment of the ego is temporary in nature and caused by acute emotional distress. Alexander designated therapeutic tasks in supportive methodology as follows: (1) gratifying dependency needs of the patient during stress situations, thereby reducing anxiety; (2) reducing stress by giving the patient an opportunity for abreaction; (3) giving intellectual guidance by objectively reviewing with the patient his acute stress situation and assisting him in making judgments, thereby enabling him to gain proper perspective of the total situation; (4) supporting the patient's neurotic defenses until the ego can handle the emotional discharges; and (5) actively participating in manipulation of the life situation when this might be the only hopeful approach in the given circumstances.

Psychoanalysis and psychoanalytic psychotherapy require many years of intensive training on the part of the therapist; this in itself has limited the number of therapists available. Both methods may require that the individual remain in therapy over an extended period of time, often for years. The obligation of time as well as expense for such extensive treatment also limits its availability for many.

BRIEF PSYCHOTHERAPY

Brief psychotherapy as a treatment form developed as the result of the increased demand for mental health services and the lack of personnel trained to meet this demand. Initially, much of it was conducted by psychiatric residents as part of their training. Later, psychiatric social workers and psychologists became involved in this form of treatment.

Brief psychotherapy has its roots in psychoanalytic theory but differs from psychoanalysis in terms of goals and other factors. It is limited to removing or alleviating specific symptoms when possible. Intervention may lead to some reconstruction of personality, although it is not considered as the primary goal. As in more traditional forms of psychotherapy, the therapy must be guided by an orderly series of concepts directed toward beneficial change in the patient. It is concerned with the degree of abatement of the symptoms presented and the return to or maintenance of the individual's ability to function adequately. To attain this goal the individual may choose to involve himself in a longer form of therapy. Another goal is assistance in preventing the development of deeper neurotic or psychotic symptoms after catastrophies or emergencies in life situations.

Free association, interpretation, and the analysis of transference are also used successfully in a modified manner. According to Bellak and Small (1965), free association is not a basic tool in short-term therapy. It may arise in response to a stimulus from the therapist. Interpretation is modified by the time limit and the immediacy of the problem. Although it may occur in brief psychotherapy, it is commonly used with medical or environmental types of intervention.

Bellak also believes that positive transference should be encouraged. It is crucial in brief therapy that the patient sees the therapist as being likeable, reliable, and understanding. The patient *must* believe that the therapist will be able to help him. This type of relationship is necessary if treatment goals are to be accomplished in a short period of time. This does not mean that negative transference feelings are to be ignored, but it does mean that these feelings are not analyzed in terms of defenses.

The therapist assumes a more active role than in the traditional methods. He avoids picking up trends not directly related to the presenting problem. The positive is accentuated, and the therapist presents himself as an interested, helpful person. The difficulties faced by the patient are circumscribed. The environmental position in which the patient finds himself is used by the therapist to help the patient evaluate the reality of his situation in an attempt to modify and change it. Productive behavior is encouraged.

Diagnostic evaluation is extremely important in short-term therapy. Its aim is to understand the symptoms and the patient dynamically and to formulate hypotheses that can be validated by the historical data. The result of the diagnosis will enable the therapist to decide which factors are most susceptible to change and to select the appropriate method of intervention. Part of the evaluation should be the degree of discrepancy or accord between the patient's fantasies and reality. His probable ability to tolerate past and future frustrations should also be considered; the adequacy of his past and present relationships is also pertinent. The question "Why do you come now?" must be asked and means not only "What is it that is going on in your life that distresses you?" but "What is it that you expect in the way of help?" It is reasonable to assume that a request for help is motivated by emotional necessities, both external and internal, which are meaningful to the patient. Short-term goals can be beneficial for *all* patients.

After determining the causes of the symptoms, the therapist elects the appropriate intervention. Interpretation in order to achieve insight is used with care. Direct confrontation is used sparingly. An attempt is made to strengthen the ego by increasing the patient's self-esteem. One facet of this approach is to help the patient feel that he is on a level with the therapist and that he is no less worthwhile nor are his problems more unusual than those of others. This technique not only relieves the patient's anxiety but also facilitates communication between the patient and the therapist. Other basic procedures used include the following: catharsis, drive repression and restraint, reality testing, intellectualization, reassurance and support, counseling and guidance to move the patient along a line of behavior, and conjoint counseling (Bellak and Small, 1965:52-56).

The ending of treatment is an important phase in brief therapy. The patient must be left with a positive transference and the feeling that he may return if the need arises. The learning that has taken place during therapy must be reinforced in order to encourage the patient to realize that he has begun to understand and solve his own problems. This has a preventive effect that will help the patient to recognize possible future problems.

As an adjunct, drug therapy may be used in selected cases. This is in contrast to pure psychoanalysis, where such is seldom utilized. Environmental manipulation is considered when it is necessary to remove or modify an element causing disruption in the patient's life pattern. Included might be close scrutiny of family and friends, his job and job training, education, and plans for travel (Bellak and Small, 1965:74-85).

Brief psychotherapy is indicated in cases of acutely disruptive emotional pain, in cases of severely destructive circumstances, and in situations endangering the life of the patient or others. Another indication involves the life circumstances of the individual. If he cannot involve himself in the long-term therapeutic situation, which implies a stable residence, job, and so forth, brief therapy is advocated to alleviate disruptive symptoms.

It is imperative that the patient feel relief as rapidly as possible, even during the first therapeutic session. The span of treatment can be any reasonable, limited number of sessions but usually is more than six. Most clinics expect the number of visits to be under twenty. Treatment goals can be attained in this short period of time if the patient is seen quickly and intensively after requesting help. Circumstances associated with disrupted functioning are more easily accessible if they are recent. Only active conflicts are amenable to therapeutic intervention. Disequilibrated states are more easily resolved *before* they have crystallized, acquired secondary gain features, or developed into highly maladaptive behavior patterns.

CRISIS INTERVENTION

Crisis intervention extends logically from brief psychotherapy. The minimum therapeutic goal of crisis intervention is psychological resolution of the individual's immediate crisis and restoration to at least the level of functioning that existed before the crisis period. A maximum goal is improvement in functioning above the precrisis level.

Caplan emphasizes that crisis is characteristically self-limiting and lasts from 4 to 6 weeks. This constitutes a transitional period, representing both the danger of increased psychological vulnerability and an opportunity for personality growth. In any particular situation the outcome may depend to a significant degree on the ready availability of appropriate help. On this basis the length of time for intervention is from 4 to 6 weeks, with the median being 4 weeks (Jacobson, 1965).

Since time is at a premium, a therapeutic climate is generated that commands the concentrated attention of both therapist and patient. A goal-oriented sense of commitment develops in sharp contrast to the more modest pace of traditional treatment modes.

Methodology

Jacobson and associates (1968) state that crisis intervention may be divided into two major categories, which may be designated as individual or generic. These two approaches are complementary.

Generic approach

A leading proposition of the generic approach is that there are certain recognized patterns of behavior in most crises. Many studies have substantiated this thesis. For example, Lindemann's (1944) studies of bereavement found that there is a well-defined process that a person goes through in adjusting to the death of a relative. He refers to these sequential phases as "grief work" and found that failure of a person to grieve appropriately or to complete the process of bereavement could potentially lead to future emotional illness.

Subsequent studies of generic patterns of response to stressful situations have been reported. Kaplan and Mason (1960)* and Caplan (1964)* studied the effect on the mother of the birth of a premature baby and identified four phases or tasks that she must work through to ensure healthy adaptation to the experience. Janis (1958)* suggests several hypotheses concerning the psychological stress of impending surgery and the patterns of emotional response that follow a diagnosis of chronicity. Rapoport (1963)* defines three subphases of marriage, during which unusual stress could precipitate crises. These are only a few of the broad research studies being done in this field.

The generic approach focuses on the characteristic course of the *particular kind of crisis* rather than on the psychodynamics of each individual in crisis. A treatment plan is directed toward an adaptive resolution of the crisis. Specific intervention measures are designed to be effective for all members of a given group rather than for the unique differences of one individual. Recognition of these behavioral patterns is an important aspect of preventive mental health.

Tyhurst (1957:149-172) has suggested that knowledge of patterned behaviors in transitional states occurring during intense or sudden change from one life situation to another might provide an empirical basis for the management of these states and the prevention of subsequent mental illness. He cites as examples the studies of individual responses to community disaster, migration, and retirement of pensioners.

Jacobson and associates (1968) state that generic approaches to crisis inter-

---

*These studies are also discussed in Chapters 6 and 7 of this text.

vention include "direct encouragement of adaptive behavior, general support, environmental manipulation and anticipatory guidance. . . . In brief, the generic approach emphasizes (1) specific situational and maturational events occurring to significant population groups, (2) intervention oriented to crisis related to these specific events, and (3) intervention carried out by non-mental health professionals."

This approach has been found to be a feasible mode of intervention that can be learned and implemented by nonpsychiatric physicians, nurses, social workers, and so forth. It does not require a mastery of knowledge of the intrapsychic and interpersonal processes of an individual in crisis.

Individual approach

The individual approach differs from the generic in its emphasis on assessment, by a professional, of the interpersonal and intrapsychic processes of the person in crisis. It is used in selected cases, usually those nor responding to the generic approach. Intervention is planned to meet the unique needs of the individual in crisis and to reach a solution for the particular situation and circumstances that precipitated the crisis. This differs from the generic approach, which focuses on the characteristic course of a particular kind of crisis.

Unlike extended psychotherapy, there is relatively little concern with the developmental past of the individual. Information from this source is seen as relevant only for the clues that may result in a better understanding of the present crisis situation. Emphasis is placed on the immediate causes for disturbed equilibrium and on the processes necessary for regaining a precrisis or higher level of functioning. Jacobson cites the inclusion of family members or other important persons in the process of the individual's crisis resolution as another area of differentiation from most individual psychotherapy.

In comparison with the generic approach he views the individual approach as emphasizing the need for greater depth of understanding of the biopsychosocial process, intervention oriented to the individual's unique situation and carried out only by mental health professionals.

Morley and associates (1967) recommend several attitudes that are important adjuncts to the specific techniques. In essence these comprise the general philosophical orientation necessary for the full effectiveness of the therapist.

1. It is essential that the therapist view the work that he is doing not as a "second-best" approach but as the treatment of choice with persons in crisis.

2. Accurate assessment of the presenting problem, *not* a thorough diagnostic evaluation, is essential to an effective intervention.

3. Both the therapist and the individual should keep in mind throughout the contacts that the treatment is sharply time limited and should persistently direct their energies toward resolution of the presenting problem.

4. Dealing with material not directly related to the crisis has no place in an intervention of this kind.

5. The therapist must be willing to take an active and sometimes directive role in the intervention. The relatively slow-paced approach of more traditional treatment is inappropriate in this type of therapy.

6. Maximum flexibility of approach is encouraged. Such diverse techniques as serving as a resource person or information giver and taking an active role in established liaison with other helping resources are often appropriate in particular situations.

7. The goal toward which the therapist is striving is explicit. His energy is directed entirely toward returning the individual to at least his precrisis level of functioning.

Steps in crisis intervention

There are certain specific steps involved in the technique of crisis intervention (Morley and others, 1967). Although each cannot be placed in a clearly defined category, typical intervention would pass through the following sequence of phases:

1. The first phase is the assessment of the individual and his problem. This requires the use of active focusing techniques on the part of the therapist to obtain an accurate assessment of the precipitating event and the resulting crisis that brought the individual to seek professional help. The therapist may have to judge whether the help-seeking person presents a high suicidal or homicidal risk. If the patient is thought to be a high level of danger to himself or to others, referral is made to a psychiatrist for consideration of hospitalization. In the event that hospitalization is not deemed necessary, the intervention proceeds.

The initial hour may be spent entirely on assessing the circumstances directly relating to the immediate crisis situation.

2. Planning of therapeutic intervention: After accurate assessment is made of the precipitating event(s) and the crisis, intervention is planned. This is not designed to bring about major changes in the personality structure but to restore the person to at least his precrisis level of equilibrium. In this phase, determination is made of the length of time since onset of the crisis. The precipitating event usually occurs from 1 to 2 weeks before the individual seeks help. Frequently it may have occurred within the past 24 hours. It is important to know how much the crisis has disrupted the individual's life and the effects of this disruption on others in his environment. Information is also sought to determine what strengths the individual has, what coping skills he may have used successfully in the past and is not using presently, and what other people in his life might be used as supports for him. Search is made for alternative methods of coping that for some reason he is not presently using.

3. Intervention: The nature of intervention techniques is highly dependent on the preexisting skills, creativity, and flexibility of the therapist. Morley suggests some of the following, which have been found useful:

a. *Helping the individual to gain an intellectual understanding of his crisis.* Often the individual sees no relationship between a hazardous situation occurring in life and the extreme discomfort of disequilibrium that he is experiencing. The therapist could use a direct approach, describing to the patient the relationship between crisis and the event in his life.

b. *Helping the individual bring into the open his present feelings to which he may not have access.* Frequently the person may have suppressed some of his very real feelings, such as anger or other inadmissible emotions, toward someone he "should love or honor." It may also be denial of grief, feelings of guilt, or incompletion of the mourning process following bereavement. An immediate goal of intervention is the reduction of tension by providing means for the individual to recognize these feelings and bring them into the open. It is sometimes necessary to produce emotional catharsis and reduce immobilizing tension.

c. *Exploration of coping mechanisms.* This approach requires assisting the person to examine alternate ways of coping. If for some reason the behaviors he used in the past for successfully reducing anxiety have not been tried, the possibility of their use in the present situation is explored. New coping methods are sought, and frequently the person devises some highly original methods that he has never tried before.

d. *Reopening the social world.* If the crisis has been precipitated by loss of someone significant to the person's life, the possibility of introducing new people to fill the void can be highly effective. It is particularly effective if supports and gratifications provided by the "lost" person in the past can be achieved to a similar degree from new relationships.

4. The last phase is the resolution of the crisis and anticipatory planning. The therapist reinforces those adaptive coping mechanisms that the individual has used successfully to reduce tension and anxiety. As his coping abilities increase and positive changes occur, they may be summarized to allow him to reexperience and reconfirm for himself the progress he has made. Assistance is given as needed in making realistic plans for the future, and there is discussion of ways in which the present experience may help in coping with future crises.

SUMMARY

A differentiation between psychoanalysis, brief psychotherapy, and crisis intervention methodology has been explored. No attempt has been made to state that one type of therapy is superior to another. In Table 1 we have provided the reader with a succinct profile of some of their major differences.

Table 1 □ Major differences between psychoanalysis, brief psychotherapy, and crisis intervention methodology

	Psychoanalysis	Brief psychotherapy	Crisis intervention
Goals of therapy	Restructuring the personality	Removal of specific symptoms	Resolution of immediate crisis
Focus of treatment	1. Genetic past	1. Genetic past as it relates to present situation	1. Genetic present
	2. Freeing the unconscious	2. Repression of unconscious and restraining of drives	2. Restoration to level of functioning prior to crisis
Usual activity of therapist	1. Exploratory 2. Passive observer 3. Nondirective	1. Suppressive 2. Participant observer 3. Indirect	1. Suppressive 2. Active participant 3. Direct
Indications	Neurotic personality patterns	Acutely disruptive emotional pain and severely disruptive circumstances	Sudden loss of ability to cope with a life situation
Average length of treatment	Indefinite	From one to twenty sessions	From one to six sessions

In psychoanalysis the goal of therapy is that of restructuring the personality; the focus of treatment is on the genetic past and the freeing of the unconscious. Psychoanalytic psychotherapeutic procedures are usually divided into two functional categories: the supportive (suppressive) and uncovering (exploratory or expressive) procedures. The therapist's role is nondirective, exploratory, and that of a passive observer. Indications for this type of therapy are for those individuals with neurotic personality patterns. Length of the therapy is indefinite and depends on the individual and the therapist.

Brief psychotherapy has as its goal removing specific symptoms and aiding in the prevention of developing deeper neurotic or psychotic symptoms. Its focus is on the genetic past as it relates to the present situation, repression of the unconscious, and restraining of drives. The role of the therapist is indirect, suppressive, and that of a participant observer. Basic tools used are psychodynamic intervention coupled with medical or environmental types of intervention. Indications for brief psychotherapy are acutely disruptive emotional pain, severely disruptive circumstances, and situations endangering the life of the individual or others. It is also indicated for those who have problems that do not require psychoanalytic intervention. The average length of treatment is from one to twenty sessions.

The goal of crisis intervention is the resolution of an immediate crisis. Its focus is on the genetic present, with the restoration of the individual to his precrisis level of functioning or possibly to a higher level of functioning. The therapist's role is direct, suppressive, and that of an active participant. Techniques are varied and limited only by the flexibility and creativity of the therapist. Some of these techniques include: helping the individual gain an intellectual understanding of his crisis, assisting the individual in bringing his feelings into the open, exploring past and present coping mechanisms, finding and using situational supports, and anticipatory planning with the individual to reduce the possibility of future crises. The indications for this type of therapy are an individual's (or family's) sudden loss of ability to cope with a life situation. The average length of treatment is from one to six sessions.

REFERENCES

Alexander, F: Psychoanalysis and psychotherapy, New York, 1956, W. W. Norton & Co., Inc.

Alexander, F., and French, T. M.: Psychoanalytic therapy, New York, 1946, The Ronald Press Co.

Bellak, L., and Small, L.: Emergency psychotherapy and brief psychotherapy, New York, 1965, Grune & Stratton, Inc.

Caplan, G.: Principles of preventive psychiatry, New York, 1964, Basic Books, Inc., Publishers.

Freud, S.: Collected papers, vol. 1. (Translated by Joan Riviere, Alex Strachey, and James Strachey, London, 1924, The Hogarth Press Ltd.)

Jacobson, G.: Crisis theory and treatment strategy; some sociocultural and psychodynamic considerations, J. Nerv. Ment. Dis. **141**:209, 1965.

Jacobson, G.: Strickler, M., and Morley, W. E.: Generic and individual approaches to crisis intervention, Am. J Public Health **58**:339, 1968.

Janis, I. L.: Psychological stress; psychoanalytical and behavioral studies of surgical patients, New York, 1958, John Wiley & Sons, Inc.

Kaplan, D. M., and Mason, E. A.: Maternal reactions to premature birth viewed as an acute emotional disorder, Am. J. Orthopsychiatry **30**:539, 1960.

Lindemann, E.: Symptomatology and management of acute grief, Am. J. Psychiatry **101**:101, Sept., 1944.

Mason, E. A.: Method of predicting crisis outcome for mothers of premature babies, Public Health Rep. **78**:1031, 1963.

Morley, W. E., Messick, J. M., and Aguilera, D. C.: Crisis; paradigms of intervention, J. Psychiatr. Nurs. **5**:537, 1967.

Rapoport, R.: Normal crises, family structure, and mental health, Fam. Process **2**:68, 1963.

Stone, L.: Psychoanalysis and brief psychotherapy, Psychoanal. Q. **20**:217, 1951.

Tarachow, S.: An introduction to psychotherapy, New York, 1963, International Universities Press.

Tyhurst, J. A.: Role of transition states — including disasters — in mental illness, Symposium on Preventive and Social Psychiatry sponsored by Walter Reed Institute of Research, Walter Reed Medical Center, and National Research Council, April 15-17, Washington, D.C., 1957, U.S. Government Printing Office.

ADDITIONAL READINGS

Bateson, G.: Steps to an ecology of mind, New York, 1973, Ballantine Books, Inc.

Brandon, S.: Theory and possibilities of therapeutic intervention, Br. J. Psychiatry **117**:627, Dec. 1970.

Caplan, G.: Emotional crisis. In Deutsch, A., and Fishbein, H., editors: The encyclopedia of mental health, vol. 2, New York, 1963, Franklin Watts, Inc.

Caplan, G., and Grunebaum, H.: Perspectives on primary prevention, Arch. Gen. Psychiatry **17**:331, Sept. 1967.

Decker, J. B., and Stubblebine, J. M.: Crisis intervention and prevention of psychiatric disability; a follow-up study, Am. J. Psychiatry **129**:725, Dec. 1972.

Dressler, D. M., and Nash, K. B.: An approach to crisis intervention through team expension, Am. J. Orthopsychiatry **42**(2):317, 1972.

Ford, D. H., and Urban, H. B.: Systems of psychotherapy, New York, 1963, John Wiley & Sons, Inc.

Fromm-Reichmann, F.: Psychoanalysis and psychotherapy, Chicago, 1959, University of Chicago Press.

Hankoff, L. D.: Emergency psychiatric treatment, Springfield, Ill., 1968, Charles C Thomas, Publisher.

Langsley, D. G., and Kaplan, D. M.: The treatment of families in crisis, New York, 1968, Grune & Stratton, Inc.

Raphael, B.: Crisis intervention; theoretical and methodological considerations, Aust. N.Z. J. Psychiatry 5:183, 1971.

Rapoport, L.: The state of crisis; some theoretical considerations, Chicago, 1972, University of Chicago Press.

3 □ Group therapy concepts in crisis intervention

GROUP CONCEPTS

From birth on, the individual is a member of a group composed of himself and his parents. His life becomes a succession of group memberships, expanding from the basic family unit to peer groups, play groups, and groups in school, business, and church. An individual may remain in some groups permanently or temporarily, voluntarily or involuntarily, and in some directly or indirectly, but he will usually participate in some form of group activity until death.

A helpless infant depending on the actions of others for survival progresses through intellectual, emotional, and social development. Forms of behavior that communicate feelings, needs, and ideas develop through interactions with others. At the same time, perceptions and reactions toward the feelings, needs, and ideas of others develop.

It has been suggested that an individual's behavior can be controlled and influenced by the forces of groups of which he is a member and that he becomes what he is because of the roles, status, and functions that are taken or given in them (Asch, 1951:177-190; Merton, 1968). Interpersonal skills are neither inherited nor instinctive but are acquired through a continual learning process involving use of all the senses. Facial expressions, vocal tones, body movements, odors, touch, and so forth are all a part of the language of interpersonal communications. Since man communicates through nonverbal as well as verbal clues, deprivation of any one of the senses could lead to distorted perceptions of the actions and responses of others.

Experiences that bring feelings of comfort and satisfactions are usually tried again, whereas those that result in frustration and discomfort are avoided whenev-

29

er possible so that progressive learning is based on past experiences. If a child's first important group, the immediate family, fails to provide him with gratifying, positive interpersonal learning experiences, his future psychosocial development could be impaired. For example, the child who has never learned how to obtain gratifying feelings of approval from within his family may be less than secure in establishing relationships with authority figures in other groups later, such as a teacher-pupil relationship in school. He may also experience added difficulties in his early peer groups, where beginning competition and leadership skills are first learned.

In recent years practical and scientific knowledge has been synthesized to form new concepts about the manipulation of group structures and group processes to effect change, both on the group and on its individual members. In psychiatry there has been a shift of emphasis from considering man as a biological entity to considering him as a biopsychosocial entity. Movement has been increasingly away from an organism-centered to a social-centered conceptualization of personality dynamics. Other professions and social institutions have also been increasingly aware of the effects of group influences upon the individual.

During and immediately after World War II there was an increased recognition of the necessity to meet the special needs of groups of people for whom individual care was impossible. This contributed to a rapid rise in the development and acceptance of group therapy and other therapeutic groups in the military, veterans' hospitals, and state and private institutions and clinics. Since then, an increasing variety of therapy groups has been developed in community and institutional settings, not only for patients with psychiatric problems but also for people unable to cope with many situational and maturational problems and stresses in daily life.

THERAPY GROUPS

Any simple definition of the term group therapy would be difficult because of a wide variety of concepts, methods, and interpretations of its meaning. In reference to people a group means, primarily, more than one person. If combined with the word therapy, it could mean, simply, a treatment given simultaneously to more than one person. When the group goal of effecting a change is included, it becomes more complicated because consideration must then be given to the methods and processes of group action, of individual action, and of the wide differences in group accomplishments.

Corsini and Rosenberg (1955) proposed a classification of group therapies in terms of involvement of intellectual, emotional, or action factors. Luchins (1964) suggests classifications based on concrete activities. According to Hinckley and

Hermann (1951), one approach to understanding the differences between the many types of therapy groups has been to focus on their purposes and results. They suggest two main categories: *social group work* and *group therapy*.

Social group work

In social group work the purpose is to achieve a common group goal with the aid of a leader. A project or an activity is used to unite the members, and the chief result is socialization. Examples of this are recreational groups, calling for teamwork and sportsmanship, or rhythm and games groups; another example is sociodrama, in which symptomatic behavior is indirectly touched on by participants through playacting. In this way discussions of feelings and behavior can be directed toward the *part* that is acted out, not toward the participant himself. Scouting and camping groups for children and adolescents are other means of fostering socialization and group-unifying activities.

In any of these social groups the leader serves as a director, discussant, or counselor. He must have skills in special areas, and his understanding of the dynamics of personality is secondary in importance to his understanding of group action and cultural patterns and mores. He is usually directive in his method of leading group activities along a prescribed course.

Slavson's (1964) approach to classifying therapy groups is to focus on the concept of depth in therapy for differentiating between types of psychotherapies. He acknowledges the concept of depth in therapy to be a controversial one, and there is apparently no absolute criterion for determining the absolute values of any one method in relation to another. The absence of accurate measuring devices makes it difficult to measure quantitatively changes in the psyche, functions, or attitudes resulting from therapy, and comparisons between methods could be misleading.

If the choice of method and course of psychotherapy is determined by the nature and intensity of individual needs, Slavson suggests a differentiation of psychotherapies based on the level of a person's psyche that requires change. Using this concept he has differentiated psychotherapy into the main categories of counseling, guidance, and psychotherapy.

Counseling

Counseling is reality oriented and focuses on solving specific problems arising from situational or interpersonal difficulties. The counselor is not required to be a trained psychotherapist but should have a greater knowledge than the counselee of the factors affecting the situation. His role is to direct actively toward the finding and acceptance of a solution to an immediate difficulty while not intentionally exposing the counselee's feelings or attitudes for the purpose of changing them. It is assumed that once the solutions are made clear, the ego will be able to function adequately toward solving the problem. The length of time in interviews is comparatively brief, and the sessions terminate as soon as the immediate specific difficulty is resolved. This method is least effective in group use.

Guidance

Guidance is a reality-oriented approach that may be used when a person finds himself incapable of coping with increased stresses because the emotional significance of a specific problem begins to affect his simple ego functioning. The aims and techniques are toward holding or reducing anxiety to a tolerable level and preventing disorganization. The focus is on correcting feelings and requires a professionally trained person with a sound understanding of psychodynamics and experience in psychotherapy that will enable him to work at this deeper level. The therapist's role is to supply clarification and support through empathy, acceptance, and permissiveness, thus enabling a client to bring conflictual feelings about the specific problem into conscious awareness and to ventilate them without increasing anxiety, guilt, or fear.

This approach may require a much longer period of time and more sessions than in the counseling approach because there is a need to prevent additional stress and discomfort, since the client is confronted with his feelings and may be expected to change some of his perceptions, attitudes, and behaviors.

The use of groups appears to accelerate the guidance process, particularly when people with problems of a similar nature are brought together. There is mutual identification with the problem area, and interactions occur rapidly, members possibly providing each other with greater support of self-esteem through empathy, acceptance, and permissiveness than the therapist along could provide. Negative feelings of being uniquely alone in needing help with a problem are alleviated.

Guidance has been found particularly effective in dealing with adolescents, persons with marital problems, families, parents of handicapped children, and so on. The therapist's role in the group requires the ability to use skills necessary for psychotherapy, recognizing and avoiding threatening areas for each member while working with the group as a whole. Feelings and behaviors are explored only as they are significant to the reality of each member's life situation; unrestricted exploration of feelings is avoided.

Group psychotherapy

Group psychotherapy is intended to make fundamental personality changes and to investigate reasons for personal emotional problems (Hinckley and Hermann, 1951). Unlike counseling or guidance it does not aim to solve a single specific situational problem; rather, it aims toward correction of intrapsychic processes that will make the person more capable of dealing with many problems.

The group approach is based on concepts of individual psychotherapy. Free association and unrestricted exploration of emotions are encouraged. Unlike social or guidance groups there is no one specific group goal, and each member has his own specific aims and expectations as to what the group experience can offer. Cohesiveness of members develops from the stresses and pain they experience as they focus on emotional problems, traumatic memories, and uncovered feelings, and possibly from mutual identification with any specific reality problem area. Efforts to minimize these feelings by resorting to gamelike activities are not permitted. Rather than avoiding threatening areas, the therapist takes relatively few precautions and encourages ventilation or catharsis of feelings. General therapeutic goals for patients with functional illness are to relieve tensions and anxiety, help them to gain some insights into their problems, assist them to resolve some of their conflicts, and support them in replacing or changing maladaptive behaviors for adaptive ones.

Group therapy utilizes a variety of techniques to obtain its general aims, and therapists often differ in their leadership roles. Some actively direct, whereas others may deem it more therapeutic to take a passive, indirect role to a degree that the group appears to be self-directed.

Although there is a relationship between technique and theory, few present-day techniques have been derived *solely* from theory. The therapist will undoubtedly be testing out certain theories and hypotheses of psychodynamics and group dynamics; this is an intrinsic part of a professional-scientific role. At the same time, he also has the role of "healer," assuming responsibilities to help individuals solve concrete problems encountered in their daily living.

Some therapists may focus on the psychodynamics of individual behavior; others may focus on group dynamics. Sometimes the focus will remain on the theoretical, intellectual level rather than on the specific individual behavioral responses taking place within the immediate interactions of the group; more often than not there is a combination of both going on, and no one method can be criticized as being better or worse than another.

A most important responsibility for the therapist is interpreting to patients the purpose for bringing the group together and the principles or rules under which they will operate. The patient's acceptance of this mode of therapy is determined in large part by whether he sees it as meeting his needs and whether he will be able to function under the principles of the group's operation. For example, the basic difficulties of a person may stem from early negative experiences in his primary family, and resultant avoidance reactions to group contacts could further increase his anxieties. Not only might this lead to increasing areas of conflict but the necessary positive transference phenomena would be unlikely. Selection criteria for members vary widely according to their needs, the availability and special areas of expertise of qualified therapists, and the purpose of the groups. These factors may also influence the size of membership, and there is no general agreement as to the number of sessions needed to accomplish specific goals.

The group process provides more than one person with whom the individual may identify and test out reactions to past experiences. In addition to the parental role figure that the therapist is most likely to be seen as, there are the sibling role figures of other members with whom interactions take place. In this way it provides on a small scale a situation in which a problem in interpersonal relationships can be exposed, a setting for action, reaction, and interaction within a therapeutic environment, and distorted perceptions of interpersonal experiences in the past can be revealed and examined. Varied interpersonal stimuli will be received from more than one source, and increasing opportunities for transference phenomena to take place and to be worked through will occur. Briefly, a transference phenomenon occurs when a person reacts to someone in the present as he did to someone in the past. This is because there is a tendency in everyone to carry over, into the present, attitudes and impressions gained from past interpersonal experiences. Although the present person may possess only one or two of the characteristics of the past person, a generalized distortion of the relationship can be triggered off. He becomes the recipient of the emotional responses and reactive behaviors that, in reality, were learned in the past relationship.

One therapeutic goal is to modify and clarify feelings, and feelings must be labeled and then verbalized in order for this to take place. The group provides an incentive in this area by open discussion during which patients are stimulated by the fact of emotions expressed by others and by the opportunity to relate their own problems to others in the group. Changed or new behavior responses can be tried out, observed in action, reflected back, and the dynamics explored for cause-and-effect reactions. Providing opportunities to increase coping capacities is important because this reflects the ability to resolve emotional issues and interpersonal problems that create conflicts.

For the individual, group experience is primarily an emotional one, and through interactions with other members he is confronted by relationships that may be supportive, critical, or a combination of both. Members are encouraged to both criticize and support each other, support occurring most often through mutual acceptance and empathic responses from other members. The presence of others is perceived as a protection against being the only object of the therapist's attention. Acceptance by a peer group rather than by just one person, the therapist, is reassuring, and feelings of being different and isolated are counteracted by the discovery that these same feelings and problems may be shared by others. It seems generally agreed that intergroup support is essential to the growth of a therapy group. Group interaction should assist the members to achieve insight into past behavior and to gain self-awareness in learning to adapt to more positive and satisfying interpersonal experiences in the future.

CRISIS GROUPS

Since the term group therapy may mean any two individuals who are in therapy together with a therapist, certain terms that may be unfamiliar to those who have not been involved in conducting therapy will be clarified. When *individual* crisis intervention therapy is mentioned, it means that an individual is in therapy on a one-to-one relationship with the therapist (Case study: Status and role change, Chapter 6, p. 81). *Conjoint* therapy refers to therapy that is conducted with a husband and wife who are seen by the therapist together (Case study: Prematurity, Chapter 6, p. 76). *Family* therapy includes those members of the family who are involved or affected by the crisis situation (Case study: Prepuberty, Chapter 7, p. 137). *Collateral* therapy could include almost any combination of two individuals who are involved in the crisis: mother-son, father-son, mother-daughter, father-daughter, boyfriend-girlfriend, boyfriend-boyfriend, roommates, and so forth. (Case study: Young adulthood, Chapter 7, p. 147.) The term crisis *group* refers to a collection of individuals who are unknown and unrelated to each other who meet as a group with a therapist to work together toward resolution of their individual crisis through group interaction (Case study: Mrs. L., Chapter 3, p. 40).

Treatment goals

The goal of a crisis group is that of returning the individual members of the group to at least their precrisis level of functioning and possibly to a higher level with an increased ability in problem solving. The focus of treatment (like that of crisis intervention individual therapy) is orientated to the present and to the problem that is of concern at the time the individuals request help. It deals with the stresses and balancing factors that are either absent or ineffective in the present crisis situation and is directed toward assisting the members to achieve a resolution of their crises. With the therapist the members explore the crisis-precipitating events, the crisis, past coping skills (what they usually do when they cannot handle anxiety, tension, and so on), situational supports (whom they usually turn to for help), and what is going on at the present time that is preventing them from solving their problems. The group members quickly become a cohesive group, actively involved in helping other members develop new coping skills and find situational supports. The therapist keeps them aware that the number of sessions is limited to six, using such methods as reminding them that a certain member has only two more sessions left.

Selection of participants

The determination of whether individuals requesting help in a crisis situation would benefit more from group therapy sessions than from individual therapy sessions is initially left to the discretion of the intake worker who sees the patient first. It might be that a group is being formed or that an ongoing group is oriented toward problems similar to the one in which the individual is involved. For example, there may be groups of married couples experiencing marital discord, parents with problems that involve their children, a group whose members are trying to break the drug habit, and adolescents with problems (family, drugs, juvenile authority, and so forth). Another consideration is whether another member can be added to the group. The crisis groups are open ended—its members enter and leave at different times; some will be beginning in the group, others will be halfway through, and others will be terminating. Five to eight members is usually considered the best size for a crisis group; it can fluctuate weekly as some members are absent or are terminated and new members are added. The therapist who conducts the group can control this by limiting the number of intake interviews scheduled each week.

Other crisis groups have differing rather than common problems as their focus. The purpose of including individuals in one of these groups would be because the interviewer believes that the individual would benefit more by interaction in a group than in a one-to-one relationship. It may be decided that part of his problem is due to inadequate interpersonal relations. The individual may be a social isolate by choice or by necessity, and his problem may be that he has never been able to establish satisfactory relationships with others because of low self-esteem, poor self-concept, or a real or imagined handicap; or he may be new to the area, functioning in a new job or school and having difficulty meeting and making friends and would benefit from a group experience. This also could be true with individuals who, although they might resist accepting the "advice of experts," would be more agreeable to changing faulty coping skills through group pressure.

If it is thought that a person would benefit from group therapy, he is told the time and day the group meets and is asked if he would be willing to participate. If he agrees, he is given an appointment for a pregroup interview with the therapist who will be conducting the group. In this interview the therapist assesses the individual and makes the final decision of recommending group or individual therapy. Determinations are made of the stressful event(s) that precipitated the crisis, the symptoms that are present, and the degree of disruption that the crisis is creating in the individual's life. If group therapy is the treatment of choice, the therapist discusses the format of the sessions. Explanations are made of the time element (six weekly sessions that last for 1½ to 2 hours), the necessity for focus on immediate problems, and the fact that some members will be new to the group and others will be terminating. If the group comprises members with a common problem area, a brief explanation may be made of who is in the group; for example: Mr. and Mrs. X. who have been married for 4 years and are having problems in their marriage similar to those of other members. This technique assists those seeking help to relax and feel that their problem is not unique, that they are not alone, and that they can expect other members of the group to understand and help them reach a solution to their problem.

Format of sessions

The format of sessions is highly individual, not only with the therapist but also with the physical environment or setting where the group sessions meet. Members may be asked to wait in a reception room until the scheduled hour before bringing them into the office (or room) that has been assigned. Again, depending on the therapist and the facility, a room may be set aside, the members going directly to the room and, in some cases, "starting" the session informally before the therapist arrives.

In the first part of the group session the therapist very briefly introduces new members and asks them to tell the reason why they came for help. The other members then tell the reason why they are there and will usually add at what stage they are in therapy and what they believe is being accomplished in the group.

Role of the therapist

The role of the therapist is active and direct. He functions as a participant leader in the group sessions, assisting the members to focus on the problem areas under discussion by restricting and diverting general social conversation and lengthy discussions of past occurrences that have no relevance to the present crisis of the individuals in the group. He also acts as a group facilitator and must be alert to the quiet, passive members and encourage their participation. Conversely, he must control and direct those highly verbal and dominant members without completely silencing them as participants. The therapist must be skillful in understanding and acting on nonverbal clues from the members of the group. An example of this was the silent wife who appeared to the group to be calm and unruffled while her verbal, aggressive husband in an angry tirade told the rest of the group about the problems he was having with their son who never talked to him, refused to mind, was never home, and so on. The therapist, observing the wife's nonverbal behavior (tense posture, hands folding her handkerchief over and over, lips tightly compressed — as if she did not dare to speak), interrupted the husband politely but firmly and asked the wife directly is this was the way their son acted toward his father. The wife looked at the rest of the group; they encouraged her, saying that she should know her son better than his father because she was with him more. Thus encouraged by the therapist and the group, she replied that their son did act this way toward his father and she believed that he had every reason to because he had no respect for him. Turning to her husband she said, "Why should he? Every time he sees you you are either drunk or mad at something and you are always fighting with him."

STUDIES OF CRISIS GROUPS

There is relatively little written about the effectiveness or ineffectiveness of crisis group therapy. Strickler and Allgeyer's (1967) pilot study done at the Benjamin Rush Center in Los Angeles was one of the first to test the feasibility of conducting group therapy using the crisis intervention model. In this study, consideration was given to the unique role of the therapist, the dynamics of the group process, and the group instrument that was structured to lend itself to the characteristic phases of crisis resolution.

Selection of members and structure of the group were in most respects similar to the general admission procedures for individual crisis intervention. No one was eliminated from group therapy because of severe pathology. After the initiation of the pilot group, it was found necessary to eliminate the following two groups of individuals: (1) those whom the therapist believed were seriously suicidal or homicidal and in need of more concentrated and individualized attention; and (2) those who were unable to relate to others because of a psychotic state or who, because of a language barrier, were unable to communicate in English. In the intake interview the individual was allowed the opportunity of choosing individual therapy over group therapy if he so desired.

The study, which was conducted over a 6-month period, served thirty patients and had an average weekly attendance of four to five sessions for each member. The size of the group in each session varied from four to eight members; five to six members each session were considered to be the optimum number for treatment purposes.

The crisis group at the Benjamin Rush Center was structured to correspond to the three sequential phases of crisis resolution. The first phase involved the formulation of the crisis situation for the patient, which was accomplished in the pre-group interview. The second phase constituted the utilization of the group to help the patient attempt to solve his problem. In the third phase the group reinforced and helped sustain the patient's confidence in his new way of coping.

A study by Morley and Brown (1968) explored the disadvantages and advantages of crisis intervention groups. Their study was carried out at the Venice branch of the Benjamin Rush Center. This clinic serves those individuals who are usually underrepresented in most mental health facilities: families with an annual income of less than $4,000, blacks, those of Mexican or Spanish-American descent, or those whose main family wage earner is a blue-collar worker. The criteria for accepting individuals into the group were similar to those previously used by Strickler and Allgeyer.

Morley and Brown listed several advantages of crisis groups and individual crisis intervention not typically available in "traditional" group or individual psychotherapy. First, it brings help to a number of individuals in need of treatment who might be unwilling or unable to enter into traditional treatment. This would include individuals who are willing to accept help with a problem but who do not consider themselves in need of psychiatric treatment for a mental or emotional illness. Second, many individuals are unwilling to agree to long-term therapy but will accept help for a particular problem carried out over a short period of time. Third, the universality of crisis provides a common meeting ground between patient and therapist, and the terminology and concepts seem to be more understandable and more acceptable to many individuals.

It was concluded that there seemed to be some disadvantages that occurred in the crisis group approach when compared with a traditional group approach. First and primarily, the analysis of group process, which is a powerful tool in traditional group work, had to be sacrificed to a certain extent. The time-limited and problem-oriented crisis groups made it impossible to make as much use of process analysis as with a longer-term group. The need to focus on each individual's presenting problem limited dealing with group interaction on any but a superficial level. Second, there seemed to be some loss of spontaneity. It was often necessary for the therapist to use the technique of "going around" to be certain that all members became active participants as soon as possible. Third, there was some loss of continuity and a greater need for repetition. The members were constantly changing, and new members needed to be brought up to date on the problem areas of the other members. Finally, transference interpretation was minimized. Negative transference interpretation was minimized because there was not a long-term relationship to give the individuals support if there was a sharp focus on strong negative feelings.

The study also compared crisis groups with individual crisis intervention. On the positive side, group support was apparent to a significant degree, and members of the group offered a considerable amount of help and assurance to particularly disturbed group members, both within and outside the group therapy session; significant social relationships often grew out of the group contacts, and group members were effective in suggesting alternate coping mechanisms to others in the group. The group provided an avenue for encouraging expression of feelings, and members who saw others in the group openly expressing their feelings were thus encouraged to express their own feelings.

On the negative side the primary problem was keeping each individual's crisis in sharp focus. With members presenting a wide variety of different crises, it was often difficult to keep each person dealing solely with the specific area necessary for successful resolution of the crisis. It was also difficult to identify the "correct crisis." In the second or third hour of therapy the original area identified as the crisis might be supplanted by another. In individual crisis therapy this could be reassessed and identified easier than in a group setting. Another problem area was that of destructive coping mechanisms offered by other members of the group. Because they did not understand the underlying dynamics operating within a particular individual, the suggestions they would make might be more maladaptive than adaptive. Morley and Brown believed that the group approach offered little or no saving of professional time. The pregroup interviews and cancellations seemed to have been of primary importance in producing this result.

One of the authors (Aguilera) also conducted crisis group therapy at this same center in Venice and concurs with the findings of Strickler and Allgeyer and those of Morley and Brown. The format of the sessions and admission to the group were essentially the same as those for the other studies cited, with one exception: The selection of members was made with a specific problem area in which to work. The problem area of the group was defined as those parents who were having problems with their young adolescents. These parents were seen in one group with the therapist, and their adolescent children were seen in another group with another therapist. The sessions usually lasted from 1 to 1½ hours and were scheduled concurrently for the same evening. There was close communication between therapists, usually immediately after a session. Occasionally it was decided that the parents and adolescents would benefit from a collateral session with both therapists present. This was usually scheduled either before or immediately following the group therapy session. These crises groups seemed extremely effective because of the specific focus on a problem area, and the interaction between the group members was exceptionally high. The members were able to support each other in decisions regarding their problems and to explore alternate ways of coping. During the intake interview and the pregroup interview the parent(s) and child were seen individually, and if necessary, together, to determine their reasons for requesting help, their willingness to enter a group, and the appropriateness of their membership in the group.

In order to present a brief overview of how group therapy functions using crisis-intervention techniques, a case study is presented to depict how the therapist and the group members interrelated in resolving their crisis.

It was initially believed by the intake worker that Mrs. L. would benefit more from group therapy than from individual therapy. She was by choice a social isolate and in all probability would resist efforts to modify her behavior with her daughter because she strongly believed that she was "right" and a "good mother." Cindy, in turn, would benefit from group therapy with those of her own age group to gain their support or have her actions invalidated by them. They were scheduled for their pregroup interview with the therapist.

Case study

Mrs. L., 42 years of age and a grandmotherly appearing woman, came to a crisis intervention center for her pregroup interview with the therapist, accompanied by her 14-year-old daughter Cindy. Cindy and her mother had been referred to the center for therapy by juvenile authorities. Cindy had run away from home and had been picked up by the police while trying to hitchhike to a well-known commune in northern California. When Mrs. L. was notified that Cindy had been found and was at the police station, she refused to come down, stating to the officer, "You had better keep her; I can't do anything with her!" She was told to come to court the next morning.

Cindy was held overnight in a juvenile hall. This had apparently been a terrifying experience for her. She said that she had shared a room with two other girls but had been too frightened to sleep because they threatened to kill her if she "reported on their lesbian activities." She stated she would do anything to avoid going back to juvenile hall or a similar corrective institution.

Cindy was very attractive and mature socially as well as physically. She was soft spoken and poised, was of above-average intelligence with A and B grades in school, and enjoyed tennis and playing the piano. She was well liked by her teachers but had few friends in her peer group.

Cindy told the therapist that she thought her mother's standards were too rigid and that she tried to keep her isolated from her own age group. She refused to let her participate in social activities or dating and would even wait for Cindy to get out of school and "walk" her home.

Mrs. L. said that Cindy had been a "good" girl until recently, very obedient, and so forth, and she could not understand her present behavior. When questioned about Cindy's father, Mrs. L. became quite angry and defensive and said they had been divorced for 6 years. She implied that she had "married beneath her" and that he drank too much and had difficulty in keeping jobs. It was the small amount of alimony and support for Cindy that had forced them to move from their original "middle-class" neighborhood to their present, low socio-economic area. She was apparently attempting to isolate Cindy from the "undesirable elements and people" in the environment. She saw herself as a "good" mother who was trying to maintain middle-class morality while living among a lower class.

Group session

Phase I. Formulation of crisis situation. Mrs. L. was introduced to the other members of the group and asked by the therapist to state what problem she was having with Cindy. She repeated her previous remarks to the group about Cindy running away and what she had done and said to the officer. When asked what had preceded Cindy's running away (the precipitating event), she became quite verbal. She said Cindy has asked to go to a neighborhood teen social center where a dance was being held. Mrs. L. refused, feeling that "Cindy was too young . . . she would meet the 'wrong' kind of people . . . the events were not properly chaperoned, etc., etc." While Mrs. L. was watching television in the living room, Cindy sneaked out of the house, went to the dance, and got back without being found out. The next day a neighbor informed Mrs. L. that her daughter had seen Cindy at the dance.

Mrs. L. immediately went to school, had Cindy called out of class, and confronted with the information. Cindy admitted she had attended the dance and that she would sneak out again if she got the chance. Mrs. L. slapped her, and Cindy ran from the school crying. When Cindy failed to come home that evening, Mrs. L. reported her missing to the police. Cindy was picked up the next afternoon. Mrs. L.'s previous method of coping, by denying the reality of the situation and by trying to isolate herself and Cindy from their environment, was no longer effective: Cindy was growing up and demanding more freedom and independence.

Group response. Some of the members of the group responded to Mrs. L.'s comments by making superficial supportive statements, such as, "It sure is difficult to raise kids these days!" and, "The kids must be acting this way because of the kind of world we live in." Others suggested that she was "too rigid," and, "You have to give the girl some freedom . . . she's not a baby anymore . . . you can't keep her a prisoner." Another offered alternate ways of coping: "You don't have to give in all the way, but give her a chance; if it doesn't work, then try something else." One member reminded her that her present behavior had *caused* Cindy to run away. Others challenged her with, "If you don't like the neighborhood, move; no one is keeping you there!" and, "If you don't have the money, go to work instead of staying home and playing the good mother."

Mrs. L.'s response to group. At first Mrs. L. reacted with hostility toward the group suggestions and confrontations. She still maintained her rigidity and saw her actions and behavior as justified. She rationalized them by stating firmly that she "couldn't care less what other people think," she knew she was right. Later, when the group members began making suggestions for different ways of maintaining discipline and still allowing Cindy some freedom, she responded with, "I'll consider it." She reacted warmly to those members who made supportive statements or suggestions and directed most of her remarks toward them. To the members who made negative statements she responded in an aloof, superior, cold manner and avoided conversation with then if she could.

Phase II. Intervention. In subsequent sessions Mrs. L. became more comfortable with the group members and felt less threatened. She began to adapt some of their suggestions in coping with Cindy. When the suggestions "worked," she always expressed her thanks to the member who had made the suggestion. She soon dropped her superior attitude toward group members and was able to express her feelings of guilt over slapping Cindy. She stated that she rarely had to punish Cindy because she was usually able to reason with her. She still maintained her "good mother" role in the group, and the group accepted her as an authority figure because she was very verbal and intelligent. They still challenged her rigidity and inconsistency about not wanting to work while Cindy was in school. She believed that she and her daughter were beginning to understand each other a little better.

The group members worked cohesively and sharply focused on specific problem areas. By the end of the third session they were interacting freely, testing new coping devices and reality testing within the group. Before the fourth group session the therapist had a pregroup interview with a Mr. G. His problems with his son appeared to be so similar to Mrs. L.'s that the therapist thought he would be a valuable addition to the group and would benefit from the group experience.

In the pregroup interview with the therapist Mr. G. expressed great concern over his son's changed behavior and appeared genuinely at a loss as to why he should now be presenting problems. He had also run away from home and had been picked up by authorities. He said he had tried hard to be a "good father" since his wife had left him 5 years ago, and he stated repeatedly how much he loved his son and what a good boy the son had always been before running away. Mr. G. appeared to be a very mild-mannered man and was quiet almost to the point of shyness.

He entered the group at the fourth session. After being introduced he began talking about his son and his problems with him. Very matter-of-factly, with little emotional expression, he calmly stated: "I'm a good father, I love my son, I can't understand why he has changed. I've beaten the hell out of him since he was 5 years old, and with the buckle end of the belt half the time, and he still won't mind." The group members were shocked into silence. The therapist, recognizing this, remained silent to observe the responses of the individual members to this different attitude about disciplining a child.

Group response. The group recovered from their state of shock over Mr. G.'s announcement and immediately began to attack him verbally. Mrs. L. emerged as their "leader" in the attack. Their comments were personal and cutting. Mr. G. countered their attack by becoming hostile and just as verbally aggressive. It was obvious that the focus of the group was, at this time, shattered because the group had deviated from problem areas to attacking an individual's attitude and character. The therapist stopped the "debate" and confronted the group with their behavior. After a discussion period the group, at the insistence of the therapist, began to redirect the focus to problem areas of concern. Mrs. L., as the group leader, began to explain to Mr. G. how the group functioned and brought him up-to-date on the problems they had been working on together. Mr. G. remained mostly silent for the rest of the session, giving his opinion only if asked directly by a group member or the therapist.

(Therapist's note: Mr. G.'s attitude and statements in the pregroup interview were totally different from those displayed in the group. I was caught completely unaware by his change in behavior. It was a very valuable learning experience for the group *and* the therapist!)

Phase III. Termination. By the sixth session Mrs. L. had apparently resolved her crisis with the help of group support. She and Cindy were getting along well together. (This information was verified by Cindy and her therapist.) She admitted that occasionally minor problems occurred but that she and Cindy were usually able to reach an agreeable compromise. She became quite friendly with several members of the group. They even visited at each other's homes. Thus, Mrs. L. was able to overcome her illogical isolation of herself and Cindy from the low-income community. The most dramatic and encouraging change in behavior in Mrs. L. was apparent when she announced in the last session that through the encouragement and help of another member, she had gotten a part-time job as a secretary at a local junior college. She had worked 3 days and, as she stated it, "I love it! I've never been happier and Cindy is so proud of me!"

It was at this session that the therapist and the group reviewed the progress and work they had done in the previous sessions to help Mrs. L. resolve her problem. Mrs. L. expressed some reluctance over terminating with the group. She was reassured by the members that they would "keep in touch." In an attempt to overcome her feeling of loss, Mrs. L. invited the entire group to her house for cake and coffee after the session. Everyone accepted the invitation.

SUMMARY

The behavior and personality of the individual may be changed by the forces of any group in which he is a member. Since World War II, the increasing awareness of the need to treat large groups of people has contributed to the rapid advances in the development and acceptance of group therapy and other therapeutic groups. An overview of therapeutic groups and group therapy has been presented to show the basis from which crisis groups evolved.

Two representative studies have been utilized for the purpose of showing their implementation, advantages, and disadvantages. A case study has been presented to demonstrate the use of crisis intervention techniques in a group therapy session.

REFERENCES

Asch, G.: Effects of group pressure upon the modification and distortion of judgment. In Guetzkow, H., editor: Groups, leadership and men, Pittsburgh, 1951, Carnegie Press.

Corsini, R. J., and Rosenberg, B.: Mechanisms of group psychotherapy, J. Abnorm. Soc. Psychol. **51:**406, 1955.

Hinckley, R. G., and Hermann, L.: Group treatment in psychotherapy, Minneapolis, 1951, University of Minnesota Press.

Luchins, A. S.: Group therapy; a guide, New York, 1964, Random House, Inc.

Merton, R. K.: Social theory and social structure, enlarged edition, New York, 1968, The Free Press.

Morley, W. E., and Brown, V. B.: The crisis-intervention group; a natural mating or a marriage of convenience? Psychother. Theory, Res. Prac. **6:**30, Winter 1968.

Slavson, S. R.: A textbook in analytic group psychotherapy, New York, 1964, International Universities Press.

Strickler, M., and Allgeyer, J.: The crisis group; a new application of crisis theory, Soc. Work **12:** 28, July 1967.

ADDITIONAL READINGS

Allgeyer, J.: The crisis group; its unique usefulness to the disadvantaged, Int. J. Group Psychother. **20:**235, April 1970.

Barten, H. H.: Children and their parents in brief therapy, New York, 1972, Behavioral Publications.

Berns, E.: Principles of group treatment, New York, 1966, Oxford Book Co., Inc.

Bloch, H. S.: An open-ended crisis-oriented group for the poor who are sick, Arch. Gen Psychiatry 18:178, Feb. 1968.

Christ, J.: The adolescent crisis syndrome; its clinical significance in the outpatient service. Psychiatric Forum 3(1):25, 1972.

Eisler, R., and Hersen, M.: Behavioral techniques in family-oriented crisis intervention, Arch. Gen. Psychiatry 28(1): 111, 1973.

Fallom, C. W.: Providing relevant brief service to couples in marital crises, Am. J. Orthopsychiatry 43(2):235, 1973.

Gazda, G. M., editor: Basic approaches to group psychotherapy and group counseling, Springfield, Ill., 1968, Charles C Thomas, Publisher.

Goldstein, S., and Giddings, J.: Multiple impact therapy; an approach to crisis intervention with families. In Specter, G.: Crisis intervention, New York, 1973, Behavioral Publications, No. 210, pp. 193-204.

Jew, C. C., and others: The effectiveness of group psychotherapy in a correctional institution, Am. J. Psychiatry 129(5):602, 1972.

Katz, M.: Family crisis training; upgrading the police while building a bridge to the minority community, J. Police Sci. Admin. 1(1):30, 1973.

MacGregor, R., and others: Multiple impact therapy with families, New York, 1964, McGraw-Hill Book Co.

Masserman, J., editor: Current psychiatric therapies, vol. 8, New York, 1968, Grune & Stratton, Inc.

Moreno, J. L., and others, editors: The international handbook of group psychotherapy, New York, 1966, Philosophical Library, Inc.

Pattison, E. M.: Group psychotherapy and group methods in community mental health programs, Int. J. Group Psychother. 20:516, 1970.

Pool, M., and Frazier, J.: Family therapy; a review of the literature pertinent to children and adolescents, Psychother. Theory, Res. Prac. 10(3):256, 1973.

Satir, V. M.: Conjoint family therapy, Palo Alto, Calif., 1964, Science & Behavior Books, Inc.

Sheff, A., and Wedge, B.: Crisis intervention in groups; some underlying considerations. In Miller, L.: Fourth International Congress of Social Psychiatry, abstract of papers, Jerusalem, 1972, Ahva Cooperative.

Slavson, S. R., editor: The fields of group psychotherapy, New York, 1966, John Wiley & Sons, Inc.

Small, L.: The briefer psychotherapies, New York, 1971, Brunner/Mazel, Inc.

Stratton, J.: Crisis intervention counseling and police diversion from the Juvenile Justice System; a review of the literature, Juvenile Justice, 25(1): 44, 1974.

Tarsh, M.: Community service with young adults. In Miller, L.: Fourth International Congress of Social Psychiatry, abstract of papers, Jerusalem, 1972, Ahva Cooperative.

Ten Broeck, E.: The extended family center, Child. Today 3(2): 2, 1974.

Toomim, M.: Structured separation with counseling; a therapeutic approach for couples in conflict, Fam. Process 11((3): 299, 1972.

Torop, P., and Torop, K.: Hotlines and youth culture values, Am. J. Psychiatry 129(6):730, 1972.

Zilbach, J. J.: Crisis in chronic problem families, Int. Psychiatry Clin. 2(8):87, 1971.

4 □ Sociocultural factors affecting therapeutic intervention

In a discussion of some of the sociocultural factors that can act as barriers in the psychotherapeutic process there are two aspects to be considered. First, there are the professionals who are frustrated when trying to give help to someone from a different and unfamiliar sociocultural background; and second, there are those in need of help who are frustrated when they do not receive the kind of assistance they feel they need.

The following will not attempt to cover the gamut of specific ethnic and cultural factors present in today's society, but an effort will be made to discuss certain key areas that are usually considered to be problems and to help the reader become aware of the nature of these difficulties.

The inability to understand and accept the attitudes and values of those who are not in our same educational, economic, and ethnic group is a major barrier. Professionals are aware of its existence, since they experience difficulty and are uncomfortable when trying to communicate with those who do not share their same standards and ideas.

One reason for this is the sociocultural background of the professionals. The majority are from the middle-class culture and have no difficulty in understanding and working comfortably with members of their own class culture. They speak the same language, have the same values ethically and morally, and share essentially the same expectations from life. When confronted with someone from a different sociocultural background seeking help, the professionals are frustrated in their desire to help because they may not understand what is being asked of them. Language and terminology are a mutual problem because codes of conduct and behavioral expectations are not always understood. Mutual suspicion is aroused, with the professional feeling that the individual does not really want his help, and the individual in need of help, not understanding what is expected of him, is uncomfortable and aggravates the situation of noncommunication.

Behavior and beliefs that are acceptable and highly valued in one cultural group may be unacceptable and devalued in another, or what is viewed as normal in one group could be abnormal in another.

Normal is the term society uses for social behaviors that are preferred, and *abnormal,* for those to which it objects (Benedict, 1934; Opler, 1956; Redlich, 1952). One of the big problems for social psychiatry is to determine just which feelings, thoughts, and actions are normal and which are abnormal. Who or what determines this? The term normal has several definitions. *Statistically* it can mean average, or the "norm." This is most likely to be seen in mathematical samples. When the term *adaptive* is used to mean normal behavior, it is more likely to be used psychiatrically. For example, normal behavior is the ability of the individual to adapt to ordinary environmental conditions without undue stress or anxiety. If the individual has more difficulty adapting to ordinary environmental conditions than the general group, his behavior could be labeled as being abnormal or maladaptive.

Benedict suggests that normality is culturally defined and cites as an example the behavior of the mystic who experiences trancelike states and catalepsy. In our general culture this could be considered abnormal behavior; in some cultures the greatest prestige is awarded to those who have trancelike experiences. They are considered blessed and are accorded the reverence due them as shaman in their communities. Their behavior is given cultural approval, and their roles as counselors and diviners are a necessary part of the social structure of their communities. It can be demonstrated in all cultures that honorable roles are assigned by society to those behaviors it needs and accepts, and devalued roles are assigned to those it no longer needs and rejects. From this frame of reference normality is defined by culture.

Consider the traditional Chinese culture, where the grandparents were revered by their descendants, bowed to, and given full obedience to their demands. Such expectations from grandparents in our culture would be considered abnormal. In some cultures suicide is considered to be a traditionally normal and honorable way to resolve problems. In Western culture it is generally considered abnormal to the degree that there are laws against it, religious as well as societal, and any attempts may be punishable as a crime against society. The same extremes of views among cultures may be held toward such actions as homicide, homosexuality, and polygamy.

DIFFERING CULTURAL VALUES

Widely divergent cultural perceptions are also found between the values accorded family roles, child-rearing methods, and the roles and status given individuals relative to their age, sex, occupation, marital status, religion, education, and so forth. Changes vary with the conditions under which society must function. There are constant problems facing every culture in adapting to the environs and attempting to maintain cultural equilibrium. Most of their norms are directed toward their basic needs for survival (Opler, 1956).

It is important to avoid stereotyping if there is to be understanding and communication between members of different cultural classes. Preconceived ideas about who does what, and why it is done, are the strongest barriers to understanding behavior and effecting change.

An example of this is the traditional middle-class culture. It has been both attacked and supported in recent decades. Its values and ideals have been called the backbone of our society and the cause of our weaknesses. Both opinions probably hold elements of truth. Because of its pervasive influence on all facets of our society, it has been scrutinized, criticized, praised, and derogated. Today, many think it an insult to be accused of "middle-class thinking." Values and ideals that were once considered to be inviolate are now being challenged.

Traditional middle-class culture

Before the depression years of the 1930's the traditional middle-class ideals and values were based on the Protestant ethic — the idea that hard work and self-control would lead to success. Traditions of social behavior were strongly adhered to, with emphasis on self-discipline, individualism, and clearly defined roles in the family and community (Haas, 1963; Seward, 1956). Social stability was the key word.

This was the culture in which proverbs were lived, not hung on the walls as "pop-art" decorations. "Early to bed and early to rise makes a man healthy, wealthy, and wise" was a way of life. So, also were "A stitch in time saves nine," "A rolling stone gathers no moss," "Virtue is its own reward," and the dozens of others that emphasized the goodness of industriousness, stability, and self-discipline, and the evils of laziness, instability, and lack of self-control.

The father was expected by society to reign unchallenged in his role as patriarch and breadwinner in his family. His wife obeyed him, and her role was relegated to the family, kitchen, and church. The children were expected to be obedient to both parents. Impulsive actions and aggressive hostility were frowned on. Family roles were clearly defined and were reinforced by the social institutions of the times (Seward, 1956). Traditional education emphasized discipline, order, and authority. Christian morality still held the puritanical tenets of fear of God's judgment for any real or imagined sins against His teachings. Sex was only a three-letter word, not acceptable for use in mixed company or "polite" conversation.

This was the era of strong conscience and of fear of punishment and social disfavor if any deviance were discovered. Today it would be said that the middle-class culture of that era was ruled by overly severe superegos. These were a tradition-bound, hard-working people who were, in many ways, the necessary source of stability in the rapidly changing society in the United States. As progressive changes occurred in the overall society, cultural changes followed.

New middle-class culture

The values and ideals of any culture reflect the attitudes and needs of its society. With technological advances the United States has become increasingly industrialized and urbanized. The core of the "old" middle class decreased in numbers. The predominating cultural values and needs of the rural independent farmers and the small-town entrepreneurs were supplanted by the changing needs of the urban middle class (Riessman and Miller, 1964). The children no longer were expected to be the tradition bearers of their rural home communities. They moved on to less stable urban areas, and the old ideals, attitudes, and values failed to meet their changing needs. Industriousness no longer was a guarantee of personal success. Too often a man was working for someone else, and self-employment was the exception rather than the rule. Authoritarianism and self-control were coming into conflict with the changing values of an increasingly technological society. Creativity, individual autonomy, and self-expression grew in cultural value.

Child-rearing and education goals reflected these changing ideals, attitudes, and values. Permissiveness and self-expression gained in favor (Riessman and Miller, 1964). Individualism gave way to the concepts of group membership, cooperation, and teamwork. High value was placed on the individual's ability to interrelate with others. Cultural emphasis on these last factors was exemplified by the never-failing request for evaluations of a person's interpersonal and communication skills in reference questionnaires sent out by employers.

The "new" middle-class culture shows the effects of the vast changes introduced into American society since World War II. Yet is retains the basic high valuation of thrift, industriousness, and self-control, which still permeate the structure of its institutions. Socioeconomic stratification of classes has diffused these values into other sociocultural classes.

TRADITIONAL TREATMENT METHODS

Federal legislation has made increased funding available for the development of community programs and facilities. Professional disciplines have refocused their activities to include consideration of the sociocultural components of mental illness. The accumulation of data over the past decade suggests that there are several important factors that are considered barriers to effective therapeutic intervention. Until ways are found to overcome these barriers, successful programs will be limited in the scope of their activities.

One of the main criticisms of the traditional psychiatric treatment methods is that they have become self-limiting by the very nature of their origins. Theories and techniques have been developed by professionals who come predominantly from the middle class and identify with its cultural values and goals. For example, Freud's psychoanalytic theories were based on his observations made in a middle-class continental culture with a relatively stable environment (Seward, 1956). His norms were a reflection of the norms of his culture, and his therapy was focused toward adaptation to those norms. One of his basic assumptions was that a patient would have enough time and money to continue in a long course of private therapy sessions. A prevailing theme in literature is the dominant middle-class character of the mental health movement (Haas, 1963; Riessman and Scribner, 1965; Yamamoto and Goin, 1965).

A number of studies (Heine and Trossman, 1960; McMahon, 1964; Myers and associates, 1968) have attempted to identify the character traits of the patient who might be most likely to "succeed" in psychodynamic-based therapies. The consensus describes him as a person who feels a strong need to relate to people, particularly when he has problems. He is psychologically oriented, has the intellectual capacity to deal with abstracts, is sophisticated in the jargon of psychiatry, and has some idea of the values and goals of psychotherapy. This makes it easier for him to communicate his feelings to the therapist. A basis for mutual understanding is more readily established. He is introspective in nature and probably has a strong tendency to blame himself, rather than others, for his problems. He is highly motivated to find out why he feels the way he does and how he can change his life-style to make things better for himself. He places a high value on self-control and on his ability to accept delayed gratification of his needs, and he expects to have to put much of his own efforts into getting those needs met. For these reasons he accepts the lengthy time that he may have to spend in therapy and has positive feelings that it will be well worth his efforts. These characterological traits reflect many of the basic ones reported for the middle-class culture.

Until the early 1940's the main focus of treatment was derived from theories stressing the organic and psychological causes of mental illness. This was followed by a shift, which included the effects of interpersonal relationships on behavior and personality. Current emphasis on sociocultural factors influencing mental health has stimulated broad research in this area, particularly in the relatively new field of social psychiatry.

The basis of psychiatric treatment is the establishment of meaningful communication between the therapist and his patient. If unable to accomplish this, the therapist has few alternatives to offer. In order to establish a meaningful base of communication the therapist's responsibility is to have some awareness, if not a full understanding, of the needs, values, and goals of his patient.

Members of one socioeconomic class may not actually understand or be aware of the needs, values, and goals of another. As a result of the increasing number of mental health programs being maintained by state and local governments, more individuals from substandard sociocultural groups are having their first contacts with mental health professionals. At the same time, many of the mental health professionals are having *their* first contacts with these groups in their home environments. The appropriateness of treatment modalities is being questioned not only by the professionals but also by the public receiving them.

CLASS STRATIFICATION SYSTEMS

Since Hollingshead and Redlich (1958) completed their study of the relationships between social class and mental illness, further studies in the field have supported their findings (Albronda and associates, 1964; Brill and Storrow, 1960; Haas, 1963; Myers and associates, 1968). Relationships have been found to exist between social class and the development, type, prevalence, and treatment of mental illness. It appears that the lower a person's location is on the socioeconomic class scale, the more restricted is the range of available therapies.

Defining social classes might be done through either of two main approaches. The first, the *statistical* approach, can be drawn from the socioeconomic levels of education, income, occupation, and place of residence. This is most frequently seen in industrial- and government-type reports. Although this will convey a concrete differentiation between the American system of socioeconomic classes, it does not include any criteria for the sociocultural life styles of different groups of people. If only the statistical method is used, there may be a strong tendency to stereotype people into classes using only the available economic information about them. Poverty level in one part of the country might well be a comfortable lower middle-class level in another.

The second method of defining social classes, *life-styles,* recognizes and accounts for the influences of the less well-defined, systematized behavior patterns, values, and life-styles of groups of people, and their interrelated effects on the socioeconomic classifications. In their study of a selected population group that was receiving psychiatric treatment, Hollingshead and Redlich (1958) utilized a classification format that took into consideration the values the subjects placed upon their education, income, occupation, and place of residence. They also developed a two-factor index (occupation and education) to determine social position. Occupation presumably reflected the skill and power that individuals possessed in society; education reflected not only knowledge but also cultural tastes. The proper combination of these two factors, using statistical techniques, enabled them to determine approximately the social position occupied by an individual in the structure of society.

In the collection and organization of their data they used a pattern of vertical divisions such as race, religion, and ethnic groupings. In addition they classified subjects in horizontal divisions according to their commonly held values attached to places of residence, occupations, educational backgrounds, and associations. This meant that, regardless of his race, religion, or ethnic grouping, an unskilled laborer with little formal education who lived in a poverty area of the community was ranked low in all of the vertical divisions' groupings.

Class I. This class consisted of the communitiy's business and professional leaders. Its members lived in the best areas of the community; the men were college graduates, and their wives usually have completed from 1 to 4 years of college. Income was the highest of any class, and members of the core group were descendants of the pioneers who settled in New England. The core group family was stable, secure, and socially responsible for its members and the welfare of the community. These families dominated the private clubs, and play was a prominent part of this group's use of leisure time.

Class II. Most of the adults in this class had some formal education beyond high school. The men occupied managerial positions, and many were engaged in lesser-ranking professions. Its members lived in one-family houses in the better residential areas. The families were well-to-do, but there was no inherited or acquired wealth. The nuclear family was composed predominantly of married adults and their minor children. They belonged to neighborhood clique groups, local church organizations, political clubs, and so on. Family members of all ages were "joiners."

Class III. The typical Class III man or woman was a high school graduate. The men were employees in various salaried positions: clerical, semiprofessional, or technical. The women also worked in clerical, sales, or technical positions. They tended to live in the "good" sections of the residential areas. The family included father, mother, and minor children but no other relatives or nonrelatives. Most members belonged to community organizations of one kind or another: fraternal orders, church clubs, athletic clubs, lodges, or veterans' groups. More men and women were dissatisfied with their present living conditions and less optimistic about the future than were those in Class II.

Class IV. The median years of school completed by the men was 9.4 years and by their wives, 10.5 years. The men were primarily semiskilled employees, skilled manual employees, or clerical and sales workers. Almost all of the women were working as semiskilled factory workers, clerical workers, or sales workers. The majority of the families lived in two-, three-, or multiple-family dwellings in the working-class sections of the city. The family income was spent, for the most part, as it was earned. The family constellation differed from that of Class III in four ways: There were more broken homes, more households had boarders and roomers, the families were larger, and there were more three-generation families living under one roof. Recreation consisted of "working around the place," watching television, listening to the radio, and family visiting. The husband belonged to the union but no other organization; the wife belonged to no formal organization but was a member of informal neighborhood women's groups.

Class V. This class had the poorest education in the population. The median years of school for men was 6 years and slightly less than 8 years for the women. The men worked as semiskilled and unskilled workers, and some had never had a regular job. Jobs in this class were poorly paid, requiring long hours for 6 or 7 days a week and in industries that were not unionized. Over two thirds of Class V persons lived in crowded tenement areas, the tenements housing from ten to fifty families. Family ties were more brittle in this class. Five types of families existed; the nuclear family of father, mother, and children; the three- or four-generation family; the broken nuclear residual families consisting of widows, widowers, or elderly couples; mixed families of one parent, children, and roomers; and the common-law groups. Only a small number of family members belonged to organized community institutions. Their social life took place in the household, on the street, or in neighborhood social agencies. Adults were resentful of the way they were treated by employers, clergymen, teachers, physicians, police, and other representatives of organized society.

An individual, for example, from Class IV or Class V could not invest the money or the time for extensive psychotherapy. His education level would limit his understanding of the psychotherapeutic goals and terminology. He would be more concrete and direct in his thinking, and not particularly introspective. If he sought help, he would want it immediately, not 6 months from now. He is inclined to regard authorities with suspicion and dislike and will only seek their help as a last resort. In the follow-up study by Myers and associates (1968), individuals in Class V of the Hollingshead and Redlich study were the ones who had remained institutionalized and usually ended up dying there or had repeated admissions. This validates their suspicions that they should not ask for help unless absolutely forced to because the only help available to them is in institutions.

LOWER SOCIOCULTURAL GROUPS

Current literature puts various labels on the lower sociocultural groups. These are, for the most part, indications of the specific areas within the lower-class structure being studied. Designations have been made such as the "underprivileged," the "poor," the "culturally disadvantaged," the "culturally deprived," the "migratory worker," the "blue-collar worker," the "disenfranchised," ad infinitum. The one fact that they all seem to hold in agreement is that there are people who, for one reason or another, will always be found clustered at the lower level of any class-stratification system. A clear-cut criterion for just exactly "who" these people are has not been developed, and inconsistencies in results of studies of similar populations bear out this fact.

There are many scales of class measurement, and a person does not necessarily fall into all lower categories at the same time. Just because an individual is the unemployed head of a household and living on the fringes of a poverty area is no reason to categorize him with the culturally deprived. If this were so, there would be a large mass of college students eligible for cultural poverty programs! On the other hand, a blue-collar laborer making a good salary could feasibly be described as culturally deprived if there were a lack of cultural programs available to him.

Societies are usually structured around institutions that they have created to provide for the "normal" needs of their population. Judgments as to its "abnormal" needs are most often made by the same group that has determined the norms for their culture. Only in the recent history of the United States has there been active recognition of the high variability of cultural norms and values, and values of the dominant sociocultural class are no longer being left unchallenged as being "good" or "bad" for all of the society's members.

BARRIERS TO THERAPY

All of the groups (ethnic, racial, occupational, age, and so forth) who live in the culturally and economically lower margins of society have been categorized as "lower class." Much of the tone of literature about them tends to have a negative quality. In terms of socioeconomic programs there has always seemed to be more interest in what could be done for them rather than with them. This was particularly evident in programs to effect changes in their ways of life; little confidence was expressed in their ability to change. Only recently has there been emphasis on a new theme — that of recognizing their strengths rather than just their weaknesses and of going into their communities and working in a cooperative effort with them to make changes they *they* feel are most necessary.

Mental health professionals are well aware that the attitudes of the general community toward mental illness are a keystone in the development of any treatment program and that they should be recognized as determining the goals of the services offered. To be effective, a program should be meaningful and seen as needed by the community groups it is meant to reach.

Crisis intervention is by *no* means restricted to those of the lower sociocultural levels; however, because of certain inherent factors it is thought that its techniques are more effective for those at this level than are the techniques of other types of therapy.

Jacobson (1965) has stated that motivating forces have universal elements and precede cultural differences. Typically, people are wary of strangers, and time is needed to assess new situations and strangers in the environment. Under such circumstances they are usually guarded in their speech and controlled in their actions. In emergency situations such as fires, earthquakes, and other catastrophes, individuals work together freely, barriers to communication are lowered, and sociocultural levels are disregarded. This occurs similarly when a person is in a crisis and comes for help. The element of strangeness is quickly overcome as the individual and the therapist concentrate on relieving the symptoms of stress even though they may be from different sociocultural backgrounds.

The time-limiting factor of crisis intervention is a distinct advantage with those individuals in the lower sociocultural group, who are focused on the here and now and want relief of their symptoms as soon as possible. Crisis intervention is directed toward helping the individual solve a specific problem. Major characterological and behavioral changes are not expected, nor are they dwelt on in the therapy sessions. This lessens the threat to him because he does not have to expose his complete pattern of living, which may be different from that of the therapist.

A community mental health center conceivably serves individuals from different sociocultural levels. Psychotherapy for an extended period of time may be too expensive for an average middle-class family or person, and it may not be needed if a crisis situation exists. Those who may now be considered middle class may have originally come from a lower sociocultural background and may retain its views regarding the value of psychotherapy and misconceptions about mental illness.

Referrals to a community mental health center come from multiple sources. Family physicians may decide that certain individuals need help with an emotional problem and make the referral; attorneys, juvenile authorities, clergymen, family service agencies, and others may also make referrals. The community itself is usually aware through publicity (radio, television, newspapers, word-of-mouth, and liaison personnel) of a community center's function and the services available. Because of this publicity and location in the community they may serve many who "walk in" for help.

Conversely, referrals from a community mental health center are also diversified and are usually highly individualized. A person may be referred directly for hospitalization if dangerously suicidal or homicidal, for longer-term therapy after crisis intervention for chronic problems, to a family service agency if needed, or to a rehabilitation center.

The prevalent attitudes toward mental illness in our society are less than favorable. There is still an aura of fear and anxiety surrounding overt mental disturbance. Much of this is due to the distorted ideas about what happens when a person "goes crazy" or "insane," which have been reinforced by the mass media (Tershakovek, 1964). Basic to many movies, television programs, or fiction that have been put out for the public are elements of fear, loss of control, and questionable "recovery" — believable yet grossly exaggerated for impact and saleability.

The lower sociocultural groups, in particular, fear mental illness (Riessman and Schribner, 1965; Myers and Roberts, 1959; Myers and associates, 1968). Often they fail to even admit its presence until there is overt psychotic behavior present. Frequently, outside help is asked only when a person becomes a threat and a danger to himself or others. And, just as frequently, the first "help" they receive is from the police who are called in for protection from the mentally ill person. Too often the family tries to keep the disturbed member at home until it is too late and he becomes unmanageable.

There are many cultural reasons for this. Many still consider mental illness to be inherited and passed on from generation to generation. To admit it is "in the family" could destroy any pending marriages, business associations, and, most certainly, the family status in the community.

Realistically there is good reason for the lower classes to fear it. Hollingshead and Redlich's study (1958) shows that Class V individuals had the greatest percentage who were in state hospitals and receiving custodial care.

Class V individuals saw mental illness as craziness, not as being sick. For this they saw only institutionalization as the answer. Fearing this end, they avoided seeking any help, even when it was obviously needed.

Other factors have been recognized as pertinent, basic needs of the lower sociocultural groups that must be met in treatment programs (Bloch, 1968; Hartog, 1967; McMahon, 1964; Riessman and Schribner, 1965; Yamamoto and Goin, 1965). Generally, they are oriented to the here and now; they cannot afford to wait for tomorrow and later. Too often theirs is a day-by-day existence. They have no reason to save up for a rainy day because for them it may rain every day.

Long-term therapy is not for them if for no other reason than its cost. If a day laborer has to choose between keeping a clinic appointment and getting a few hours' work, he will have to have concrete proof that he will get help if he keeps the appointment and will expect immediate feelings of relief for his symptoms.

The lower sociocultural families have had long experience with help from outsiders, and the past history of social intervention from outsiders has not done much to build their trust. Many have learned to mistrust the well-intentioned social welfare agencies that saw fit to move the aged or infirm away from their homes and into institutions "for their own good." They are familiar with situations in which children have been taken from "unfit" parents and placed in foster homes or similar child-care agencies. Too often their families have been measured against middle-class norms and found lacking in stability. Ineffective outside action has led only to further instability. How can they be expected to trust the mental health profession? Historically it has taken either adverse actions against them or neglected them completely.

Even more concretely, until they have active proof that conversation or "talking treatment" will help them, their basic needs for survival will outweigh any appeals from them for their emotional needs. Not knowing what to expect or value from psychiatry, they cannot be expected to immediately feed back their needs.

The following case study illustrates how a therapist worked effectively in crisis intervention with a married couple who sociocultural background was different from her own.

Case study

Tony and Marta, a young married couple with four small children, came to a crisis intervention center and requested help. They had originally gone to their parish priest for advice, and he had recommended that they seek professional help at a nearby community center. Tony was an unskilled laborer who worked for an airline as a maintenance man. He had finished the eighth grade in school; Marta had finished 9 years of school and had worked in a garment factory until right before the birth of their first child. They lived in a poor section of town in a house owned by Tony's mother. Their only recreation was watching television. Tony usually worked 6 to 7 days a week.

Tony was very angry and suspicious at the beginning of the session, whereas Marta appeared frightened and was reluctant to talk. When asked by the therapist as to "why they had come to the center," Tony replied that he thought his wife was crazy; he then began to explain her "crazy" behavior. The afternoon before, Marta had caught their oldest son (Joe, 9 years old) playing with matches behind the house. She flew into a rage, pulled him into the house, and burned his arm by holding it over the flame of the kitchen stove. Tony's mother had walked in while Joe was screaming. The grandmother learned what had happened, and she had grabbed Marta and forced her arm over the flame so she "could see how it felt." When the therapist asked Marta if this were "true," she nodded her head and began to cry. The therapist asked if she could see her arm. Together they removed the bandage; it was a rather large, second-degree burn. Marta said she had put a patented burn medicine on it and a dressing. The therapist told Marta that she would like the doctor to see her arm to give her an antibiotic prescription and some medicine to help her control herself. A medical consultation was arranged and while Marta saw the physician, the therapist met with Tony.

(Therapist's note: This maneuver served two purposes: first, it showed Marta and Tony that she wanted to provide immediate help; and, second, by her non-judgmental attitude and acceptance of their behavior, she established a basis for rapport.)

When Tony was alone with the therapist, he dropped his defensive attitude and showed his true concern for Marta's irrational behavior. When questioned about Marta's usual manner of coping with problems, he stated that he really did not know—usually she just "blew up" at him, and since it did not bother him, he ignored it. He stated that he loved his wife and children and he believed that she loved him and the children, too. When asked what he and Marta usually did together and with the children for pleasure, he said, "Are you kidding? I work 6 or 7 days a week . . . hard! I come home and I'm tired; I have a few beers, eat, and usually fall asleep in front of T.V." When asked what Marta usually did, he stated that she "took care of the house and kids."

When Marta returned from the medical consultation, the therapist repeated what Tony had told her. Marta said, "That's true . . . that's *all* I do: take care of his mother's crummy house and the kids!" Tony jumped on this immediately and said, "You have never gotten along with my mother . . . you hate her!" Marta said that she did not hate her . . . she just did not like her "always butting into our business and you always taking her side against me and the kids! I've told you I don't like living in her house, where she can walk in and out anytime she wants to; I want a place I can call my own. We pay her rent; we can pay rent someplace else . . . and get a better house too!"

Tony said, "You never told me you didn't want to live in Mother's house." Marta said, "I have . . . but you never listen!"

When asked about the possibility of moving, since Marta was unhappy with the living arrangements, Tony said his mother would "not understand," but "Marta and the kids mean more to me than anything."

The therapist thought at this time she could refocus on the problem that had brought them into the center. She asked Marta about burning Joe's arm. Marta said, "I was tired and upset; all I ever hear are the kids yelling and Tony's mother butting in and telling me everything I'm doing wrong . . . with the kids and the house; and Tony never tries to help or even listen to me. I just felt like I was cracking up!"

Tony was asked if there were any way he could help Marta. It was explained that it can be very exhausting taking care of four small children every day without a few hours "off." The therapist went on to tell Tony that his work kept him in contact with people all day, whereas Marta had no contact with anyone except his mother (who was an added irritant) and the children. Marta said that if only she could look forward to talking with him when she was upset, or even if she could go over to a friend's house for a few hours once or twice a week, "anything to get away for a few hours!" she knew she would be all right.

Tony very reluctantly said that he would put the kids to bed one night for her so she could go to a friend's house. The therapist said that it sounded like a wonderful idea and that what would really be good for them both would be if they could get out for a few hours together to talks things over. Their reaction was a cautious silence.

When Tony and Marta came for their next session, it was very obvious that they had had a good week. They were talking together quite animatedly when the therapist came into the waiting room to get them for their appointment. She remarked how well they looked, and how happy. Marta started talking about their week: Tony had put the kids to bed one night, as he had said he would, and she had gone to a friend's house to visit. She said it was really great to be out for a few hours. When Tony was asked how he had managed with the children, he looked embarrassed and said, "It was a mess! I don't know how she ever manages them all; no wonder she gets so tired!" It seemed that Tony could not get the children to go to sleep—or even stay in bed—without Marta there to control them. What he finally did was bring them all into the living room to watch television, and when they fell asleep, he carried them one by one to bed. The highlight of the week came when Tony told his mother not to come to the house and bother Marta. He had said that if she did, he and Marta would find another house and move. This made Marta feel so much better that she backed down a bit and told her mother-in-law that she could visit them but that she ought to call in advance to say that she was coming. The therapist told them how well they were doing in working toward solving their problem but cautioned them that there would be good weeks and bad weeks and if they began to talk *with* each other when problems arose rather than *at* each other, they could work out solutions more easily.

At the next session Marta had apparently stabilized, and Tony and she were relaxed and comfortable with each other and the therapist. Tony began by saying that they both really felt that they were capable of handling their problems now and did not want to return for more visits. He said that he could really understand Marta's feelings of being "hemmed in" and "trapped" when she was with the children constantly, all day and every day. He said a friend at work had invited them over for dinner the Saturday before, and instead of refusing as he usually did he had accepted. He asked his mother to stay with the children, and he and Marta went to dinner. He said that as he watched Marta laughing and talking, he realized how much he had missed their being together, alone, "like before we were married. I watched her and realized how pretty and young she really is and how much I love her. I'm going to do everything I can to help her with the kids . . . I know we can make it now!" The therapist agreed and wished them luck and told them that if they needed help again to feel free to return to the center.

Summary of case study

The therapist in this situation, even though from a middle-class background, was aware of the sociocultural background of her patients, and this knowledge was invaluable in the approach. Her attitude was nonjudgmental, concentrated on getting some immediate "help" (the medical consultation), and focused on assisting them with their problem. No attempt was made at characerological or insightful changes in their behavior, but she worked on the "here and now" and was very directive. Although she offered suggestions, no attempt was made at major changes in behavior. The terminology was kept at a concrete level, so she was able to talk with them in language they could understand. She attempted to give them the feeling that she was there to help them and that she would be there in the future if necessary.

CONCLUSIONS

It is our contention that crisis intervention is a logical treatment modality that transcends sociocultural classes. It can fulfill needs for immediate problem solving, it is direct and short term, and the therapist's role in it is an active one. No attempt is made to produce drastic behavioral changes. Its object is to reduce the symptoms of disequilibrium and to restore the individual to a precrisis level of functioning, with improved abilities to solve problems and more effective coping skills.

Community mental health centers, rather than large, isolated institutions, are where the "people" are. If therapists are to work successfully with people from all sociocultural levels, they should understand and accept the possibility that those who seek their help may have different attitudes and values. It should be the therapists' commitment to learn how to communicate with and meet the needs of those who seek help. The burden should not be placed upon them to change their life-style and patterns of living in order to get the help they are seeking.

REFERENCES

Albronda, H. F., Dean, R. L., and Starkweather, J. A.: Social class and psychotherapy, Arch. Gen. Psychiatry 10:276, 1964.

Benedict, R.: Anthropology and the abnormal, J. Gen. Psychol. 10:59-82, 1934.

Bloch, H. S.: An open-ended crisis-oriented group for the poor who are sick, Arch. Gen. Psychiatry 18:178, Feb. 1968.

Brill, N. Q., and Storrow, H. A.: Social class and psychiatric treatment, Arch. Gen. Psychiatry 3:340, 1960.

Haas, K.: The middle-class professional and the lower-class patient, Ment. Hyg. 47:408, 1963.

Hartog, J.: The mental health problems of poverty's youth, Ment. Hyg. 51:85, Jan. 1967.

Heine, R. W., and Trossman, J.: Initial expectations of the doctor-patient interaction as a factor in continuance in psychotherapy, Psychiatry 23:275, Aug. 1960.

Hollingshead, A. B., and Redlich, F. C.: Social class and mental illness, New York, 1958, John Wiley & Sons, Inc.

Jacobson, G. F.: Crisis theory and treatment strategy; some sociocultural and psychodynamic considerations, J. Nerv. Ment. Dis. 141:209, Aug. 1965.

McMahon, J. T.: The working class psychiatric patient; a clinical view. In Riessman, F., and others, editors: Mental health of the poor, New York, 1964, The Free Press.

Myers, J. K., Bean, L. L., and Pepper, M. P.: A decade later; a follow-up of social class and mental illness, New York, 1968, John Wiley & Sons, Inc.

Myers, J. K., and Roberts, B. H.: Family and class dynamics in mental illness, New York, 1959, John Wiley & Sons, Inc.

Opler, M. K.: Culture, psychiatry and human values, Springfield, Ill., 1956, Charles C Thomas, Publisher.

Redlich, F. C.: The concept of normality, Am. J. Psychother. 6:551, 1952. Republished in Bergen, B. J., and Thomas, C. S., editors: Issues and problems in social psychiatry, Springfield, Ill., 1966, Charles C Thomas, Publisher.

Riessman, F., and Miller, S. M.: Social change versus the psychiatric world view, Am. J. Orthopsychiatry 34:29, Jan. 1964.

Riessman, F., and Scribner, S.: The underutilization of mental health services by workers and low income groups; causes and cures, Am. J. Psychiatry 121:798, Feb. 1965.

Seward, G.: Psychotherapy and culture conflict, New York, 1956, The Ronald Press Co.

Tershakovek, A.: An observation concerning changing attitudes toward mental illness. Am. J. Psychiatry 121:353, Oct. 1964.

Yamamoto, J., and Goin, M. L.: On the treatment of the poor, Am. J. Psychiatry 122:267, Sept. 1965.

ADDITIONAL READINGS

Adams, P. L., and McDonald, F.: Clinical cooling out of poor people, Am. J. Orthopsychiatry 38:457, April 1968.

Barocas, H. A.: Urban policemen; crisis mediators or crisis creators? Am. J. Orthopsychiatry 43(4):632, 1973.

Blum, J. D., and Smith, J. E.: Nothing left to lose; studies on street people, Cambridge, 1972, Sanctuary Publishers.

Chilman, C. S.: Growing up poor, Washington, D.C., 1969, U.S. Department of Health, Education, and Welfare.

Cobb, C. W.: Community health services and the

lower socioeconomic classes; a summary of research literature on outpatient treatment (1963-1969), Am. J. Orthopsychiatry **42**:404, April 1972.

Craig, T. J., Huffine, C. L., and Brooks, M.: Completion of referral to psychiatric services by inner city residents, Arch. Gen. Psychiatry **31**(3):353, 1974.

Lavletes, R. L.: Crisis intervention with ghetto children; mythology and reality, Am. J. Orthopsychiatry **44**(2):241, 1974.

Lazare, A., Cohen, F., Jacobson, A. M., Williams, M. W., Mignone, R. J., and Zisook, S.: The walk-in patient as a "customer"; a key dimension in evaluation and treatment, Am. J. Orthopsychiatry **42**(5):872, 1972.

Lilienfeld, D.: Mental health information and moral values of lower-class psychiatric clinic patients, J. Soc. Psychiatry **15**:264, 1969.

Massie, H. N.: Neighborhood psychiatry in a mobile health unit; a report on psychiatric contact with adolescents and young adults in the Judson Mobile Health Unit in New York's Lower East Side in 1969 and 1970, Compr. Psychiatry **13**(5):420, 1972.

Torop, P., and Torop, K.: Hotlines and youth culture values, Am. J. Psychiatry **129**(6):730, 1972.

5 □ Problem-solving approach to crisis intervention

According to Caplan (1964:38), man is constantly faced with a need to solve problems in order to maintain equilibrium. When he is confronted with an imbalance between the difficulty (as he perceives it) of a problem and his available repertoire of coping skills, a crisis may be precipitated. If alternatives cannot be found or if solving the problem requires more time and energy than is usual, disequilibrium occurs. Tension rises and discomfort is felt, with associated feelings of anxiety, fear, guilt, shame, and helplessness.

One purpose of the crisis approach is to provide the consultation services of a therapist skilled in problem-solving techniques. This does not mean that the therapist will have an answer to every problem. However, he will be expected to have a ready and knowledgeable competency in problem solving, guiding and supporting his client toward crisis resolution. The therapeutic goal for the individual seeking help is the establishment of a level of emotional equilibrium equal to or better than his precrisis level.

Problem solving requires that a logical sequence of reasoning be applied to a situation in which an answer is required for a question and in which there is no immediate source of reliable information (Black, 1964:247-248). This process may take place either consciously or unconsciously. Usually the need to find an answer or solution is felt more strongly where such a resolution is most difficult.

The problem-solving process follows a structured, logical order of steps, each depending on the one preceding. In the routine decision making required in daily living, this process is rarely necessary. Most people are unaware that they may follow a defined, logical sequence of reasoning in making decisions, often only remarking that some solutions seem to have been reached more easily than others. Finding out the time or deciding which shoe to put on first rarely calls for long, involved reasoning, and more often than not the question arises and the answer is found without any conscious effort.

FACTORS AFFECTING THE PROBLEM-SOLVING PROCESS

Depending on the past experience related to the immediate problem, some people will be more adept at finding solutions than others. Both internal and external factors affect the process at any given time, although initially there may be only a temporary lack of concrete information. For example, when a driver finds himself lost because of a missing road sign, how much finding the right directions means to him in terms of his physical, psychological, and social well-being could affect the ease with which he finds an answer to the problem. Anxiety will increase in proportion to the value he places on finding a solution. If he is only out driving for pleasure, for example, he may feel casually concerned; but if he is under stress to be somewhere on time, his anxiety may increase according to the importance of his arrival to his immediate goals.

When anxiety is kept within tolerable limits, it can be an effective stimulant to action. It is a normal response to an unknown danger, experienced as discomfort, and helps the individual to mobilize his resources in meeting the problem. But as anxiety increases, there is a narrowing of perceptual awareness, and all perceptions are focused on the difficulty. When problem-solving skills are available, the individual is able to use this narrowing of perceptions to concentrate on the problem at hand.

If a solution is not found, anxiety may become more severe. Feelings of discomfort become intensified, and perceptions are narrowed to a crippling degree. The ability to understand what is happening and to make use of past experiences gives way to concentration on the discomfort itself. The individual becomes unable to recognize his own feelings, the problem, the facts, the evidence, and the situation in which he finds himself (Peplau, 1952:127-128).

Although problem solving involves a logical sequence of reasoning, it is not *always* a series of well-defined steps. According to Myer and Heidgerken (1962), it usually begins with a feeling that something has to be done. The problem area is generalized rather than made specific and well defined. Next, there is a search of the memory in an attempt to come up with ideas or solutions from similar problems in the past. March and Simon (1963) refer to this as "reproductive problem-solving," and its value is greatly dependent on past successes in finding solutions.

When no similar past experiences are available, the individual may next turn to "productive problem solving," Here he is faced with the need to construct new ideas from more or less raw data. He will have to go to sources other than himself to get his facts. For example, the driver looking for the road sign may find someone nearby who can give him the needed new data; directions to the right road. If there is no one nearby, he will have to find some other source of information. He may resort to trial and error and with luck and patience find the way himself. Finding a solution in this way may meet a present need, but the information gained may not always be applicable to solving a similar problem in the future.

PROBLEM SOLVING IN CRISIS INTERVENTION

John Dewey (1910) proposed the classical steps or stages represented in different episodes of problem solving: (1) a difficulty is felt, (2) the difficulty is located and defined, (3) possible solutions are suggested, (4) consequences are considered, and (5) a solution is accepted. With minor modifications, these steps in problem solving have been persistent over the years. Johnson (1955) simplified problem solving by reducing the number of steps to three: preparation, production, and judgment.

In 1962 Merrifield and associates conducted extensive research on the role of intellectual factors in problem solving. They advocated return to a five-stage model, with preparation, analysis, production, verification, and reapplication. The fifth term was included in recognition of the fact that the problem solver often returns to earlier stages in a kind of revolving fashion.

According to Guilford (1967), the general problem-solving model involves the following process. (1) *input* (from environment and soma), (2) *filtering* (attention aroused and directed), (3) *cognition* (problem sensed and structured), (4) *production* (answers generated), (5) *cognition* (new information obtained), (6) *production* (new answers generated), (7) *evaluation* (input and cognition tested, answers tested; new tests of problem structure, new answers tested).

Assessment of the individual and his problem

When professional help is sought because a person is in crisis, the therapist must use logic and background knowledge to define the problem and plan intervention. The model for problem solving in the crisis approach will be readily familiar to mental health professionals.

The crisis approach to problem solving involves an assessment of the individual and his problem, planning of therapeutic intervention, intervention, and resolution of the crisis and anticipatory planning (Morley and others, 1967).

Assessment begins when the individual requesting help is seen by a therapist. The first therapy session is directed toward finding out what the crisis-precipitating event was and what factors are affecting his ability to solve problems.

It is important that both therapist and patient be able to define a situation clearly before taking any action to change it. Questions are asked such as "What do I need to know?" and "What must be done?" The more specifically the problem can be defined, the more likely it is that the "correct" answer will be sought.

Clues are investigated to point out and explore the problem or what is happening. The therapist asks questions and uses observational skills to obtain factual knowledge about the problem area. It is important to know what has happened within the immediate situation. How the individual has coped in past situations may affect his present behavior. Observations are made to determine his level of anxiety, expressive movements, emotional tone, verbal responses, and attitudinal changes.

It is important to remember that the therapist's task is that of focusing on the immediate problem. There is not enough time and *no need* to go into the patient's past history in depth.

One of the therapist's first questions usually is, "Why did you come for help today?" It is important to be emphatic about using the word *today*. Sometimes the individual will try to *avoid* stating why he came by saying: "I've been planning to come for some time." The usual reply is, "Yes, but what happened that made you come in *today?*" Other questions to ask are, "What happened in your life that is *different? When* did it happen?"

In crisis the precipitating event usually has occurred within 10 to 14 days before the individual seeks help. Frequently it is something that happened the day before or the night before. It could be almost anything: threat of divorce, discovery of extramarital relations, finding out their son or daughter is on drugs, loss of boyfriend or girlfriend, loss of job or status, an unwanted pregnancy, and so forth.

The next area on which to focus is the individual's perception of the event: What does it mean to him? How does he see its effect on his future? Does he see the event realistically, or does he distort its meaning?

The patient is then questioned about available situational supports: What person in the environment can the therapist find to support the person? With whom does he live? Who is his best friend? Whom does he trust? Is there a member of the family to whom he feels particularly close? Crisis intervention is sharply time limited, and the more people involved in helping the person the better. Also, when therapy is terminated, if others are involved and familiar with the problem they can continue to give support.

The next area of focus is to ascertain what the person usually does when he has a problem he cannot solve: What are his coping skills? He is asked the following: Has anything like this ever happened to him before? How does he usually abate tension, anxiety, or depression? Has he tried the same method this time? If not, why not, if it usually works for him? If his usual method was tried and it did not work, the therapist asks, *why*. What does he feel would reduce his symptoms of stress? Something is usually thought of; coping skills are so very individual. Methods of copying with anxiety that have not been used in years may be remembered. One man recalled that he used to "work off tensions" by playing the piano for a few hours, and it was suggested that he try this method again. Since he did not have a piano, he rented one; by the next session his anxiety had reduced enough to enable him to begin problem solving.

One of the most important parts of the assessment is to find out whether the individual is suicidal or homicidal. The questions must be very *direct* and *specific:* Is he planning to kill himself or someone else? How? When? The therapist must find out and assess the seriousness of the threat: Is he merely thinking about it or does he have a method selected? Is it a lethal method—a loaded gun? Is a tall building or bridge picked out? Can he tell you when he plans to do it—for example, after the children are asleep?

If the threat does not seem too imminent, the individual is accepted for crisis therapy. If the intent is carefully planned and details are specific, hospitalization and psychiatric evaluation are arranged in order to protect him or others in the community.

Planning of therapeutic intervention

After identifying the precipitating event and the factors that are influencing the individual's state of disequilibrium, the therapist plans the method of intervention. Determination must be made as to how much the crisis has disrupted the individual's life. Is he able to work? Go to school? Keep house? Care for his family? Are these activities being affected? This is the first area to examine for the degree of disruption. How is his state of disequilibrium affecting others in his life? How does his wife (or husband, boyfriend, girlfriend, roommate, or family) feel about this problem? What do they think he should do? Are they upset?

This is basically a search process in which data are collected. It requires the use of cognitive abilities and recollection of past events for information relative to the present situation. The last phase of this step is essentially a thinking process in which alternatives are considered and evaluated against past experience and knowledge as well as in the context of the present situation.

Tentative solutions are advanced as to *why* the problem exists. This requires familiarity with theoretical knowledge and the anticipation of more than one answer. In the study of behavior it is important to seek casual relationships. Clues observed in the environmental conditions are examined and related to theories of psychosocial behavior to suggest reasons for the individual's disturbed equilibrium.

Intervention

In the third step invervention is initiated. Action is taken with the expectation that if _____ is taken, the _____ will occur.

(planned action)   (expected result)

After the necessary information is collected, the problem-solving process is continued to initiate intervention. The therapist defines the problem from the information that has been given and reflects it back to the individual. This clarifies the problem and encourages focusing on the immediate situation. The therapist then explores possible alternate solutions to the problem to reduce the symptoms produced by the crisis. At this time, specific directions may be given as to what should be tried as tentative solutions. This enables the individual to leave the first session with some positive guidelines for going out and testing alternate solutions. At the next session the individual and therapist evaluate the results, and if none of these solutions has been effective, they work toward finding others.

The therapist may validate observations and tentative conclusions by reviewing the case with another therapist when deeming that it may be helpful or necessary. Briefly, the therapist identifies the crisis-precipitating event, symptoms that the crisis has produced in the individual, the degree of disruption evident in the individual's life, and the plan for intervention. Planned intervention may include one technique or a combination of several techniques. It may be helping the individual to gain an intellectual understanding of the crisis or helping him to explore and ventilate his feelings. Other techniques may be helping the individual to find new and more effective coping mechanisms or utilizing other people as situational supports. Finally, a plan would be presented for helping the person to establish realistic goals for the future.

Anticipatory planning

Evaluation is made to determine whether or not the planned action has produced the expected results. Appraisal must be objective and impartial in order to be valid. Has the individual returned to his usual or higher level of equilibrium in his functioning? The problem-solving process is continued as the therapist and the individual work toward resolution of the crisis.

PARADIGM OF INTERVENTION

According to Caplan (1964:40-41), there are four developmental phases in a crisis:

1. There is an initial rise in tension as habitual problem-solving techniques are tried.

2. There is a lack of success in coping as the stimulus continues and more discomfort is felt.

3. A further increase in tension acts as a powerful internal stimulus and mobilizes internal and external resources. In this stage emergency problem-solving mechanisms are tried. The problem may be redefined or there may be resignation and the giving up of certain aspects of the goal as unattainable.

4. If the problem continues and can neither be solved or avoided, tension increases and a major disorganization occurs.

Whenever a stressful event occurs, there are certain recognized balancing factors that can effect a return to equilibrium; these are perception of the event, available situational supports, and coping mechanisms as shown in Fig. 1.

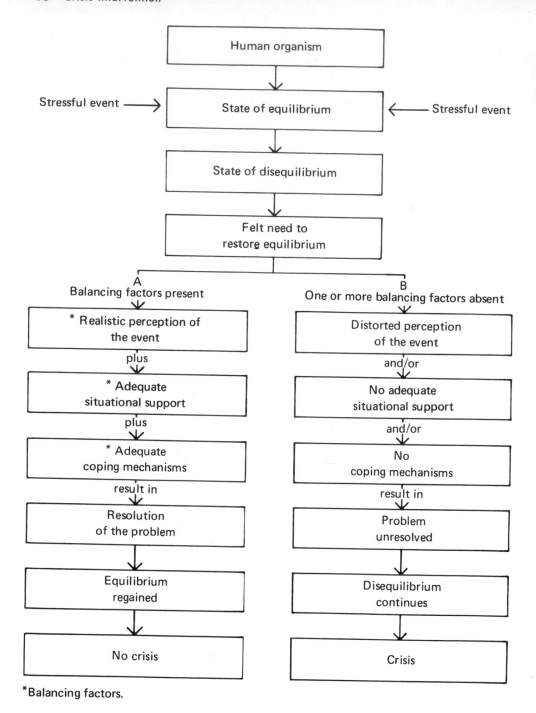

*Balancing factors.

Fig. 1. □ Paradigm: effect of balancing factors in a stressful event.

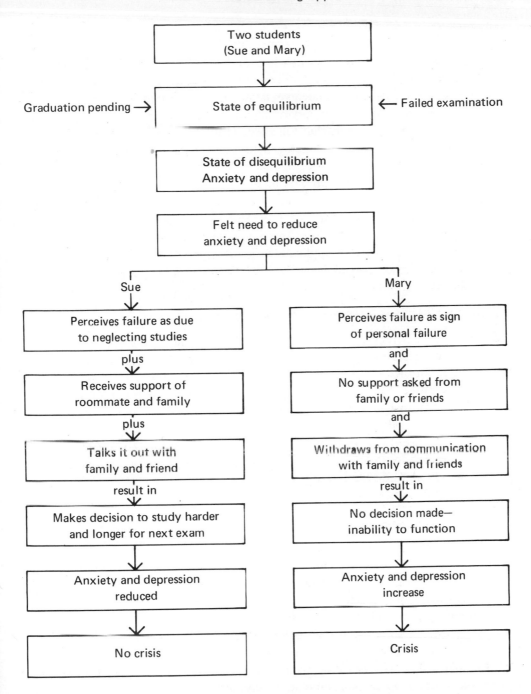

Fig. 2. □ Paradigm applied to case studies.

The upper portion of the paradigm illustrates the "normal" initial reaction of an individual to a stressful event.

A stressful event is seldom so clearly defined that its source can be determined immediately. Internalized changes occur at the same time as the externally provoked stress, and as a result, some events may cause a strong emotional response in one person, yet leave another apparently unaffected. Much is determined by the presence or absence of factors that can effect a return to equilibrium.

In column *A* of Fig. 1 the balancing factors are operating and crisis is avoided. However, in column *B* the absence of one or more of these balancing factors may block resolution of the problem, thus increasing disequilibrium and precipitating crisis.

Fig. 2 demonstrates the use of the paradigm for presentation of subsequent case studies. Its purpose is to serve as a guideline to focus the reader on the problem areas. An example of its applicability is presented in the cases of two people affected by the same stressful event. One resolved the problem and avoided crisis; the other did not.

BALANCING FACTORS AFFECTING EQUILIBRIUM

Between the perceived effects of a stressful situation and the resolution of the problem are three recognized balancing factors that may determine the state of equilibrium. Strengths or weaknesses in any one of the factors can be directly related to the onset of crisis or to its resolution. These are perception of the event, available situational supports, and coping mechanisms.

Why do some people go into crisis when others do not? In Fig. 2 this is illustrated by the cases of two students, Sue and Mary. Both fail a final examination. Sue is upset but does not go into crisis. Mary *does* go into crisis. Why does Sue react one way and Mary differently to the same stressful event? What "things" in their present lives make the difference?

Perception of the event

If the event is perceived realistically, there will be recognition of the relationship between the event and feelings of stress. Problem solving can be appropriately oriented toward reduction of tension, and successful solution of the stressful situation will be more probable.

If the perception of the event is distorted, there may be no recognition of a relationship between the event and feelings of stress. Thus attempts to solve the problem will be ineffective, and tension will not be reduced.

In other words, what does the event mean to the individual? How is it going to affect his future? Can he look at it realistically, or does he distort its meaning? For example, Sue sees failing the examination as the result of not studying enough or of concentrating on the wrong material and decides it will not happen again. Mary, on the other hand, thinks that failing the examination makes *her* a failure; she feels threatened and believes she will never graduate from college.

Situational supports

By nature, man is social and dependent on others in his environment to supply him with reflected appraisals of his own intrinsic and extrinsic values. In establishing his life patterns, certain appraisals are more significant to him than others because they tend to reinforce the perception he has of himself. Dependency relationships may be more readily established with those whose appraisals tend to support the individual against feelings of insecurity and who reinforce feelings of ego integrity.

Loss, threatened loss, or feelings of inadequacy in a supportive relationship may leave the individual in a vulnerable position, so that when confronted with a stressful situation, the lack of situational support may lead to a state of disequilibrium and possible crisis.

Situational supports mean those persons who are available in the environment who can be depended on to help solve the problem.

Sue talked to her roommate about her feelings over failing the exam; she even cried on her shoulder. She also called home for reassurance from her family. In effect; *someone* had been found for support during this stressful event.

Mary did not feel close enough to her roommate to talk about the problem. She had no close friends whom she trusted. Fearing their reaction, she did not call home to tell her family about failing. Mary did not have *anyone* to turn to for help; she felt overwhelmed and alone.

Coping mechanisms

Through the process of daily living the individual learns to use many methods to cope with anxiety and reduce tension. Life-styles are developed around patterns of response, which in turn are established to cope with stressful situations. These life-styles are highly individual and quite necessary to protect and maintain equilibrium.

Tension-reducing mechanisms can be overt or covert and can be consciously or unconsciously activated. They have been generally classified into such behavioral responses as aggression, regression, withdrawal, and repression. The selection of a response is based on tension-reducing actions that successfully relieved anxiety and reduced tension in similar situations in the past. Through repetition it may pass from conscious awareness during its learning phase to a habitual level of reaction as a learned behavior. In many instances the individual may not be aware of *how,* let alone *why,* he reacts to stress in given situations. Except for vague feelings of discomfort, the rise and consequent reduction in tension may pass almost unnoticed. When a novel stress-producing event arises and learned coping mechanisms are ineffectual, discomfort is felt on a conscious level. The need to "do something" becomes the focus of activity, narrowing perception of all other life activities.

Available coping mechanisms are what people *usually* do when they have a problem. They may sit down and try to think it out or talk it out with a friend. Some cry it out or try to get rid of their feelings of anger and hostility by swearing, kicking a chair, or slamming doors. Others may get into verbal battles with friends. Some may react by temporarily withdrawing from the situation in order to reassess the problem. These are just a few of the many coping methods people use to relieve their tension and anxiety when faced with a problem. Each of these has been used at some time in the developmental past of the individual, found effective to maintain emotional stability, and become part of his life-style in meeting and dealing with the stresses of daily living.

Sue used her roommate to talk it out; this reduced her tension and anxiety. She was able to solve the problem and decided that for the next exam she would study more, over a longer period of time. Her tension and anxiety were reduced, equilibrium was restored, and she did not have a crisis.

Mary withdrew. She had no coping skills to use, and her tension and anxiety increased. Unable to solve the problem and unable to function, she went into crisis.

REFERENCES

Black, M. Critical thinking; an introduction to logic and scientific method, Englewood Cliffs, N. J., 1946, Prentice-Hall, Inc.

Caplan, G.: Principles of preventive psychiatry, New York, 1964, Basic Books, Inc., Publishers.

Dewey, J.: How we think, Boston, 1910, Heath Co.

Guilford, J. P.: The nature of human intelligence, New York, 1967, McGraw-Hill Book Co.

Johnson, D. M.: The psychology of thought and judgment, New York, 1955, Harper & Row, Publishers.

March, J. G., and Simon H. A.: Organizations, New York, 1963, John Wiley & Sons, Inc.

Merrifield, P. R., Guilford, J. P., Christensen, P. R., and Frick, J. W.: The role of intellectual factors in problem-solving, Psychol. Monogr. 76(10), 1962.

Morley, W. E., Messick, J. M., and Aguilera, D. C.: Crisis; paradigms of intervention, J. Psychiatr. Nurs. 5:538, Nov.-Dec. 1967.

Myer, B., and Heidgerken, L. E.: Introduction to research in nursing, Philadelphia, 1962, J. B. Lippincott Co.

Peplau, H. E.: Interpersonal relations in nursing, New York, 1952, G. P. Putnam's Sons.

6 □ Situational crises

Whenever stressful events occur in a person's life situation that threaten his sense of biological, psychological, or social integrity, there is some degree of disequilibrium resulting and the concurrent possibility of a crisis. Several determining factors affect the positive balance of equilibrium, and the absence of one or more could make a state of crisis more imminent.

According to Rapoport (1962), when an instinctual need or a sense of integrity is threatened, the ego usually responds characteristically with anxiety; when loss or deprivation occur, the response is usually depression. On the other hand, if the threat or loss is viewed as a challenge, there is more likely to be a mobilization of energy toward purposeful problem-solving activities.

That which may create only a feeling of mild concern in one person may create a high level of anxiety and tension in another. Recognized factors influencing a return to a balance of equilibrium are the perception of the event, available coping mechanisms, and available situational supports. Crises may be avoided if these factors are operating at the time the stressful event(s) is intruding into the individual's life-style.

Studies have been made of behavior patterns that might be anticipated in response to common stressful situations. These have provided valuable clues to anticipatory planning for prevention as well as intervention in crisis situations. Some of these are combat neurosis (Glass, 1957), relocation through urban renewal (Brown and associates, 1965), rehabilitation of families after tornado disasters (Moore, 1958), hospitalized children and adolescents (Vernick, 1963), unwed mothers (Bernstein, 1960), separation anxiety of hospitalized children (Bowlby, 1960), and death and dying (Kübler-Ross, 1969, 1974). These studies suggest that there are certain patterned phases of reactions to unique stressful situations through which select groups of people can be expected to pass before equilibrium is restored. Preventive techniques of community psychiatry focus on anticipatory intervention; this is to prevent crises that could result from maladaptive responses as individuals attempt to return to equilibrium.

In this chapter, stressful events that could precipitate a crisis have been selected on the premise that each could affect some member of a family, regardless of its socioeconomic or sociocultural status. The case studies selected are not to be considered all-inclusive of the many situational crises with which a therapist may come in contact.

It is also important to recognize that the theoretical material preceding each case study is presented as an overview, relevant to the crisis situation. Those therapists already trained in crisis intervention will recognize the need for much greater depth of theoretical knowledge than is presented in this chapter. The intent is only to provide guidelines; further study of problem areas is suggested for more comprehensive knowledge.

In order to clarify the steps in crisis intervention, much extraneous case study material has been eliminated. In crisis a person may be confronted with *many* stressful events occurring simultaneously. He may have no conscious awareness of *what* occurred, let alone which event requires priority in problem solving. The studies may appear oversimplified to anyone who has struggled through the phases of defining the problem and planning appropriate intervention.

The paradigm is a means we devised to keep the reader focused on the problem area and on the balancing factors that influence the presence or absence of crisis. We doubt if it could be successfully used as a form that could be quickly completed after the initial assessment interview; rarely are stressful events so easily defined. It is the very nature of a crisis that interrelated internal and external stresses compound the problem area and distort the causes of objective and subjective symptoms.

One responsibility essential in assuming the role of a therapist in this method of intervention is recognition of the need for knowledge of the generic development of crises.

PREMATURITY
Theoretical concepts

The birth of a premature baby is a stressful situation for any family. Even when anticipated, there is a sense of emergency both at home and in the hospital when labor begins. In the hospital, both staff and parents feel anxiety for the potential welfare of the newborn infant.

Researchers have identified the following four phases or tasks the mother must work through if she is to come out of the experience in a healthy way (Mason, 1963; Kaplan, 1965).

1. She must realize that she may lose the baby. This anticipatory grief involves a gradual withdrawal from the relationship already established with the child during the pregnancy.

2. She must acknowledge failure in her maternal function to deliver a full-term baby.

3. After separation from the infant due to its prolonged hospital stay she must resume her relationship with it in preparation for the infant's homecoming.

4. She must prepare herself for the job of caring for the baby through an understanding of its special needs and growth patterns.

After delivery the infant is hurriedly taken to the premature nursery. The parents have barely had a glimpse of their new son or daughter and certainly have had no opportunity to reassure themselves about its condition. The infant is isolated from all except the medical personnel during its hospital stay, and the parents, denied physical contact with the child, cannot allay their anxieties. There is a realistic danger that the baby will not live or that it will not be normal. Often physicians and nurses talk about the baby in guarded terms, not wanting to give false reassurance, so that the feeling of anxiety may last for days or weeks.

The way in which the family react to this period of stress is crucial in determining whether or not a crisis will develop. These studies of families who have experienced the stress of a premature birth show that some have managed very well; the mother was not apprehensive about caring for the baby, despite the special attention it required. In these families the relationship between husband and wife was found to be good; they seemingly had adjusted to the new member of the family, and their relationship was not threatened by the increased responsibility.

Other families studied appeared to be in a state of crisis, although the premature infant was out of danger. In those cases the relationship between the husband and wife was determined to be unstable. The baby was cared for by an overly apprehensive mother who often seemed unconcerned about important things such as his weight gain, whether or not he was eating adequately, and his immediate prognosis.

It has been hypothesized that women who were most disturbed during the period when there was real danger to the baby dealt with this stress more effectively (Caplan, 1964:290). Women who showed symptoms of a crisis were those who seemingly denied the existence of any danger. They did not question the information given them nor the reassurances of the treating personnel. In fact, they seemed to encourage a conspiracy of silence, avoiding any confrontation with feelings of fear, guilt, and anxiety.

Many emotions develop in parents when a new baby arrives, even when the child is full term. The mother is called upon to meet additional demands on her time and may feel hostility toward the new baby. Usually, however, the strong feeling of mother love ensures repression of any resentment she may feel and the guilt it inspires. The usual activities of the father are not as directly interrupted, so that his resentment is usually less than that of the mother and is more often aroused by jealousy of the attention that the mother gives to the baby.

The following case study concerns a young mother of a premature baby. Clues from the initial assessment interview indicated that she was acknowledging herself to be a failure for not delivering a full-term baby. Intervention focused on relieving the immediate causes of her anxiety and depression and assisting her to adapt to subsequent phases in the characteristic responses to a premature birth.

Case study: Prematurity
Assessment of the individual and his problem

Laura and Peter G. were a young couple who had been married for 3 years. Peter, 5 years older than Laura, was the oldest of four children. Laura, a petite young woman, was an only child. They had a daughter 2 years old and a son 2 months of age who was born prematurely.

Peter's company had transferred him to another city when Laura was 7½ months pregnant; she went into labor the day after moving into their new home 100 miles from their home town, where both their families lived. She delivered their son in a private hospital with excellent facilities but under the care of an obstetrician previously unknown to her due to their recent move. She was upset by the strangeness of the hospital, by the new physicians and by the precarious physical condition of the son she and Peter had been hoping for. Laura did not want to discuss her fears with Peter, because she knew he was also concerned about the baby, and she did not want to add to his worries. Laura did not feel free to discuss her fears with her physician, because she did not know him, or with the nurses, because they "always seemed so busy." She also thought that since she had had a baby before, she should know the answers to all the questions she had in mind.

After she and Peter brought their son home from the hospital, Laura had episodes of crying and was experiencing symptoms of anxiety, including insomnia. She felt physically exhausted and increasingly fearful concerning her ability to care for her son. No matter what she did, the baby slept only for short periods and was more fretful when awake than their daughter had been. Because of the baby's small size, Peter was afraid to help with his care, so Laura was responsible for all his physical care.

Peter's mother arrived for a visit "to see how the new baby was doing." she had been critical of Laura's intention to move at the time of Peter's transfer, advising that Laura should wait until after the baby's birth. Laura had now begun to think that she should have followed that advice. Her mother-in-law and she often had talks about the rearing of children. Laura had begun to have confidence in her own mothering abilities as a result of her daughter's good health and average development, but now she was doubtful again because of her apparent inability to care for her new son.

Planning of therapeutic intervention

The event that precipitated the crisis was the visit of a mother-in-law who was critical of Laura's ability to care for her new baby. "I can't understand why the baby cries so much. You must be doing something wrong. My children always slept through the night by 2 months of age and took long naps during the day," were typical of her constant comments. Peter seemed reluctant to take sides against his mother, so Laura received little support from him in dealing with these criticisms. She was finally unable to cope with her feelings of inadequacy, which were intensified by her mother-in-law's visit, and as a result became extremely upset, cried uncontrollably, and was unable to care for the baby at all. Peter's employer commented to him that he seemed upset and asked if there was anything wrong at work. Peter told him that the problem was not his job but Laura's behavior since the birth of the baby. His employer recommended that they seek help at a nearby crisis center.

The goal of intervention determined by the therapist at the crisis center was to assist both Laura and Peter in exploring their feelings regarding the premature birth of their son, their changed communication pattern, and the lack of support Peter was giving Laura.

Intervention

During the first few weeks, Laura was able to discuss her feelings of inadequacy in the mothering role and to tell Peter of her anxieties regarding their son, of her fears that he would be abnormal, and of her belief that the premature birth was her fault because she had insisted on moving with Peter at the time of his transfer. Peter, in turn, could tell Laura of his feelings of guilt at not being able to help more during the move, and also of the blame he placed on himself because the labor was premature. The therapist assisted them in seeing the reality of the situation. Although the move may have been a factor in the premature onset of labor, there could have been other causes.

Peter discussed his insecurities regarding the handling of such a small baby; Laura was then able to tell him that she felt the same way, and she feared she might be doing something wrong with this baby. The therapist gave them information about the differences in the behavior of a normal child and the care required for a premature infant. She reassured Laura that she was doing well and that in time the baby would adjust to more regular hours. She also encouraged Peter to help his wife so that she could get more rest; in turn Laura helped Peter to gain confidence in holding and caring for their new son.

Anticipatory planning

As Peter became comfortable in caring for the baby, he was encouraged to share the responsibility of caring for him in the evenings. This enabled Laura to

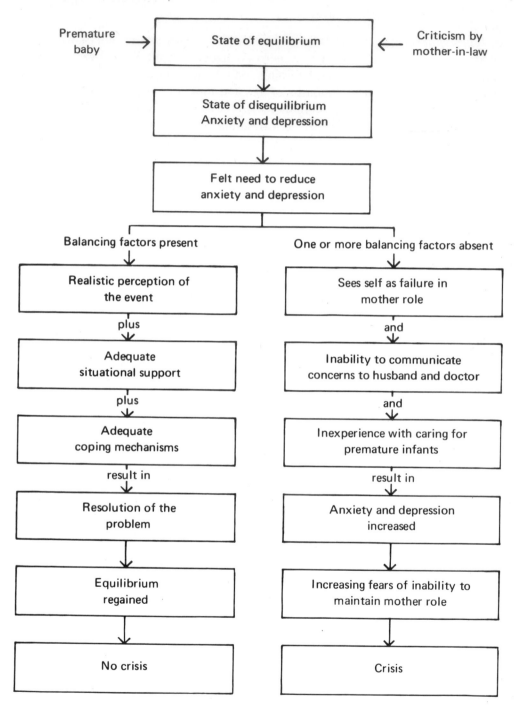

Fig. 3. □ Case study: Laura.

get more physical rest. Peter's emotional support helped her to relax, and she began to sleep better.

The therapist discussed their need to continue to improve communications between them. It was stressed that they must reestablish a pattern of social activities with each other. They were assured that their new son could survive for a few hours with a competent baby-sitter while they went out to dinner or to play cards with other couples.

Most of the energies and concern during the past 2 months had been concentrated on their son. It was recommended that they also devote some additional time to their 2-year-old daughter. This was a stressful time for her, too! Since her mother and father could not give her their sole attention, she would be competing for time with her new brother, and the feelings of sibling rivalry would emerge. She would need to feel that her position in the family was also unique and important—that is, a daughter and their firstborn. Time should be planned for her to have some activities with her parents. This would emphasize that she was "old" enough to be included in their activities.

They were warned to expect some acting-out behavior and possibly some regressive behavior in her bids for "equal" attention.

During their last visit Laura and Peter were assured they could return to the Center if they felt the need for help with a problem.

Summation of the paradigm

This case study concerned a young mother unable to cope with problems of an unexpectedly premature baby. Assessment of the stressful events precipitating the crisis indicated that Laura regarded herself as a failure for not delivering a full-term baby. This was reinforced by the criticisms of her mother-in-law and the lack of situational support from her husband.

In the assessment phase the therapist maintained focus on the immediate area of stress that could have precipitated the crisis. After determining a possible cause-effect relationship, a goal for intervention was established. Laura was encouraged to ventilate her feelings of guilt and inadequacy in the present situation. Realistic perception of the event developed as the therapist provided information leading to an intellectual understanding of the relationship between the event and the resulting symptoms of stress. The husband was brought in as a situational support, and new as well as previously successful coping skills were utilized in resolving the crisis.

STATUS AND ROLE CHANGE
Theoretical concepts

Throughout his life the individual is constantly in the process of joining and leaving social groups related to family, occupation, recreation, education, church, and so forth. *Status* within each of these groups is determined by the relative rights and duties that society assigns to the position. *Role* is determined by the expectations of society that the individual will carry out the duties of his position. If the member's position is changed within the group, his status and role will also change (Linton, 1956:42-63).

Allport (1961:184) cites four interrelated meanings of the term role. The first, *role expectation,* is what society expects of the individual. *Role conception* means *how* the individual perceives the effect of the role on his self-concept. He defines the role according to his perception and his needs, which are influenced by life goals, basic values, and congruency with other roles he is expected to perform. *Role acceptance,* like role conception, is a highly subjective matter. Not all roles are willingly accepted, nor are they willingly altered. The political process is one example of the kind of pressure that society can exert to force a role change. Reciprocal role changes will occur for all dependent on the winner's (and loser's) new status.

Role performance depends on role expectation, conception, and acceptance. The performance of the role will meet the expectations of society only to the degree that there has been mutual communication and understanding throughout the process. The greater the disagreement in any area of understanding, the greater the possibility of failure in the performance.

A person tends to perceive a role from his view of how it relates to his self-concept. The "self" might be defined as the image that the individual builds of himself through interpretation of what he thinks others are judging him to be. It is also derived from the reflected values that others place on him and the values that he places on himself in his societal roles. As new evaluations are perceived, he is obliged to reconcile these new concepts with preexisting ones. Increasing conflictual appraisals of the self result in increased tension and anxiety, leading to a state of disequilibrium.

A person tries to avoid accepting a role that might threaten the security of his self-concept. Various defensive mechanisms are used to escape conflict and to ensure the integrity of self. Danger occurs when an unacceptable change in role is forced by society and cannot be avoided. For example, in the sudden death of a husband, the existing role of wife ceases to exist; the position is gone and its status with it. Without a husband there is no wife role. Similar loss situations may occur in occupations and other groups; a business closes or a position is abolished, so that the need for certain roles no longer exists.

The individual's feelings of loss are in accordance with the value that he places on the role. Effects of the loss are viewed in relation to the self-image, and this involves consideration of the negative factors that might cause conflicting appraisals from others. The greater the conflict between self-concept and expectations due to role change, the more painful is the decision-making experience.

Changes in roles related to loss of status are particularly critical because they represent a direct threat to self-esteem and may encourage the development of a negative self-concept. If defensive coping mechanisms (such as projection or rationalization) prove ineffective in protecting the integrity of the self, anxiety and tension will rise, and the balance of equilibrium will be disturbed.

The following case study illustrates a depressive reaction to a negative change in role status and loss of self-esteem. It was important in the initial interview to determine if Mr. E. was suicidal before intervention was initiated. Intervention focused on clarifying the problem area and assisting him to explore and ventilate unrecognized feelings. The therapist acted as situational support until other supports could be found in his environment.

Case study: Status and role change
Assessment of the individual and his problem

Mr. E. requested help at a crisis center on the advice of his attorney. He was in a state of severe depression and anxiety. He described his symptoms as insomnia, inability to concentrate, and feelings of hopelessness and failure. He was a well-dressed man, 47 years old, who looked older than his stated age because of tense posture, a dull, depressed facial expression, and a rather flat, low tone of voice. Married for 22 years, he had three children, a daughter 13 years old and two sons 8 and 10 years old.

His symptoms had begun about 3 weeks previously when his company closed their West Coast branch and he lost his job. His symptoms had increased in intensity during the past 2 days to the point where he remained in his room, lying in bed, and not eating. He became frightened of his depressed thoughts and feared losing complete control of his actions.

During the initial session he stated to the therapist that he had never been without a job before. Immediately following graduation from college, 22 years before, he had started his own advertising agency in New York City. It had expanded over the years, and he had incorporated, retaining controlling interest and the position of company president. On several occasions he had been approached by larger companies with merger proposals. About a year ago one of the "top three" advertising companies offered him the presidency of a new West Coast branch, which he could run with full autonomy, gaining a great increase in prestige and salary. All expenses were to be paid for his family's move to the West Coast.

Mr. E. saw this as a chance to "make it big" — an opportunity that might never come his way again. His wife and children, however, did not share his enthusiasm. Mrs. E. had always lived in New York City and objected to his giving up his business where he was "really the boss." She liked the structured security of their life and did not want to leave it for one that she thought would be alien to her. The children sided with her, adding personal objections of their own. They had known

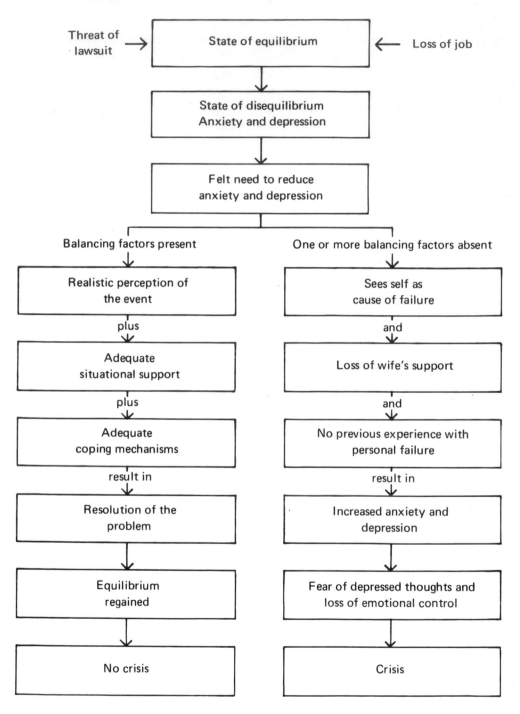

Fig. 4. □ Case study: Mr. E.

only city life, had always gone to the same schools, and did not want to move "way out West." Despite resistance from his family, he made the decision to accept the job offer. His business friends admired his decision to take the chance and expressed full confidence in his ability to succeed. Selling out his shares in his own company to his partner, he moved West with his family within a month.

In keeping with his new economic status and the prestige of his job, he leased a large home in an exclusive residential area. He left most of the responsibility for settling his family to his wife and became immediately involved in the organization of his new business. He described her reaction to the change as being "everything negative that she told me it would be." The children disliked their schools, made few friends, and did not seem to adjust to the pace of their peer group activities. His wife could not find housekeeping help to her liking and consequently felt tied down with work in the home. She missed her friends and clubs, was unable to find shops to satisfy her, and was constantly making negative comparisons between their present life-style and their previous one. He felt that there had been a loss of communication between them. His present work was foreign to her, and he could not understand why she was having so many problems just because they had moved to a new location. Her attitude was one of constantly blaming everything that went wrong on his decision to move West and into a new job.

About a month ago the company suddenly lost four big accounts. Although none of these losses had been a result of his management, immediate retrenchment in nationwide operations was necessary to save the company as a whole. The decision was made to close the newest branch office — his branch on the West Coast. There was no similar position available in the remaining offices, and he was offered a lesser position and salary in the Midwest. He was given 2 months in which to close out his office and to make a decision.

Mrs. E.'s attitude toward these sudden events was a quick "I told you so." She blamed him for their being "stranded out here without friends and a job." He said that he was not a bit surprised by her reaction and had expected it. He had been able to "tune out" her constant complaints in the past months because he had been so occupied by his job, but now he was forced to join her in making plans for his family's future and in considering their tenous economic status. He felt that he had been able to hold up pretty well under the dual pressures of closing out the business and planning for his family's future security. A week ago his wife had found a smaller home that would easily fit into their projected budget during the interim until he decided on a new job. He had felt a sense of relief that she had calmed down and was "working *with* me for a change."

Two days ago, however, their present landlord had sent an attorney, threatening a lawsuit if Mr. E. broke the lease on their present home. His wife became hysterical, blaming him for signing such a lease and calling him a self-centered failure who had ruined his family's lives. "Suddenly I felt as though the bottom had fallen out of my world. I felt frozen and couldn't think what to do next, where to go, and who to ask for help. My family, my employees, everyone was blaming me for this mess! Maybe it *was* all my fault."

Until now, Mr. E. had always experienced a series of successes in his business and home life. Minor setbacks were usually anticipated and overcome with little need for him to seek outside guidance from others. Now, for the first time, he felt helpless to cope with a stressful situation alone. The threat of having to fulfill the lease on a house he could no longer afford not only destroyed his plans for his family, but also broke off what little support he had been receiving from his wife. His feelings of guilt and hopelessness were reinforced by the reality of the threatened lawsuit and the loss of situational support.

Planning of therapeutic intervention

Because of his total involvement in his new work, Mr. E. had withdrawn from his previous business and family supports. The sudden loss of his job threatened him with role change and loss of status for which he had no previous coping experiences. Perceiving himself as a self-made success in the past, he now perceived himself as a self-made failure, both in business and in his parent-husband roles.

When asked by the therapist about his successful coping methods in the past, he said that he had always had recourse to discussions with his business friends. He now felt ashamed to contact them, "to let them know I've failed." He had always felt free to discuss home problems with his wife, and they usually had resolved them together. Now he seemed no longer able to communicate at home with his wife. When questioned if he was planning to kill himself he said "No, I could never take *that* way out. That never entered my mind." After determining that there was no threat of immediate suicide, the therapist initiated intervention.

One goal of intervention was to assist Mr. E. in exploring unrecognized feelings about his change in role and status. His loss of situational supports and lack of available coping mechanisms for dealing with the present stressful situation were recognized as areas in need of attention.

Intervention

In the next 4 weeks, through direct questioning, he began to see the present crisis as a reflection of his past business and family roles. Mr. E. had perceived himself as being a strong, independent "self-made" man in the past, feeling secure in his roles as "boss," husband, and father. He now felt shame at having to depend on others for help in these roles. Coping experiences and skills learned in the past were proving to be inadequate in dealing with the sudden, unexpected, novel changes in his social orbit. The loss of situational support from his wife had added to his already high level of tension and anxiety. This resulted in the failure of what coping skills he had been using with marginal success, and in precipitation of the crisis.

After the fourth session, Mr. E.'s depression and feelings of hopelessness had diminished. His perception of the total situation had become more realistic, and he realized that the closing of the branch office was not due to any failure on his part. It was, in fact, the same decision that he thought he would have made had he been in charge of the overall operation. He further recognized what great importance he had placed on the possibility that this job would have been his "last chance to make it big." His available coping skills had not lessened in value but had, in fact, been increased by the experience of the situation.

By the fifth week Mr. E. had made significant changes in his situation, both in business and in his family life. He had been able to explore his attitudes about always feeling the need to be "the boss" and a sense of shame in being dependent on others for support in decision making. He was now able to perceive the stressful events realistically and to cope with his anxieties.

He met with his former landlord and resolved the impending lawsuit, breaking the lease with amicable agreement on both sides. His family had already decided to move into a smaller home, and his wife and children were actively involved with the planning. He had contacted business friends in the East and accepted one of several offers for a lesser position. He would return East alone, his family choosing to follow later when he had reestablished himself. His wife and children made this choice rather than repeat the sudden move into an unsettled situation as they had a year ago.

He felt pride that his friends had competed for his services rather than giving him the "I told you so" that he had been dreading.

Anticipatory planning

Before termination Mr. E. and the therapist reviewed the adjustments and the tremendous progress Mr. E. had made in such a short period of time. It was emphasized that it had taken a great deal of strength for him to resolve such an extremely ego-shattering experience. He was also complimented on his ability to recognize the factors he could change, those he would be unable to change, and his new status in life.

He viewed the experience as having been very disturbing at the time, but felt he had gained a great deal of insight from it. He believed that he would be able to cope more realistically if a similar situation occurred in the future. He was quite pleased with his ability to extricate himself from a seemingly impossible situation.

In discussing his plans for the future, he stated that he no longer believed he had lost his chance for future advancement. He was realistic about past happenings and the possibility that such a crisis could occur again. He was relieved about his family's rapid adjustment to the lesser status of his new position. They were happy to be returning to family and friends on the East Coast.

He expressed optimism about again rising to a high position in business, concluding with, "I wonder if I could ever really settle for less?"

Summation of the paradigm

Mr. E.'s crisis was precipitated by a sudden change in role status (loss of his job) and threatened economic, social, and personal losses. Assessment of the crisis situation determined that he was depressed but not suicidal. Because he was overwhelmed by a sense of failure in both business and family roles, his perceptions of the events were distorted. Having no previous experience with personal failure of this scope, he was unable to cope with his feelings of guilt and depression. His wife's actions reinforced his low self-esteem, and she withdrew as situational support.

Realisitc perception of the event developed as the therapist assisted him in exploring and ventilating unrecognized feelings; he was able to gain insight into relationships between his symptoms of depression and the stressful events. Mrs. E. resumed her role of situational support as his new coping skills were successfully implemented in resolving the crisis.

RAPE
Theoretical concepts

The word *rape* arouses almost as much fear as the word *murder*. In a sense it kills both the rapist and his victim. The rapist dies emotionally because he can no longer express or feel tenderness or love, and his victim suffers severe emotional trauma.

Women have nightmares about being sexually assaulted; they anguish over what to do. They can either resist, hoping to fend off the rapist, or they can obey his commands, hoping he will leave without seriously injuring or killing them.

Rape is defined in numerous ways, usually including terms such as *forcible carnal knowledge* (McDonald, 1971:24) *unlawful carnal knowledge* (Amir, 1971: 48), and *against the will* or *without the consent* (McDonald, 1971:75) of the victim. For our purposes rape is defined as forcible carnal knowledge of a woman without consent and against her will.

Rape, although an overtly sexual act, is properly considered an act of violence with sex utilized as the weapon (Burgess and Holmstrom, 1974). Viewing the victim of rape as a victim of violence might assist in a more objective and nonjudgmental approach to the victim. The victim of any other type of physical violence is never treated with the same type of emotional, superstitious approach that the victim of rape must endure.

The victim of rape is the victim of medical and cultural myths. The medical myth insists that a healthy adult woman cannot be forcibly raped with full penetration of the vagina unless she actively cooperates (Amir, 1971:163).

The medical myth does not seem to consider emotional reactions, such as fear and panic, or logical reations, such as submissiveness, to ensure life. Neither does the use of weapons, fists, or threats by the offender seem to have a role in the medical myth. The medical myth must spring from the cultural myth that "whatever a man does to a woman she provokes" (McDonald, 1971:74). The low esteem that society in general holds for women is reflected in both the medical and cultural myths.

Sociological studies reflect that the most typical victim is between 15 and 24 years of age, of the same race as the offender, and of the lower socioeconomic group of the society. The initial contact for the rape or the rape itself occurs in the approximate neighborhood of the offender and the victim (Amir, 1971:45).

The victim's emotional reactions to rape have been classified into phases by both McDonald and Burgess and Holmstrom. McDonald (1971) classifies the emotional reactions of victims into phase I: acute reaction, phase II: outward adjustment, phase III: integration and resolution. Burgess and Holmstrom (1974) classify the rape trauma syndrome into the acute phase: disorganization, and the long-term process: reorganization.

McDonald's "acute reaction" and Burgess and Holmstrom's "acute phase" are very similar. The victim is seen in a disorganized, emotionally active state, weeping, distraught, unable to think clearly; or, conversely, as emotionally contained with only occasional signs of emotional pressure, such as inappropriate smiling and increased motor activity.

McDonald's "outward adjustment phase" is described as a period where the victim goes through a denial of the emotional impact of the rape. She goes back to work, restores her social life, rejects any attempts at assisting her, and in general attempts to carry on as if nothing had happened.

Burgess and Holmstrom's "long-term process: reorganization" seems to contain elements of McDonald's "phase II" and "phase III." The emphasis in both studies is on the necessity of emotional confrontation with the experience, changes in life space because of the trauma, the resultant dreams, and deterioration of sexual relationships.

The treatment of the rape victim is not well studied or documented. McDonald emphasizes traditional short-term psychotherapy, whereas Holmstrom and Burgess(1975) emphasize the crisis intervention model. Perhaps McDonald's finding of depression in the third phase and Burgess and Holmstrom's lack of emphasis on depression are due to the different modes of treatment utilized. Crisis intervention seems to be an ideal model for use with rape victims. Rape is a sudden, overwhelming experience for which the usual coping mechanisms probably are inadequate. The victim needs an opportunity for emotional catharsis, reality testing for self-blame, active support on a short-term basis, and someone who will assist in identifying the situational supports available. Crisis intervention seems to be well defined to reach this group of people.

Crisis intervention is also increasingly available in the area where rape victims are initially brought to the attention of the health care system—the emergency room. Prompt referral and active intervention in the emergency room may well prevent deterioration of the victim's emotional status (Burgess, 1973).

The crisis precipitated by rape seems to be approachable by the generic type of crisis intervention. There are recognized patterns of behavior; a characteristic course of behavior results, and specific interventions seem to be effective with the majority of the victims. The exceptions to the generic approach are those victims with compounded reactions because of a history of physical, psychological, or social problems. In those instances the usual physician, therapist, or agency probably should handle the case.

To be a genuine victim in our society means that one must have people available who can accept and acknowledge that something extremely disruptive has occurred in one's life. In other words, the victim's claim to having been victimized needs to receive confirmation from others.

There are three basic types of rape. The first type is rape involving persons who know one another, for example, neighbors, separated husbands and wives, fathers and daughters, and prostitutes and dissatisfied clients. The second type of rape is gang rape, in which two or more men, usually young men, rape one woman. These encounters follow different patterns. It is the third type, the stranger-to-stranger rape, that women fear most, and it is this type of rape that follows an identifiable pattern.

First, a potential rapist looks for a woman who is vulnerable to attack. Rapists differ in defining who is vulnerable. Some look for victims who are handicapped or who cannot react appropriately or swiftly to the threat of rape. Such a man might prey on retarded girls, old women, sleeping women, or women who are intoxicated.

Other rapists look for environments that are easily entered and relatively safe. They make certain that the victim is alone and that they will not be interrupted. This type often commits his crime in the run-down sections of town, where many women live alone.

Rapists often select their victims long before they approach them, and they usually are very consistent in how they do it; they repeat the same pattern over and over again. Rapists seem to have a sixth sense for identifying women who live alone, and they are especially good at finding streets, laundromats, or theater rest rooms that are isolated but that draw unsuspecting victims.

Housing that is easy to enter and the isolation of the victim are two obvious factors that make women particularly vulnerable to rape, but women who are usually friendly and who like to help others are also courting danger. Teachers, nurses, volunteers, and other women who have learned to serve others, to be charitable, and to give of themselves are especially vulnerable to sexual exploitation.

A woman's first act of resistance should be to refuse to help—or be helped by—strange men. It is not wise to stop on a street to give a man a light or to explain street directions. It may be rude but much safer to state firmly while continuing to walk, "I don't have a match," or "I don't know." Do not smile and say, "I'm sorry but . . ." and so forth.

Women should refuse to let a stranger in their apartments or homes to make an emergency phone call or for any other reason. These may be ploys, and there are hundreds of clinical case histories and police reports to validate this method of entry for the purpose of rape.

After finding a vulnerable target, the rapist proceeds, in essence, to ask his victim, "Can you be intimidated?" If she can, he then threatens her life. For example, a rapist may approach a victim on the street and ask her for a light. If she provides it, he may ask her an intimate question. If she reacts submissively or fearfully, he knows he has intimidated her and that she likely will submit to his demands.

This testing phase is crucial for the rapist. If he guesses wrong about whether a woman can be intimidated, he will lose the opportunity to rape her, and if he is incorrect about the victim's situation, he may be caught, convicted, and sentenced to a penitentiary. The rapist tests his victim's responses to threats for intimidations such as: "Don't scream!" "Don't shout!" or "Take your clothes off!"

The safest stance for a woman alone either on the street or in her home is to be aloof and unfriendly. This is her first line of resistance to rape.

When a rapist attacks a woman without warning, that is, climbs into her bedroom while she is asleep, or pulls her into a dark alley, she must decide whether to use direct methods of resistance or to submit.

In the third, or "threat," stage of rape we find the rapist telling his victim what he wants from her and what he will do to her if she refuses to cooperate. Most important, he tells her what reward she will receive if she submits. Typically he says he will kill her if she does not cooperate and that he will not hurt her if she does. If the victim is terrified, immobilized, or hysterical, the rapist may reassure her. He will repeatedly promise her that nothing will happen to her if she does as he tells her. He may express concern for her health or future relationships with her husband or boyfriend.

The final stage of rape is the sexual transaction itself. Vaginal intercourse occurs in less than half of rape victims — anal or oral intercourse is common. In this stage we see the rapist's fantasy life in full bloom. Here he imprints his unique personality on the crime. Some rapists will create a false identity and describe a nonexistent person to the victim; others will reveal their split personalities by telling the victim, "It isn't really me doing this," or "I can't help it."

Most rapists fall into two categories. One type includes those who are usually victims of what analysts call ego splits. They are married, young, employed, and living a life that you could not describe as typical of a person who is mentally ill. However, their family life is disturbed; they cannot relate successfully to their wives or parents, and as youngsters they had problems with an older sister, cousin, or aunt.

After the crime these men will deny their behavior. Typically they will say, "I don't remember . . . it wasn't me," or "I felt like I was watching a movie." If they do not harm their victims, these rapists often get a suspended sentence or are sent to reformatories where they can get work releases and return to the communities in a matter of months. The courts generally give them a second chance on the condition that they receive psychotherapy. Most rapists fall into the first category.

The other type of rapist is a predator. Often he is a man who goes into a place to rob it. In the course of the crime he enteres a bedroom where he finds a lone woman sleeping. On the spur of the moment he decides to rape her. These men are out to exploit or manipulate others, and sometimes they do it through rape.

The rapist who requires his victim to pretend to respond sexually has often failed to please his wife or lover. On a deeper level he may be trying to maintain his shaky defenses about his own sexual inadequacy.

Most rapists have narcissistic and self-centered relationships with women. They have only a minute awareness of their partner's social needs or of the social situation itself.

A rapist also writes his diagnostic signature in the sign-off, or termination, stage of rape. A rapist who assumes the victim will report the crime terminates the rape by trying to confuse the woman. He will say, "Don't move until you count to 100." Then he will go into another room and wait to see if she moves. A minute later he will reenter the room, and if the victim has moved, he will berate her for failing to follow his directions. He may do this several times. Other offenders act guilty or apologetic when they leave. They plead for the victim not to call the police. Still others threaten future harm if she calls for help.

Unfortunately most rapists can neither admit nor express the fact that they are a menace to society. Even convicted rapists who are serving long prison terms deny their culpability; they tenaciously insist that women encourage and enjoy sexual assault. These men will tell you they are the greatest lovers in the world.

Case study: Rape
Assessment of the individual and the problem

Ann, an attractive, 26-year-old legal secretary, was brought to the crisis center by her employer. That morning on her way to work, she had been raped by a man. She returned to her apartment after being raped, showered, changed her clothes, and calmly went to work.

At approximately 11:30 AM she matter-of-factly announced to her employer that she had been raped and told him the details. He was shocked and horrified. He asked her to go to the hospital for treatment and to notify the police. She stated very unemotionally that she was "fine" and had only numerous superficial cuts on her breasts and abdomen and would continue working. By midafternoon she appeared to her employer to be in a state of shock and was acting disoriented and confused. He drove her to the crisis center where she was seen immediately as an emergency by a female therapist who had expertise in working with rape victims.

The therapist offered Ann a cup of coffee, and she accepted. While they were drinking their coffee, the therapist quietly asked Ann to tell her what had happened. Ann began to sob. The therapist handed her some tissues, put her arms around her shoulders, held her close, and told her that she understood how she was feeling. Gradually Ann calmed down and stopped crying. She then said, "I feel so filthy . . . I feel I should have resisted more . . . I am so confused." She was reassured that these feelings were normal and was asked to tell what happened.

Ann stated that she always got up early and took the bus to work since it was very convenient, and she arrived before anyone else was in the office. She liked to get her desk "in order" for the day and make the coffee so that she could serve coffee to the attorney she worked for when he arrived. She smiled slightly and said, "He isn't fit to talk to until he has finished his second cup of coffee in the morning . . . he commutes in from a suburb, and he has to battle the traffic for at least an hour or an hour and a half." The therapist smiled and asked her to continue. She took a deep breath and stated that this morning she had gotten up as usual and rode the bus to work. As she was walking from the bus stop to her office building, approximately three blocks, a man walked toward her. He was tall, attractive, and well dressed. When he approached her, he smiled and said, "Can you tell me where Fifth Street is?" She returned his smile and said, "You are going the wrong way. It's the next street up" (pointing in the direction she was walking). He said, "thank you" and, turning around, fell into step with her and started talking about the weather—"what a beautiful morning"—and other "small talk." They had walked approximately 100 yards when he suddenly pulled out a knife, shoved her against a car, put the knife to her throat, and said, "Don't scream or I'll kill you. Get in the car." Ann began to tremble and tears rolled down her cheeks. The therapist said, "How frightening! What did you do?" Ann said, "I was so shocked and terrified, I thought he *would* kill me. So when he opened the car door, I got in."

Ann continued to tell what had happened. He made her slide over to the driver's seat, keeping the knife firmly at her waist, ordered her to start the car, and told her where to drive (an isolated area near the river). He then made her get in the back seat and undress. He started caressing her and talking obscenities to her, telling her how he was going to make love to her "like no other man could." Ann said that she began to cry and plead with him, but it only seemed to make him angry. He began making small cuts on her breasts and abdomen and kept saying he would kill her if she did not "cooperate." Ann said that he acted "spaced out" and had a glazed look in his eyes, as if he was not really raping her *personally*—just somebody.

Ann stated that after he raped her, he seemed to "come to" and started to cry, saying, "I'm so sorry . . . I didn't mean to hurt you . . . please forgive me . . . I just can't help it . . . please don't tell anyone." Ann got dressed, and he helped her into the front seat and kept asking her if she was all right and generally expressed concern for her well-being. He asked if he could drive her someplace, and Ann asked him to drop her off approximately four blocks from her apartment, telling him she was going to a girl friend's to "clean up." He dropped her off and again begged her not to tell anyone and to please forgive him. Ann said that when she was certain he had driven away, she walked to her apartment in a daze. All she could think about was taking a shower to "get clean again" and to change her clothes completely to try to erase her feelings of degradation. She stated that she thought she should go to work "to keep her mind off it." It was only later in the afternoon as she "relived" the events in her mind that she began to feel terribly guilty over not "resisting" or "fighting back" when he first pulled the knife. She said (with a tone of great remorse), "I didn't even scream!"

Planning of therapeutic intervention

The therapist felt that Ann should go to the hospital immediately for treatment of her numerous cuts and to determine the presence of spermatozoa in the vagina and then report the incident to the police. After this was done, she should return to the center to meet with the therapist and continue her mental catharsis. The therapist explained to Ann that someone from the rape hot line would go with her to the hospital and remain with her constantly at the hospital and while she gave her report to the police. She was assured that the therapist would contact the hospital to arrange that Ann be examined by a female physician and that she would be interrogated by a female police officer. Ann agreed to go, and a member of the rape team was called to be with her and then to return her to the center.

Intervention

When Ann returned, she was pale and trembling but apparently in control of her emotions. Again she was offered coffee, which she accepted, and she and the therapist discussed how things "had gone" at the hospital and with the police interrogation. Ann stated it was definitely *not* pleasant but that it was not as bad as she had thought it would be and added, "Thank God I didn't take a douche!"

The therapist asked Ann if there was a friend or family member that she would like to contact and possibly have spend the night with her since she was still very frightened by her experience. Ann turned even paler and exclaimed, "Oh my God . . . Charles!" She was asked, "Who is Charles?" She replied, hesitantly,

"My fiance." The therapist asked Ann if she could call Charles and tell him what happened. Ann began to cry and said, "I am so ashamed . . . he will probably hate me . . . he probably will never want to touch me again . . . what have I done!" She was comforted by the therapist and told that *she* had done nothing wrong. She continued to cry and berate herself. The therapist gave her a mild sedative and asked her to lie down and rest. Twenty minutes later Ann asked the therapist if she would call Charles and tell him what had happened *but* that she did not want to see him until she knew how he felt about her being raped. The therapist agreed and asked for Charles's telephone number.

The call was placed to Charles, and a brief explanation was given by the therapist about Ann being raped and that she was physically unharmed but psychologically very traumatized. Charles responded with concern and anger and asked if he could see Ann. He was told to come to the center and to ask for the therapist.

Charles arrived and was extremely upset and angry. The therapist took him to her office and explained fully what had happened to Ann and what had been done for her. He started to cry and to curse, stating, "My God—poor Ann" and "I'll find that dirty bastard and kill him!" The therapist allowed him to ventilate his feelings of pity and anger, and he began to calm down. When he seemed calmer, he was asked, "Does this change your feelings for Ann?" He appeared startled and said, "No, I love her. We are getting married!" He was told that Ann was afraid he would not love her anymore, and so forth. He replied, "It wasn't *her* fault. Of course I still love her!"

It was explained that after being raped women usually felt "guilty," "unclean," and very fearful of intimacy with another man, even though they loved them very much. The therapist added that Ann needed his strength, love, and constant reassurance that nothing had changed between them. He listened and said, "I'll do *anything* I can to help her forget this."

The therapist asked if he sometimes stayed overnight at Ann's apartment, and he answered, "Yes, often." He was asked if Ann agreed, would he spend the night with her and hold her (if she would let him), touch her, reaffirm his love for her, and speak about their coming marriage but not to attempt sexual intercourse unless she asked him to; he agreed and asked to see Ann. The therapist asked for a few minutes alone with Ann first.

Ann was lying on the couch staring at the ceiling when the therapist entered. She turned her head and looked fearfully at the door. The therapist smiled, sat down by Ann, held her hand, and said, "I like *your* Charles. He is a fine young man . . . he will probably break down that door if I don't let him in to see you!" Ann said, "What did he say?" The therapist told her that he had stated he loved her very much and that he would do *anything* to help her forget, that it was not her fault, and that he would like to "kill the bastard who hurt you." Ann said, hesitantly, "Are you *sure*?" The therapist replied firmly, "*Positive!* Now comb your hair, and put some makeup on, so I can let him in!" Ann smiled weakly and complied.

Charles entered the office, took Ann in his arms, and held her gently, stroking her hair and face, saying, "I'm so sorry, my love . . . let me take care of you . . . everything is going to be all right . . . I love you . . . you are the most precious thing in my life." Ann cried softly on his shoulder. The therapist said, "Why don't you two go home and get some rest, and I'll see you both next week." Ann and Charles agreed and left with their arms around each other and Ann's head on his shoulder.

(*Note:* The therapist had listened to Ann's account of the rape and modus operandi with increasing feelings of helplessness and anger because in the past 3 months she had worked with two other rape victims who had described the exact same details but with one major difference: The first victim had only one minute cut on her throat, which she received when he pushed her against the car; the second victim had several small superficial cuts on her breast; and now the third victim [Ann] had numerous cuts on her breast and abdomen. The rapist was obviously becoming increasingly more violent with each rape.)

Anticipatory planning

The next sessions were spent in collateral therapy with Ann and Charles. The focus was on ventilation of their feelings and helping Ann begin to express anger toward her rapist. By the end of six sessions they had resumed their normal sexual activities and had advanced their wedding date 3 months. Charles felt he was really living at Ann's apartment because he wanted to be with her as much as possible; therefore, they agreed to get married sooner than they had planned.

Summation of the paradigm

Since rape is so emotionally traumatic, Ann was treated as an emergency situation by the therapist. The sooner intervention begins with a rape victim, the less psychological damage will occur.

Most women are totally unprepared for rape; therefore, it is a new traumatic experience to cope with, and previous defense mechanisms are usually ineffective to resolve the crisis.

Ann greatly feared total rejection by her fiancé (a very real and common occurrence). This is why the therapist saw both Ann and Charles in collateral sessions; thus both would have a chance to explore and ventilate their feelings together.

The event, rape, was perceived by Ann as being her fault because she did not resist immediately and did not scream. Again these feelings are common in women who have been raped. Usually everything occurs so rapidly, and the everpresent fear of being killed or seriously injured tends to immobilize the victim.

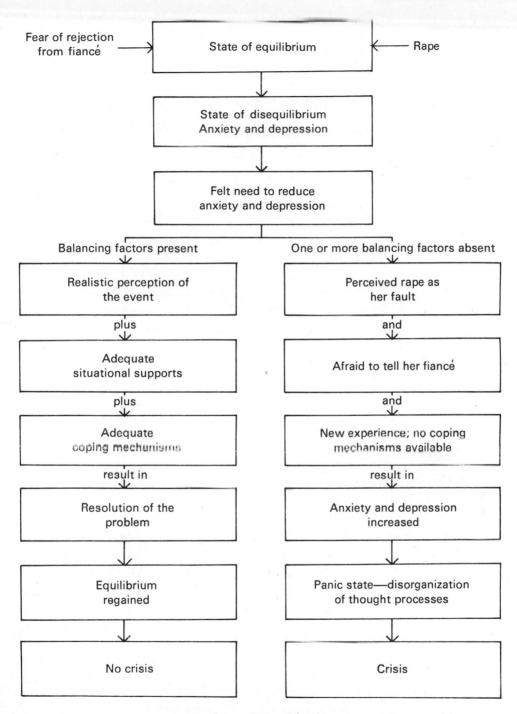

Fig. 5. □ Case study: Ann.

Addendum

Four months later a patient was referred to the center because he was on probation for rape, and he became the same therapist's patient. When questioned about how and why, as he described his modus operandi, the therapist *knew* he was the one who had raped Ann and the two other victims. After the rapist discussed his feelings — guilt, shame, and helplessness in controlling his actions — the therapist asked about his background and family. This new patient, Phillip, described his childhood as one that had been affectionally deprived. His mother had left his father, and he was reared by an "old-maid aunt" who was very cold, undemonstrative — and to him — uncaring and rigid.

When questioned about his present living circumstances, he stated that he was married (happily) and had three small children. When asked why he felt the need to rape, he stated, "I don't know." He began to cry and said, "Please help me . . . I can't help myself."

When the therapist asked if his wife knew that he was on probation for rape, he said, very hesitantly; "No, but I *know* she thinks something is wrong with me." The therapist told Phillip that she had worked with three of his victims, and she felt that he was becoming increasingly more violent, as evidenced by the increasing use of the knife and the sight of blood to stimulate him.

Phillip stared intently at the therapist and said with amazement in his voice, "My God, don't you hate me? I hate myself." The therapist was able to admit that her bias was toward his victims but that she felt he needed help because she was afraid he might kill his next victim. He admitted that he did not know whether he *would* or *would not* kill someone.

The therapist then asked him what his wife and children would feel if they found out he was a potential murderer. He shuddered and said, "Help me! I don't know what to do!" The therapist stated that he should tell his wife about being on probation and about the rapes, and then the therapist would do all she could to get him help. He agreed and called his wife and asked her to come to the center.

His wife arrived, and Phillip, with the therapist present, told her what he had done and the possibility of what he could do in the future. She began to cry and said, "I've *known* something was wrong, but I didn't know what." She turned to the therapist and asked, "What can we do?" The therapist was very candid and stated that Phillip should be at a well-known maximum security prison where he could receive consistent, intensive psychiatric therapy in order to protect the reputation of their family and to protect the community.

They agreed with this decision. The therapist then called the judge and told him the facts. He agreed that maximum security was needed and said he would send a car to transport Phillip to the facility.

It must be noted that *rarely* does a therapist work with rape victims and then with their offender. It was extremely difficult to remain "cool, calm, and collected" while Phillip related his modus operandi; however, he too was a "victim" and needed help, and help he did receive.

PHYSICAL ILLNESS
Theoretical concepts

Diseases are known to have their places as well as their times. Primitive societies have been characterized by health problems related to recurrent famines, and urban societies, until recently, by epidemics of infectious disease. Modern industrial societies are characterized by a new set of diseases: obesity, arteriosclerosis, hypertension, diabetes, and widespread symptoms of anxiety. Arising from these are two of the three greatest disablers and killers of our own place and time: coronary heart diease and stroke. In recent years increasing concern has focused investigation not only on the etiology and epidemiology of cardiac disease but on factors affecting the process of recovery.

The unexpected recognition that one has heart disease is usually a crisis event for an individual. The disease could also be a chronic condition, persisting throughout life and precipitating a series of crises both for the patient and his family.

The conceptualization of the recovery process in heart disease as a response to crisis provides strategic advantages in approaching the problem. It leads to focusing on the kinds of adaptive and maladaptive mechanisms that patients employ in coping with this illness, on the stages of recovery, and on the resources that patients use and require at each stage. Viewing response to coronary heart disease as a problem that can be approached through crisis intervention permits the utilization of concepts and formulations inherent in crisis theory.

In a discussion of the rehabilitation of patients with cardiac disease, a report by the World Health Organization in 1966 distinguishes between phases of the recovery process in terms of time and coping tasks. The first phase is categorized as one in which the patient spends approximately 3 weeks in bed, with minimal physical activity. In the next phase the patient spends approximately 6 weeks at home with a variety of sedentary activities. In the third phase, which lasts from 3 to 6 months, the patient makes a gradual reentry into the occupational world.

Lee and Bryner (1961) conceptualize phases according to the kinds of care the physician must provide for the patient at each point of the process. They specify (1) evaluation of the patient and his environment, (2) management of the patient, and (3) reestablishment of the patient in his community.

In other formulations of recovery phases, emphasis is on the kinds of therapeutic or rehabilitative relationships that predominate at each point. Hellerstein and Goldstone (1954) describe the first, or acute, phase as one in which the relationship between the physician and patient is of the utmost importance. The convalescent phase then follows, with the relationship between the patient and his family and friends becoming primary. During the recovery, or third, phase the employer or vocational counselor becomes the vital participant in the rehabilitation of the patient with cardiac disease.

Phases have also been viewed in terms of the emotional adaptation of the patient. Kubie (1955) suggests that a first phase is marked by initial shock and the second by appreciation of the full extent of the disability. In the third there is "recovery from the lure of hospital care," and in the fourth and final phase there is "a facing of independent, unsupported, competitive life."

Among the most obvious and critical determinants of the outcome of the recovery process are the severity of heart damage, the degree of impairment, and the physiological resources of the patient. While cardiac damage has much to do with setting limits on performance and affecting levels of adjustment, studies of physiological factors alone contribute only partially to understanding the recovery process. Research on the importance of the premorbid personality of the patient as a determinant of adjustment to illness suggests that this is a second important factor in the recovery process.

Other important factors bearing on the recovery process include the various psychological mechanisms that the patient uses in handling his illness. If the recovery process is viewed as a response to a crisis situation, then the individual mechanisms used by patients appear particularly important in the resolution of the crisis. The significance of emotional response to disease has often been underlined in discussing the elements that determine recovery. McIver (1960) states, "The way in which a crisis is handled emotionally may significantly influence the eventual outcome of a case in terms of the extent of recovery and the degree of rehabilitation achieved." Reiser (1951) emphasizes that it is essential to deal with the anxieties associated with the diagnosis and symptoms of heart disease if the therapy of cardiac disease is to attain its optimal effect.

A common view held is that during the acute phase of any serious illness the patient's emotional state is characterized by fear, since the illness threatens his total integrity as well as his sense of personal adequacy and worth to others.

Compared with other serious illnesses, heart disease has several unique features. Associated as it is with sudden death, it is viewed by the patient and his family as an immediate and severe threat to life. Hollender (1958) has written that even in the most stable patients the onset of heart disease is associated with an onslaught of anxiety. During the first days of illness the patient with heart disease must assume a passive role, and some believe that this tends to compound his anxiety. Physical restriction usually increases feelings of helplessness, vulnerability, and depression. The patient is then handicapped in utilizing defense mechanisms that should ultimately help him to adjust to his altered status.

Although coping responses vary widely, there appears to be a core of relatively uniform responses of adjustment. For example, depression and regression have often been reported as the initial reaction to the illness. Some patients display aggression and hostility, placing the blame for the illness on external factors. Some deal with the threat to life by denial of the illness.

It has been suggested that certain coping responses are appropriate at one stage of recovery but are inappropriate at another. When patients at the same stage of recovery are compared, similar responses may function in different ways: constructively for some patients but hindering recovery for others. There is disagreement at present as to the role denial plays in recovery. Some regard denial, which may lead to noncooperation with the physician, as a response of self-destruction. Others consider that denial arises from a belief in the integrity of the self and the invulnerability of the body. It is regarded as constructive and associated with the maintenance of health.

Since each patient will react as an individual in this life-threatening situation, it would be well to remember that the therapist will, in all probability, see a variety of coping responses being utilized. It is not the therapist's role to change the patient's pattern of coping but to understand that this reaction to his illness is part of his defense.

King (1962) has stated that "Man's basis for action in health and disease is a composite of many things. One crucial variable is the way that he sees or perceives the situation . . . and all of the social ramifications that accompany it." These perceptions are conditioned by socialization in a sociocultural context. How the patient responds to the disease is influenced by what he has learned. The content of the learning is in turn determined by the norms and values of the society in which he lives. The meaning of the disease, his attitude toward medical practitioners, his willingness to comply with medical advice, and his management of his life after a heart attack are all influenced by the attitudes and beliefs that he has learned.

Pertinent to the recovery process is the conceptualization of the "sick role," which Parsons (1951) describes as a social role, with its own culturally defined rights and obligations. While a person may be physiologically ill, he is not recognized as legitimately ill unless his illness fulfills the criteria or standards set by the society. Once defined as legitimately able to be in the "sick role," he is expected to meet certain expectations of others. He is expected, for example, to make an effort toward becoming well and to seek help. In turn he has the right to expect certain kinds of behavior in others toward him, including a willingness to permit him to relinquish his normal social role responsibilities.

Willingness to accept the sick role may mean that a patient with heart disease is likely to follow the regimen of his physician and to care for himself in ways that will maximize his recovery. At the same time, reluctance to accept the sick role may also influence the recovery process favorably. Such a patient may be anxious to avoid being defined as sick. Like the willing patient, he too may follow the therapeutic regimen in order to shorten the period of incapacity. On the other hand, reluctance to view himself as sick may lead a patient to comply minimally with medical advice and to attempt full activity before he is physically able to do so.

In essence, social and cultural standards and expectations may have a strong influence on the kinds of action a patient with cardiac disease may take in regard to his own health status.

Case study: Physical illness

Mr. Z., aged 43, was chairing a board meeting of his large, successful manufacturing corporation when he developed shortness of breath, dizziness, and a crushing, vicelike pain in his chest. An ambulance was called, and he was taken to the medical center. Subsequently he was admitted to the coronary care unit with a diagnosis of impending myocardial infarction.

Mr. Z. was married, with three children: Steve, aged 14; Sean, aged 12; and Liza, aged 8. He was president and the majority stockholder of a large manufacturing corporation. He had no previous history of cardiovascular problems, although his father had died at the age of 38 of a massive coronary occlusion. His oldest brother had died at the age of 42 from the same condition; and his other brother, still living, was a semiinvalid after suffering two heart attacks — one at the age of 44 and the other at the age of 47.

Mr. Z. was tall, slim, suntanned, and very athletic. He swam daily, jogged every morning for 30 minutes, played golf regularly, and was an avid sailor who participated in every yacht regatta, usually winning. He was very health conscious and had annual physical checkups, watched his diet, and quit smoking to avoid possible damage to his heart, determined to avoid dying young or becoming an invalid like his brother.

When he was admitted to the coronary care unit, he was conscious. Though in a great deal of pain, he seemed determined to control his own fate. While in the coronary care unit he was an exceedingly difficult patient, a trial to the nursing staff and his physician. He constantly watched and listened to everything going on around him and demanded complete explanations about any procedure, equipment, or medication he received. He would sleep in brief naps, and only when he was totally exhausted. Despite his obvious tension and anxiety, his condition stabilized. The damage to his heart was considered minimal, and his prognosis was good. As the pain diminished, he began asking when he could go home and when he could go back to work. He was impatient to be moved to a private room so that he could conduct some of his business by telephone.

Mr. Z. denied having any anxiety or concerns about his condition, although his behavior on the unit contradicted his denial. Recognizing that Mr. Z. was coping inappropriately with the stress of illness, his physician requested as consultant a

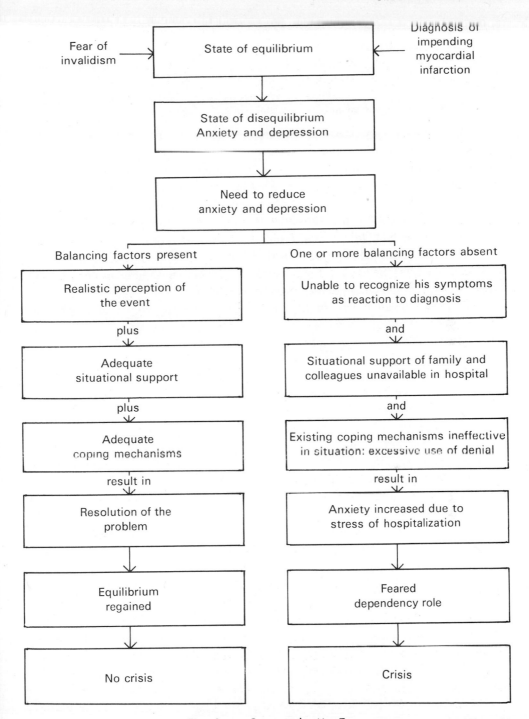

Fig. 6. □ Case study: Mr. Z.

therapist whose expertise was crisis intervention to work with Mr. Z. to help him through the crisis period.

The therapist agreed to work with Mr. Z. for 1 hour a week for 6 weeks. Their first session was scheduled the second day of his stay in the coronary care unit.

Assessment of the individual and his problem

The therapist reviewed Mr. Z.'s chart and talked with his physician before the first session in order to gain an accurate assessment of Mr. Z.'s physical condition and to gain some knowledge of factors (socioeconomic status, marital status, family history, and so on) to assist in assessing his biopsychosocial needs.

In the first session the therapist observed Mr. Z.'s overt and covert signs of anxiety and depression and determined, through discussion with him, his perception of what hospitalization meant to him, his usual patterns of coping with stress, and available situational supports. Through direct questions and reflective verbal feedback she was able to elicit the reasons for his behavior and reactions to his illness and to his confinement in the coronary care unit.

Observing his suntanned, youthful appearance, and the general physical condition of a very active and persistent athlete, the therapist questioned him about his life-style and patterns before his hospitalization. Mr. Z. was quite adamant about his "minor" condition and the possibility of curtailed activity. He stated that he was very aware of his family's tendency toward cardiac conditions, but added, "I have always taken excellent care of myself to avoid the possibility of becoming a cardiac cripple like my brother." Apparently he was not too concerned about the prospect of dying; in fact, he might prefer it to the overwhelming prospect of being a useless, dependent invalid.

He expressed concern about the length of time he might have to spend in the hospital. When questioned about his concern he stated: "I *have* to be in good shape by the second of December [approximately 3½ months]: I've entered the big yacht race, and I plan to win again!"

When he was asked how his wife and children were reacting to his illness and hospitalization, Mr. Z.'s facial expression and general body tension relaxed noticeably. He smiled and said, "My wife, Ann, is simply unbelievable; she takes everything in stride. She is always cool, calm, and collected. She even met with the board of directors and told them to delay any major decisions until I return — but that any minor decisions she could handle!"

The therapist asked if she could meet his wife. Mr. Z. replied that his wife would be in to see him soon and suggested she stay and meet her.

After meeting with them briefly, the therapist asked Mrs. Z. to stop by her office before leaving.

Session with Mrs. Z. Mrs. Z. arrived at the office and sank gratefully into a chair, losing the bright, cheerful, and optimistic manner she had maintained while with her husband. Observing her concerned expression and slumped posture, the therapist inquired, "You are very concerned about your husband, aren't you?" Mrs. Z. readily admitted that she was concerned but did not want her husband to know. When asked what specifically concerned her, she replied: "Jim's inability to accept any type of forced inactivity and his refusal to accept the possibility that he might have to change his hectic life-style. He can't *bear* the thought of being ill or being dependent upon anyone or anything!"

The therapist explained that it is difficult for many patients to accept a passive, dependent role while ill and that it takes time for them to adjust to a changed life-style. She then explained to Mrs. Z. that the physician had arranged for Mr. Z. to have therapy sessions for the next 6 weeks to help him through his crisis. Mrs. Z. seemed relieved that someone else recognized the problems confronting her husband and would help him as he worked through his feelings about his illness and unwanted, though inevitable, change in life-style.

The therapist suggested that Mrs. Z. might also need some support, as she too had to adjust to Mr. Z.'s illness. They agreed to meet for an hour each week so they could work together toward a resolution of the crisis. A convenient time was arranged each week when Mrs. Z. came to visit her husband.

Planning of therapeutic intervention

Mr. Z.'s denial of the possibility that he might die like his father and oldest brother or that he might become an invalid, "useless and dependent," like his other brother was considered of prime importance. It was felt that the first goal of intervention was to assist Mr. Z. to ventilate his feelings about his illness and hospitalization. A second goal was to assist him to perceive the event realistically. A third goal established was that of giving support to Mrs. Z. and assisting her in coping with the stress induced by her husband's hospitalization.

Intervention

It was felt that Mr. Z.'s high anxiety level would interfere with his ability to express his feelings about his illness and his hospitalization. In an attempt to reduce his anxiety, the therapist made two recommendations to his physician, which were accepted. The first recommendation was that Mr. Z. be moved out of the coronary care unit to a private room as soon as possible. The environmental surroundings in the coronary care unit, with its overwhelming and complex equipment, strange sounds, and constant activities of the staff, apparently increased Mr. Z.'s anxiety. Because of the stressful situation, he was not getting sufficient rest. After his move to a private room later that afternoon, he began to relax noticeably, became much less demanding of the staff, and began sleeping and eating better.

The second recommmmendation was that he be permitted to use the telephone for 30 minutes three times a day. Thus he was able to conduct some of his business from his bed. This apparently made him feel less dependent, and the increased mental acitvity relieved some of his anxiety about becoming a "helpless" invalid.

In the next sessions Mr. Z. began to discuss — hesitantly at first, and then more freely — his feelings about his illness and his reaction to hospitalization. He discussed his father's sudden death when he was in his teens and how lost he would have felt if his older brother had not stepped in and taken over. All three brothers were very close, and the death of the oldest one, while Mr. Z. was in college, reactivated the grievous loss he had felt for his father. He was just beginning to accept his oldest brother's death when, a year later, his other brother had a severe heart attack and was unable to continue in the family business. As Mr. Z. saw it, his brother was a "helpless" invalid. Mr. Z., the youngest son, then became the major stockholder and president of the corporation.

He stated that while he certainly didn't *want* to die, he was less afraid of dying than he was of becoming useless, helpless, and a burden to his family.

Through discussion and verbal feedback, it was possible to get Mr. Z. to view his illness and the changes it would make in his life in a realistic perspective: No, he was *not* an invalid. Yes, he *would* be able to work and live a *normal* life. No, he would *not* have to give up sailing, just have someone else do most of the crewing. Yes, he *would* be able to resume his activities but would continue them at a more leisurely pace: instead of scheduling fifteen things to do in 1 day, schedule seven and a half, and so forth. Gradually he became more accepting as he began to realize that the impending myocardial infarction was a warning he should heed and that with proper care and some diminishing of his usual hectic pace he could continue to live a productive and useful life.

The therapist continued to meet with Mrs. Z. to give her support and began anticipatory planning for her husband's convalescence at home. She discussed with her Mr. Z.'s strong need to feel independent and in control of all situations and encouraged her to continue to let her husband make decisions for the family. She assured Mrs. Z. that he would be able to continue a relatively normal life and that she did not need to protect and "coddle" him, something he would greatly resent! When asked how their children were reacting to their father's hospitalization, Mrs. Z. replied: "At first they were terribly concerned and silent; now they are beginning to ask, 'When is he coming home, and what can we do?' " It was obvious that Mr. Z. had strong situational support in his family!

Mr. Z.'s recovery progressed fairly smooth, and he began to ambulate and take care of his basic needs. While more accepting of his need for some assistance, he still became upset and impatient if the staff intervened to assist him in routine care.

Mr. Z. was discharged after the fourth week, with instructions for his convalescence at home. The therapist continued to meet with Mr. and Mrs. Z. at their home during the fifth and sixth weeks to assist the family toward stabilization as Mr. Z. adjusted to his new regimen of reduced activity and to provide anticipatory planning for their future.

Anticipatory planning

By the end of the fifth week, with the strong support of his family and the therapist, Mr. Z. was able to view his illness and his feelings about curtailing some of his hectic activities in a more accepting and realistic manner. His family still consulted him for advice and opinions regarding family decisions. This made him feel he was still an active, participating member of the family.

He was able to conduct a large part of his business from his home by having board meetings there and through periodic telephone conversations to his office. His secretary came to his home 3 days a week to take dictation and to secure his signature when needed on documents. Thus, he still remained in control of his business life, which contributed greatly to his self-esteem.

The children and Mrs. Z. were encouraged to continue in their usual daily activities so that Mr. Z. would not feel that his being at home was disrupting to their lives. It also helped Mrs. Z. to cope with her feelings and her desire to protect her husband from stress. Gradually she was able to realize that he was capable of coping with some stress and that he was not as fragile as she had believed him to be.

Before termination the therapist and Mr. Z. reviewed the adjustments he had made and the insights he had gained into his own behavior. He was able to intellectually understand his reasons for his denial and dependence/independence conflicts.

He was very optimistic about his future and felt that he could adjust to a reduced-activity schedule. He still, rather wistfully, was hoping his physician would approve his entering the yacht race.

He was realistic about his physical condition and the possibility that a coronary attack could occur again, stating, "At least now I've learned to relax and roll with the punches."

Mrs. Z. and the children felt that they would be able to cope with the occasional bouts of frustration and temper flare-ups of Mr. Z. They were now aware of how difficult it was for him to make the many adjustments necessary to his new way of life.

Summation of the paradigm

Mr. Z's fear of becoming a "cardiac cripple" like his brother distorted his perception of the event. He was unable to relax and be dependent in the coronary care unit. His anxiety and tension made him unable to accept the fact that he had had a myocardial infarction. His family and his colleagues—his usual situational supports —, were unable to be with him because of rules of the hospital and his restricted activity. He used denial excessively because he was unable to accept the fact that he might have to change his life-style. Since this was his first hospitalization and the first time he had to be in a dependent role, his anxiety increased considerably.

Addendum

Several months later the physician informed the therapist that he had permitted Mr. Z. to enter the yacht race, as a passenger, not as crew, and that his yacht had finished third.

DIVORCE
Theoretical concepts

In Western society, divorce has become a common rather than a rare occurrence. Much has been written and hypothesized about the causes and effects of divorce on individuals and family members. An estimated 494,000 decrees of divorce or annulment were granted in the United States in 1966, as compared with an estimated 481,000 for 1965. This is an increase of 13,000, or 2.7%, the highest national divorce rate since 1953 (Long, 1968:269). Since divorce rates are so high and many marriages are centers of friction and unhappiness, something must be lacking in the preparation for marriage. No event in life of equal importance is viewed with so little realism, and marriage seems to come about with little or no preparation.

Marriage and its demands on individuals can be stressful, and failure to sustain a marriage can precipitate a crisis. Rapoport (1963) delineates three subphases of marriage when stress is the most common: the engagement, honeymoon, and early marriage. Engaged couples confront major tasks on two levels, intrapersonal and interpersonal. The intrapersonal task implies a review of readiness for marriage on a conscious, preconscious, or unconscious level of psychological maturity. This readiness will be affected by the individual needs of the person and by his perceived subcultural norms. The interpersonal tasks are concerned with developing an interpersonal adjustment or accomodation that will be satisfactory in the marital relationship. The engagement period involves a process of separation from previous life patterns and of commitment of the couple to one another. The honeymoon period is a time for establishing a basic sense of harmony. The early marriage phase (the first 3 months) involves establishing a system of authority, decision-making patterns, and patterns of sexual relationships.

It is evident that individuals do not always accomplish these necessary tasks in the first few months of marriage. For some it may easily extend into the first few years of marriage. Additional stress factors may occur in this period to create even greater disequilibrium.

The largest proportion of divorces occurs in the early years of marriage among childless couples. The peak period of divorces is in the second year of marriage, after which the rate drops rapidly. A number of factors, other than those previously mentioned, are precipitating causes of divorce. Among these are urban background, early marriage (15 to 19 years of age), short courtship, short engagement, mixed racial or religious marriages, disapproval of friends and relatives, dissimilar backgrounds, and unhappy parental marriages.

Today there is greater acceptance of the possibility of divorce; because of this acceptance, divorced persons have lost some of the feelings of failure and guilt that were formerly associated with it. The higher divorce rate may reflect new values placed on marriage. Marriage is no longer accepted as an "endurance race" that is doggedly maintained "for the sake of the children." The current demands are for a "good marriage," one that meets the needs of the individuals involved. Even from the point of view of the children, who seemingly pay the highest price for marital failure, divorce may in certain circumstances create fewer psychological problems if the children are not used as pawns by the separating parents.

The rate of remarriage after divorce is quite high, and in cases where both parties had been divorced two or more times the ratio climbs even higher. Greene (1968) assumes that divorce is a repetitive phenomenon. It is apparent that an unresolved neurotic pattern, carried over from one marriage to another, would tend to reinforce the individual's failure pattern in the subsequent marriage.

This case study (Morley and others, 1967) concerns a young women, 23 years old, who sought help from a crisis center on the advice of her attorney because of an impending divorce. Neither Margie nor her husband had attained the psychological maturity or "readiness" necessary to enter marriage. Margie's impulsive marriages after brief courtships indicated her unrealistic expectations and attitudes toward marriage. Clues given in the assessment phase indicated that she felt herself a failure as a woman. These guilt feelings and lack of her usual situational supports precipitated a crisis. Intervention was planned to assist her to cope with her feelings of failure and guilt and to view her divorce in more realistic terms.

Case study: Divorce
Assessment of the individual and his problem

Margie, an extremely attractive young women in the process of divorce from her third husband, was referred to a crisis center for help because of severe depression and anxiety. This was manifested by insomnia, lack of appetite, tremulousness, inability to concentrate, and frequent crying spells. These symptoms had begun 3 weeks earlier when she was notified of the date of the divorce proceedings. She had lost her job because she was unable to control her crying spells and had subsequently developed bursitis in her shoulder, which further limited her ability to work. Her symptoms had intensified so much in the past 3 days that she felt she was losing complete control over her emotions and needed help.

During the initial session, Margie stated that she did not want a divorce and that she still loved her husband, even though he did not love her. When questioned about the increased intensity of symptoms that had begun 3 days ago, she stated that at that time she had been informed by her attorney that the only way she could receive alimony would be to countersue for divorce.

In Margie's previous two divorces she had remained a passive participant; her husbands had sued her for divorce. She had accepted these and had not contested. Now, for the first time, due to her inability to work she was forced to become an active participant in a divorce she did not want. She stated frequently that "something must be wrong with me if I can't hold a husband," and later commented, "I don't feel this is a good marriage—but I hate to fail again." This ambivalence and her expressed guilt feelings were felt to be part of the crisis-precipitating event, as was the necessity of being forced to take an active part in a divorce she did not want.

As a result of the assessment, the therapist thought that, although Margie was depressed and expressed feelings of worthlessness, she was not suicidal and did not constitute a threat to others.

Planning of therapeutic intervention

Margie had almost totally withdrawn from her social and family contacts. Her mother came occasionally to give her money for rent and bring her food. Beyond this social contact she remained isolated in the apartment she had previously shared with her husband, weeping at intervals, staring at her husband's picture, and unable to decide whether or not to contest the divorce.

Since she had not been forced into active decision making in her previous divorces, she had no coping experiences in this specific situation. When questioned about her previous methods of coping with stress, she stated that usually she had no problems because she remained involved in her work and its many social contacts, usually bowling and going to bars with friends. Her present inability to work eliminated these sources of social support, distractions from the problem, and her previous successful coping mechanisms could not be used.

The goal of intervention was established by the therapist to assist Margie to recognize and cope with her feelings of ambivalence and guilt. Unrecognized feelings about her marriage and the impending divorce were also to be explored.

Intervention

In the next 3 weeks, through direct questioning and reflection of verbal and nonverbal clues to Margie, it became possible for her to view the present crisis and its effect on her in relationship to her previous marriages and divorces.

Margie wanted desperately to marry in order to become a housewife and mother. Her usual social contacts and previous patterns of meeting men (bowling alleys and bars) and her impulsive marriages (Las Vegas, three times) and reasons

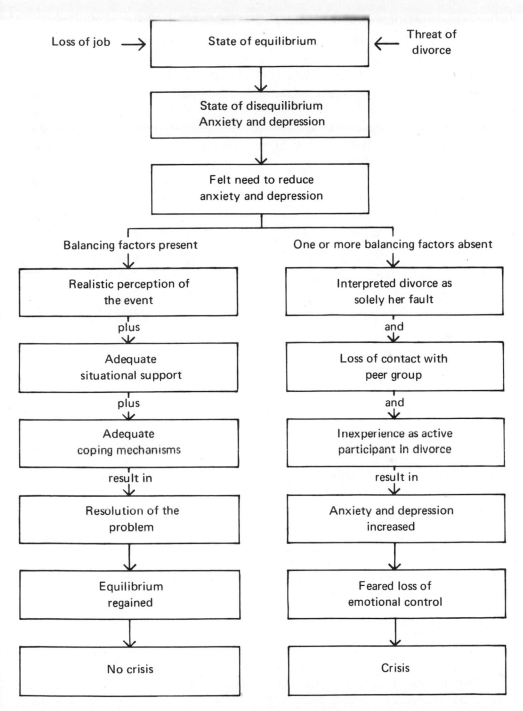

Fig. 7. □ Case study: Margie.

for marriage ("I thought I could help him . . . he needed me") were not meeting this need. The men she had met and married, and who later divorced her, were men who did not want to "settle down" with a wife and children. Instead, they wanted a gay, attractive companion to show off to their friends. Margie always hoped that they would change after marriage. However, they remained unchanged and divorced Margie when she persistently suggested "starting a family." With each marriage and subsequent divorce her guilt feelings about her ability to be a good wife magnified. With the loss of her previous patterns of coping the third divorce precipitated this crisis.

After the third session Margie's depression and symptoms had lessened as she recognized the possibility that the failure of her marriages may not have been in her "inability to be a good wife" but in the disparity between what she wanted and expected from a marriage and what the men she had married wanted and expected.

Anticipatory planning

Exploration with Margie about her usual modes of social contact and her impulsive marriages (usually after only 3 or 4 weeks' courtship) assisted her in viewing her current divorce in more realistic terms. This was an important phase in anticipatory planning.

By the fourth week Margie had made significant changes in her patterns of living. She moved from the apartment she had previously shared with her husband to a small house near her mother. She also signed the papers to contest the divorce and found a new job.

Margie was granted the divorce and was apparently able to view her past experience as a traumatic but valuable learning experience.

In discussion and review with Margie of her future plans, she was cautious but realistic. She was enjoying her new job and new friends, going to movies and occasionally dinner with girl friends. She stated that she was not accepting dates from men yet, "although I've been asked," and that if she married again, "it would not be in Las Vegas!"

Before termination Margie and the therapist reviewed and assessed the adjustments she had made in coping with the crisis, the insight she had gained into her own feelings, and her needs regarding future plans.

At termination Margie was reassured that she could obtain assistance in any future crisis that might occur.

Summation of the paradigm

Margie's inability to cope with a third divorce was precipitated by the lack of her usual situational supports, that is her involvement and social contacts at work. This was also the first time Margie was forced into the role of an active participant in the divorce process, and she had no previous coping skills. Her inability to work due to illness further isolated her from her usual contacts, and she began to introspect about her previous divorces and saw herself as a failure as a woman. As her doubts increased, her feelings of guilt and failure magnified until she feared complete loss of emotional control.

The intervention was focused on encouraging Margie to bring her feelings of failure and guilt into the open. By direct questioning and reflecting the information back to Margie it became possible for her to view her current divorce and its effect on her in more realistic terms. She was given support by the therapist as she began to explore what she wanted and expected from marriage in the future.

SUICIDE
Theoretical concepts

Each year suicide accounts for more than 20,000 deaths in the United States, which makes it the eleventh leading cause of death. It ranks second as a cause of death for adolescents and college students. Although this death rate has remained relatively stable during the past decade, suicide attempts, suicide threats, drug overdoses, and other forms of self-destructive behavior have increased dramatically. At large general hospitals a night rarely goes by in any emergency room without at least one admission for attempted suicide.

The most common form of attempted suicide is the ingestion of a sedative or hypnotic drug. Suicide attempts by other methods, such as hanging, wrist cutting or other body mutilation, gas inhalation, gunshot wounds, and jumping from high places, are less frequent.

In addition to actual suicide attempts, other persons are referred or brought to hospitals or mental health centers because they have threatened suicide or because they have demonstrated some form of self-destructive behavior, such as running into highway traffic or threatening to jump from a bridge or freeway overpass.

Regardless of how the suicidal behavior is manifested, the basic question remains, "Why suicide?" There is no single answer to this question. The complex motivations, weaknesses, and strengths that determine all types of human behavior apply also to suicide. Consequently, there are many roads that individuals may take in reaching a decision to commit suicide. Usually the process is long, and often it is complicated by other physical and emotional symptoms of distress. Despite the multiplicity of causes and patterns, suicidal behavior can usually be related to three primary motivations: loss of communication, ambivalence about life and death, and the effects of suicidal behavior on significant others.

Communication

Usually suicidal reactions are associated with feelings of hopelessness and helplessness, often related to the separation or loss of a significant or valued relationship. Suicidal behavior can best be understood as an expression of intense feelings when other forms of expression have failed. The expression of feelings can range from sad cries for help to desperate statements of despair. A suicidal person is driven to this act because he feels unable to cope with a problem and believes that others are not responding to his need. The suicidal behavior becomes a claim for the attention the person feels he has lost. Suicidal thoughts may be expressed verbally or by actions. Either directly or indirectly, the communication is frequently aimed at a specific person—the significant other. An indirect communication poses the problem of recognizing the intent of the disguised message and understanding its real content.

Ambivalence

Only a small number of people who threaten or attempt suicide actually succeed. The general explanation for an incomplete or partially effective suicidal act is that the individual is filled with contradictory feelings about living and dying. This state is termed "ambivalence." One should realize that ambivalence is a universal, human trait. We all have it at times, and it is not a weakness. Everyone experiences ambivalence over decisions at one time or another, in choosing a career, a spouse, or a place to live. The choice of a place and time to die is no exception. In making the decision of whether to live or die one would expect to find even more than the normal amount of ambivalence. This psychological characteristic accounts for the sometimes puzzling fact that a person will take a lethal or near-lethal action and then counterbalance it with some provision for rescue. The very fact that every person is divided within himself over decisions provides the chance for successful intervention with a suicidal patient. By making use of the patient's wish to live, his "cry for help," suicide may be averted. The myth that "if a person talks about suicide, he won't do it" is actually that—a myth. Every statement or ideation of the wish to die should be taken seriously and explored with the individual.

Effects on others

Suicidal behavior can further be understood in terms of its effect on those receiving the communication. A suicidal attempt may arouse feelings of sympathy, anxiety, anger, or hostility on the part of the individual's family or friends and therefore serve to manipulate relationships. The therapist may also experience similar feelings unless he or she can anticipate and counteract these reactions. The therapist must resist the desire to be omnipotent. No one is truly omnipotent, just as no one can solve all the problems and meet all the demands of every patient. This is especially true when dealing with intensely dependent patients who often attribute tremendous powers to the potential rescuer.

Many suicidal situations will arouse feelings of anxiety and self-doubts about the therapist's own ability to handle situations of this type. Although a moderate level of anxiety is appropriate, too much may seriously hamper the effort to help, especially if it is transmitted to the patient who is depending on someone to help him solve his problems. Already feeling helpless and lost, the suicidal person who perceives excessive anxiety may lose hope of being helped, and may bluntly state so. As in any form of intervention, one develops confidence in one's ability with training and experience.

Suicidal potential

Before considering the factors that influence the probability of suicide, the therapist should consider his own attitudes toward suicide and death because they definitely affect how one will function with patients. Death is a process and is a part of life and living. From the moment one is born, the process toward death begins. Unfortunately, Western cultures have surrounded death with many powerful taboos. The feelings that these taboos can arouse may very well interfere in the therapist's interactions with his patients. He must be sensitive to his own thoughts about death and suicide, and regardless of personal attitudes, he must avoid any moralistic judgments about what has happened. The professional point of view must be that death is to be prevented, if possible. A therapist will often be placed in the position of actually debating life and death questions with upset people. Although he must recognize the existence and merits of other viewpoints, his role is to represent life and to assist distressed, helpless people.

From the first conversation with a suicidal individual, a therapist immediately assumes some responsibility for preventing the suicide. In working out some plan for prevention, the therapist must first determine the individual's suicidal potential, that is, the degree of probability that the person will try to kill himself in the immediate or near future. In some individuals the suicidal potential will be minimal, whereas in others it will be immediate and great. The therapist must decide the degree of risk for each patient.

The prediction of suicide is by no means an exact science. Even the most experienced therapist can be misled in assessing a problem. However, certain criteria allow suicidal potential to be evaluated with some assurance. Assessment of suicidal potential depends on obtaining detailed information about the patient in each of the following categories.

Age and sex. Statistics indicate that women attempt suicide more often than men but that men commit suicide more often than women. Currently, this trend is changing as women are beginning to feel the same stresses in their "equal opportunity" position as men feel. They are also beginning to use more lethal methods in their suicide attempts. It is also known that the rate for completed suicide rises with increasing age. Consequently, an older man presents the greatest threat of actual suicide and a young woman, the least. Within this framework age and sex offer a general, though by no means clear-cut, basis for evaluating suicidal potential. One must remember that young women and young men do kill themselves, even though their original aim was to manipulate other people. Each case requires individual appraisal.

Suicidal plan. How an individual plans to take his life is one of the most significant criteria in assessing suicidal potentiality. One must consider the following three elements:

1. Is it a relatively lethal method? An individual who intends to commit suicide with a gun, by jumping from a tall building or bridge, or by hanging is a far greater risk than someone who plans to take pills or cut his wrists. Since the latter two methods are amenable to treatment or resuscitation, they are less lethal than the irrevocable consequences of putting a gun to one's head.

2. Does the individual have the means available? It must be determined if the method of suicide the individual has considered is in fact available to him. An actual threat to use a gun, if the person has one, is obviously more serious than the same threat without a gun.

3. Is the suicide plan specific? Can the individual tell you exactly when he plans to do it (for example, after the children are asleep)? If he has spent time thinking out details and specific preparations for his death, his suicidal risk is greatly increased. Changing a will, writing notes, collecting pills, buying a gun, and setting a time and place for suicide suggest a high risk. When a patient's plan is obviously confused or unrealistic, one should consider the possibility of an underlying psychiatric problem. A psychotic person with the idea of suicide is a particularly high risk because he may make a bizarre attempt based on his distorted thoughts. Always find out if the patient has a past history of any emotional disorder and whether he has ever been hospitalized or received other mental health care.

Stress. Find out about any stressful event that may have precipitated the suicidal behavior. The most common precipitating stresses are losses: the death of a loved one; divorce or separation; loss of a job, money, prestige, or status; loss of health through illness, surgery, or accident; and loss of esteem or prestige because of possible prosecution or criminal involvement. Not all stresses are the result of bereavement. Sometimes increased anxiety and tension are a result of success, such as a promotion with increased responsibilities. Always investigate any sudden change in the individual's life situation.

Learn to evaluate stress from the individual's point of view rather than from society's point of view. What for you may be minimal stress could be perceived by the patient as severe stress. The relationship between stress and symptoms is useful in evaluating prognosis.

Symptoms. The most common and most important suicidal symptoms relate to depression. Typical symptoms of severe depression include: loss of appetite, weight loss, inability to sleep, loss of interest, social withdrawal, apathy and despondency, severe feelings of hopelessness and helplessness, and a general atti- tude of physical and emotional exhaustion. Other persons may exhibit agitation through such symptoms as tension, anxiety, guilt, shame, poor impulse control, or feelings of rage, anger, hostility, or revenge. Alcoholics, homosexuals, and all substance abusers tend to be high suicidal risks.

The patient who is both agitated and depressed is particularly a high risk. Unable to tolerate the pressure of his feelings, the individual in a state of agitated depression shows marked tension, fearfulness, restlessness, and pressure of speech. He eventually reaches a point where he must act in some direction to re- lieve his feelings. Often he chooses suicide.

Suicidal symptoms may also occur with psychotic states. The patient may have delusions, hallucinations, distorted sensory impressions, loss of contact with reality, disorientation, or highly unusual ideas and experiences. As a baseline for assessing psychotic behavior, use your own sense of what is real and appropriate.

Resources. The patient's environmental resources are often crucial in deciding how you will manage the immediate problem. Who are his situational supports? Find out who can be used to support him through this traumatic time: family, rela- tives, close friends, employers, physicians, or clergymen. Whom does he feel close to? If the patient is already under the care of a therapist, try to contact him.

The choice of various resources is sometimes affected by the fact that the pa- tient and the family may try to keep the suicidal situation a secret, even to the point of denying its existence. As a general rule, this attempt at secrecy and denial must be counteracted by dealing with the suicidal situation openly and frankly. It is usually better, both for you and the patient, if the responsibility for a suicidal patient is shared by as many people as possible. This combined effort provides the patient with a feeling that he lacks: that others are interested in him, care for him, and are ready to help him.

When there are no apparent sources of help or support, the therapist may be the person's only situational support, his one link to survival. This is also true if available resources have been exhausted or family and friends have turned away from the individual. In most cases, however, people will respond to the situation and provide help and support if given the opportunity.

Life-style. How has the person functioned in the past under stress? First, has his style of life been stable or unstable? Second, is the suicidal behavior acute or chronic?

The stable individual will describe a consistent work record, sound marital and family relationship, and no history of previous suicidal behavior. The unstable individual may have had severe character disorders, borderline psychotic behav- ior, and repeated difficulties with major situations, such as interpersonal relation- ships or employment.

A suicidal person responding to acute stress, such as the death or loss of someone he loves, bad news, or loss of a job, which has pushed him into an unwanted and unfamiliar status, presents a special concern. The risk of early suicide among this group is high; however, the opportunity for successful therapeutic intervention is greater. If the suicidal danger can be averted for a relatively short period of time, individuals tend to emerge without great danger of recurrence.

By contrast, individuals with a history of repeated attempts of self-destruction may be helped through one emergency, but the suicidal danger can be expected to return at a later date. In general, if an individual has made serious attempts in the past, his current suicidal situation should be considered more dangerous. Although individuals with chronic suicidal behavior benefit temporarily from intervention, the emphasis should fall more on continuity of care and the maintenance of relationships.

Acute suicidal behavior may be found in either a stable or an unstable personality; however, chronic suicidal behavior occurs only in an unstable person. In dealing with a stable person in a suicidal situation, you should be highly responsive and active. With an unstable person, you need to be slower and more thoughtful, reminding the patient that he has withstood similar stresses in the past. Your main goals will be to help him through this period and assist him in reconstituting an interpersonal relationship with a stable person or resource.

Communication. The communication aspects of suicidal behavior have great importance in the evaluation and assessment process. The most important question is whether or not communication still exists between the suicidal individual and his significant others. When communication with the suicidal patient is completely severed, it indicates that he has lost hope in any possibility of rescue.

The form of communication may be either verbal or nonverbal, and its content may be direct or indirect. The suicidal person who communicates nonverbally and indirectly makes it difficult for the recipient of the communication to recognize or understand the suicidal intent of these communications. Also, this type of communication in itself implies a lack of clarity in the interchange between the suicidal person and others. At the same time it raises a danger that the individual may "act out" his suicidal impulses. The primary goal is to open up and clarify communication among everyone involved in the situation.

The patient's communication may be directed toward one or more significant persons within his environment. He may express hostility, accuse or blame others, or he may demand openly or subtly that others change their behavior and feelings. His communication may express feelings of guilt, inadequacy, and worthlessness or indicate strong anxiety and tension.

Significant other. When the communication is directed to a specific person, the reaction of the recipient becomes an important factor in evaluating suicidal danger. One must decide if the significant other can be an important resource for rescue, if he is best regarded as nonhelpful, or if he might even be injurious to the patient.

The nonhelpful significant other either rejects the patient or denies the suicidal behavior itself by withdrawing, both psychologically and physically, from continued communication. Sometimes this other person resents the patient's increased demands, insistence on gratification of dependency needs, or the demands to change his own behavior. In other situations, the significant other may act helpless, indecisive, or ambivalent, indicating that he does not know what the next step is and has given up. His reaction of hopelessness gives the suicidal individual a feeling that aid is not available from a previously dependable source. This can increase the patient's own hopelessness.

By contrast, a helpful reaction from the significant other is one in which the other person recognizes the communication, is aware of the problem, and seeks help for the individual. This indicates to the patient that his communications are being heard and that someone is doing something to provide help.

Case study: Suicide
Assessment of the individual and his problem

Carol was referred to a crisis center for help by a physician in the emergency room of a nearby small suburban hospital. The night before, she had attempted suicide by severely slashing her left wrist repeatedly with a large kitchen knife, and she had severed a tendon as a result.

When she was first seen by the therapist at the center, her left wrist and arm were heavily bandaged. She appeared tense, disheveled, very pale, and tremulous. She described her symptoms as insomnia, poor appetite, recent inability to concentrate, and overwhelming feelings of hopelessness and helplessness.

Carol was a 30-year-old woman, single, who lived alone. She had come to a large midwestern city about 4 years ago, immediately after graduating with a master's degree in business administration from an eastern university. Within a few weeks she had obtained a management trainee position with a large manufacturing distributor company. In the next 3 years she had been advanced rapidly to her current position as manager of the main branch office. She stated that she was considered by her co-workers to be highly qualified for the position. She denied any on-the-job problems other than "the usual things that anyone in my position has to expect to deal with on a day-to-day basis." As a result of her rapid rise in the company, however, she had not allowed herself much leisure time to develop any close social relationships with either sex.

About 1 year ago Carol met John, a 40-year-old widower who had a position similar to hers with another company. His office was on the same floor as hers. Within a few weeks they were spending almost all of their leisure time together, though still maintaining separate apartments.

Carol's symptoms began about 2 weeks ago when John was offered a promotion to a new job in his company, which he accepted without mentioning it to her first. It meant that he would be transferred to another office about 30 miles away in the suburbs. She stated that she did feel upset "for just a few minutes" after he told her of his decision; "I guess that was just because he hadn't even mentioned anything about it to me first."

They went out that evening for dinner and dancing to celebrate the occasion. Before dinner was even over John had to bring her home because she "suddenly became dizzy, nauseated, and chilled" with what she described as "all of the worst symptoms of stomach flu."

Carol remained at home in bed for the next 3 days, not allowing John to visit her because she felt she was contagious. After she returned to work she continued to feel very lethargic, had difficulty concentrating, could not regain her appetite, "and felt quite depressed and tearful for no reason at all."

Convincing herself that she had not yet fully recovered from the "flu," she cancelled several dates with John so that she could get more rest. She described him as being very understanding about this, even encouraging her to try to get some time off from work to take a short trip by herself and really rest and relax.

During this same time, John had begun to spend increasing amounts of his time at his new office. Their coffee-break meetings at work became very infrequent. Within the next week he expected to be moved completely.

The night before Carol came to the crisis center she had come home from work expecting to meet John there for dinner; instead she found a note under her door written by her neighbor. It said that John had telephoned him earlier in the day and left word for her that he had "suddenly been called out of town . . . wasn't sure when he would be back . . . but would get in touch with her later."

She told the therapist, "Suddenly I felt empty . . . that everything was over between us. It was just too much for me to handle. He was never going to see me again and was too damned chicken to tell me so to my face! I went numb all over . . . I just wanted to die." She paused a few minutes, head down and sobbing, then took a deep breath and went on, "I really don't remember doing it, but the next thing I was aware of was the telephone ringing. When I reached out to answer it, I suddenly realized I had a butcher knife in my right hand and my left wrist was cut and bleeding terribly! I dropped the knife on the floor and grabbed the phone. It was John calling me from the airport to tell me why he had to go out of town so suddenly — his father was critically ill."

Through sobs she told him what she had just done to herself. He told her to take a kitchen towel and wrap it tightly around her wrist. After she had done that, he told her to unlock the front door and wait there, that he would get help to her.

He immediately called her neighbors, who went to her apartment and found her with blood-soaked towels around her wrist and sitting on the floor beside the door. They took her to the hospital, and John continued on his trip. After being treated in the emergency room, Carol went home to spend the night with her neighbors. They drove her to the crisis center the next morning.

During her initial session Carol told the therapist that she had no close relatives. Her father and mother had died within a few months of each other during her last year in college. Soon after she had fallen in love with another graduate student, and at his suggestion they had moved into an apartment together. She had believed that they would marry as soon as they had both graduated and had jobs.

Just before graduation, however, her boyfriend had come home and informed her that he had accepted a postdoctoral fellowship in France and would be leaving within the month. They went out for dinner "to celebrate" that night because, she said, "I couldn't help but be happy for him . . . it was quite an honor . . . I just couldn't tell him how hurt I felt."

The next morning after he had left for classes she stated that she "suddenly realized I would never see him again after graduation . . . that he had never intended to marry me . . . and I was helpless to do anything about it." She took some masking tape and sealed the kitchen window shut, closed the door and put towels along the bottom, and turned on all of the stove gas jets.

About an hour later a neighbor smelled the gas fumes and called the fire department. The firemen broke into the apartment, found her lying unconscious on the floor, and rushed her to the hospital. She was in a coma for 2 days and remained in the hospital for a week. Her boyfriend came only once to see her. When she returned to the apartment, she found that he had moved out, leaving her a note saying that he had gone home to see his family before taking off for France. He never contacted her again. A month later Carol moved to the Midwest.

For the first few months after meeting John, Carol was very ambivalent about her feelings toward him. She frequently felt very anxious and fearful that she was "setting myself up for another rejection." Even when John proposed marriage, she found herself unable to consider it seriously and told him that they should wait a while longer "to be sure that they both wanted it." Continuing, she stated, "Until about 2 days ago I had never felt so secure in my life . . . I'd even begun to seriously consider proposing to him! Then, suddenly, the bottom began to fall out of everything."

When John accepted the new job without telling her first, Carol saw this as the beginning of another rejection by someone highly significant in her life. As her anxiety increased, she withdrew from communication with John "because of her flu." John's well-intentioned agreement to cancel several dates so that she could get more rest further cut off her opportunities to communicate her feelings to him. His suggestion that she take a trip alone compounded her already strong fear of imminent rejection by him.

Finding the neighbor's note under the door was, for her, "the last straw," final proof that he was leaving her, "just like my boyfriend did in college."

Unable to cope with overwhelming feelings of loss and anger toward herself for "letting it happen to me again," she impulsively attempted to commit suicide.

Planning of therapeutic intervention

Carol's two suicide attempts, except for the method used, were quite similar. Both were precipitated by the threat of the loss of someone highly significant in her life; both were impulsive, maladaptive attempts to cope with intense feelings of depression, hoplessness, and helplessness; and both demonstrated an inability to communicate her feelings in stressful situations.

When asked by the therapist how she usually coped with anxiety in the past. Carol said that she would keep herself so busy at work that she did not have much time to worry about personal problems. This had been her method for coping with anxiety at school, too, until her first suicide attempt. Since she had been too ill to work full time the past 2 weeks, her previous successful coping mechanisms could not be effectively used.

The goal of intervention was to help Carol gain an intellectual understanding of the relationship between her crisis and her inability to communicate her intense feelings of depression and anxiety caused by the threat of the loss of John.

Intervention

Before the end of the first session the therapist's assessment was that Carol was no longer acutely suicidal. However, because of her continuing feelings of depression, a medical consultation was arranged and an antidepressant prescribed. A verbal contact was agreed on; Carol was to call the therapist if she felt suicidal again. Carol agreed to the suggestion that she have a friend move into her apartment to help her out until her arm was less painful. Before leaving she assured the therapist that she would call him immediately if she again began to feel overwhelmed by anxiety before her next appointment.

When Carol returned for her next session, she was markedly less depressed. She told the therapist that John had called her soon after she came home from the center the week before. Although he had expressed great concern for her, she had been unable to tell him exactly why she had attempted suicide. "I just couldn't tell him that I thought he had left me for good . . . he'd think that I was trying to blame him . . . after all, I've been telling him for months that we should both keep our independence!" However, she said she felt much more reassured of his love for her. John expected to be back in about 2 more weeks.

During this and the next few sessions the therapist explored with Carol why she found it difficult to communicate her feelings to someone so significant in her life. Carol was reluctant at first to admit that this was a problem that could have contributed to her recent cirisis. She perceived herself as someone who was completely self-sufficient and denied any dependency needs on John. As a child she had been expected to control her emotions, to appear "ladylike" and composed at all times. Efforts on her part to communicate her feelings as she passed through the normal maturational crises of childhood and adolescence were met with rejecting behavior from those most significant in her life — her parents. Slow-ly she began to gain insight into the ways in which she had learned maladaptive methods to cope with stress, such as withdrawing from contact with others when-ever she felt threatened by a stressful situation; by somatizing her anxiety rather than admit it was more than she could handle. By the end of the third session she reported that she had been able to communicate her feelings to John more openly and honestly than she had ever done in the past. She appeared to be surprised and pleased that John had responded so positively to her. When asked what she would have done if he had not responded this way, she paused thoughtfully, then answered. "It was a risk I had to take. I just had to find out for sure if I could handle it this time." She added that although she had been very anxious while talking to him, she at no time felt as though she could not go on living if things had turned out differently.

By the end of the fourth session John had returned to the city, and Carol had returned to her job full time. She no longer felt depressed, and her wrist was slow-ly regaining its functioning. They were seeing each other frequently despite the distance between their offices, and Carol now said that she felt much more com-fortable talking things out with him.

Anticipatory planning

Because Carol had attempted suicide once before under much the same crisis-precipitating stressful situations, she was continued in therapy for the full 6 weeks. The purpose was to ensure that she could depend on situational support from the therapist while adjusting the fact that she would no longer be seeing John every day. She was encouraged to telephone the therapist at any time she began to feel a recurrence of her earlier symptoms and felt unable to communicate these feelings to John.

Because she now seemed to have a better understanding of the relationship between her suicide attempts and the precipitating events, she said that she felt more secure in being able to cope with stressful situations in a more positive manner.

Summation of paradigm

Carol's distorted perception of rejection by John was compounded by her pre-vious experience in losing someone highly significant in her life. Unable to direct-ly communicate her feelings to John, her anxiety and depression increased. Lack-ing adequate coping mechanisms and situational support, she became over-whelmed with feelings of hopelessness and helplessness. Anticipating another rejection, Carol, entering a state of crisis, impulsively attempted suicide. Inter-vention was focused on getting her to understand why she was unable to com-municate and cope with her intense feelings of inadequacy in interpersonal relations.

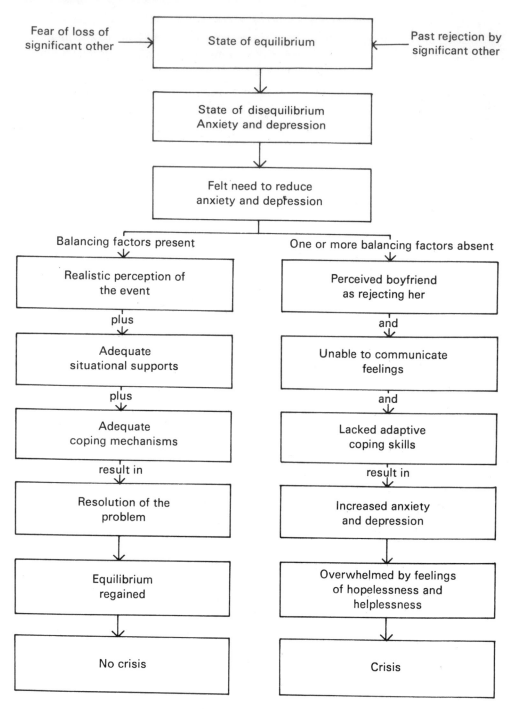

Fig. 8. □ **Case study: Carol.**

DEATH AND THE GRIEF PROCESS
Theoretical concepts

To all who are living, death is certain. This universal phenomenon has ominous presence in that it is realistic and inescapable. Since every human being will at some time be subject to death, it seems that death is most significant. Much is unknown of the process of death, and human beings are noted for their fear of the unknown. It might be said that this is a basic fear, and throughout the ages man has sought self-preservation. Advances in medical science as well as allied areas support this contention.

The critical question is not the sham dichotomy of life and death but the way in which each person relates to the knowledge that death is certain. This fear may be the prototype of human anxiety. Throughout history, death has posed an external mystery that is the core of religious and philosophical systems of thought. Anxiety relates to the fact that man is powerless; he may postpone death, he may lessen its physical pain, he may rationalize it away or deny its very existence, but he cannot escape it, and so the fight for self-preservation is inevitably lost.

The attitudes of the persons involved in the situation are basic to the process of dying. Concepts, philosophies, and attitudes about death evolve from centuries of conflicting ideas and thought.

Traditionally the attitude of a society toward death has been a function of its religious beliefs. Religion denies the finality of death and affirms the continuation of the human personality either in its psychophysical totality or as a soul. The medical and social sciences, by challenging these traditional beliefs, have indirectly caused alienation and a serious mental health problem.

Family reaction to the death of a member develops in stages varying in time. The death of a loved one must produce an active expression of feeling in the normal course of events. Omission of such a reaction is to be considered as much a variation from the normal as is an excess in time and intensity. Unmanifested grief will be found expressed in some way or another; each new loss can cause grief for the current loss as well as reactivate the grieving process of previous episodes.

Lindemann (1944) states that following the loss there are three phases of mourning.

Phase I. Shock and disbelief. There is a focus on the original object with symptoms of somatic distress occurring in waves, lasting from 20 minutes to an hour at a time, a feeling of tightness in the throat, choking with shortness of breath, need for sighing, an empty feeling in the abdomen, and lack of muscular power. There is commonly a slight sense of unreality, a feeling of increased emotional distance from other people, and an intense preoccupation with the image of the deceased.

There is a strong preoccupation with feelings of guilt, and the bereaved searches the time before death for evidence of failure to do right by the lost one, accusing himself of negligence and exaggerating minor omissions.

Phase II. Developing awareness. Disorganization of personality occurs in this phase, accompanied by pain and despair because of the persistent and insatiable nature of yearning for the lost object. There is weeping and a feeling of helplessness and possible identification with the deceased.

Phase III. Resolving the loss. Resolution of the loss completes the work of mourning. A reorganization takes place with emancipation from the image of the lost object, and new object relationships are formed.

Engel (1964) states that the clearest evidence that mourning or grieving is successfully completed is the ability to remember *completely* and *realistically* the pleasures *and* disappointments of the lost relationship.

In this phase one must also consider pathological mourning, in which there is an inability to express overtly these urges to recover the lost object. When all reactions are repressed, they will influence behavior in a strange and distorted way; for example, a schizophrenic's reaction to the death of a significant individual may be laughter. There may be a delayed reaction or an excessive reaction; or the grief reaction may take the form of a straight agitated depression with accompanying tension, agitation, insomnia, feelings of worthlessness, bitter self-accusation, and obvious need for punishment. Individuals reacting in this way may be dangerously suicidal.

Proper management of grief reactions may prevent prolonged and serious alterations in an individual's social adjustment. The essential task is that of sharing and understanding the individual's grief work. Comfort alone does not provide adequate assistance. He has to accept the pain of the bereavement. He has to review his relationships with the deceased. He will have to express his sorrow and sense of loss. He must accept the destruction of a part of his personality before he can organize it afresh toward a new object or goal. Although they are unwelcome, such phases are a necessary part of life (Lindemann, 1944).

The following case study concerns a retired widower who is threatened by a second loss before completing "grief work" from the recent death of his wife. Initial assessment of the crisis situation provided clues in the determination that he was probably in the last phase of mourning and became overwhelmed by the threat of losing another highly cathected object, his son. The goal of intervention was to assist Mr. P. in reentering his social world and in gaining an intellectual understanding of the grief process as it related to his symptoms.

Case study: Death and the grief process
Assessment of the individual and his problem

Mr. P., 67 years old and recently widowed, came for help to a crisis center on the advice of his family physician because of severe depression and anxiety. He described his symptoms as loss of appetite, inability to concentrate, restlessness, insomnia, and loss of energy. These symptoms had been first manifested a month

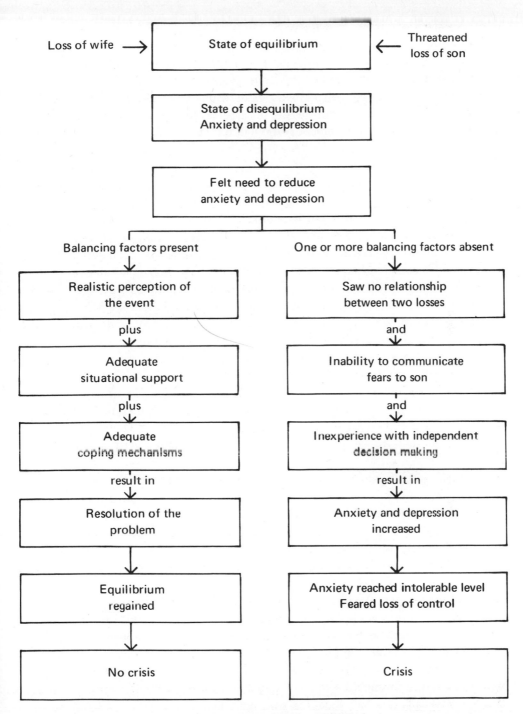

Loss of wife → State of equilibrium ← Threatened loss of son

State of disequilibrium
Anxiety and depression

Felt need to reduce
anxiety and depression

Balancing factors present / One or more balancing factors absent

Realistic perception of
the event

Saw no relationship
between two losses

plus / and

Adequate
situational support

Inability to communicate
fears to son

plus / and

Adequate
coping mechanisms

Inexperience with independent
decision making

result in / result in

Resolution of the
problem

Anxiety and depression
increased

Equilibrium
regained

Anxiety reached intolerable level
Feared loss of control

No crisis / Crisis

Fig. 9. □ Case study: Mr. P.

earlier, following the death of his wife. He thought that they had been subsiding, but they suddenly increased to an intolerable level and he feared loss of emotional control. He denied any suicidal ideas, stating "I don't want to die, it's just that I've lost all interest in life and no longer care what happens to me."

During the initial visit, Mr. P. was, at first, unable to determine any specific event that might have caused the sudden and acute rise in his symptoms. His wife's death was not unexpected, and he had felt "well prepared" for a future life without her. He viewed himself as realistic in his attitudes and planning before she died and as having experienced a "normal amount of grief" afterward.

After a mandatory-age retirement when he was 65 years old, he had devoted most of his time in helping to care for his wife, a semi-invalid with severe coronary disease. "I think I was really glad when I retired, because I'd had so little time for myself in those last few years, working all day and then coming home and trying to catch up with things I had to do there." Having little time for social activities with his business friends, he had felt little sense of their loss when he left his job.

He had one son, married and living nearby. The son and his wife had close relationships with Mr. and Mrs. P., helping them out with their household activities and the care of Mrs. P. Mr. P. had made tentative plans to move into an apartment after his wife's death, feeling fully able to care for his own needs. However, just after she died his son and daughter-in-law brought up the idea of their moving into his home with him. It was a large home, much larger than their rented one, and they would pay him monthly amounts toward eventually buying it from him. He said that he was quite pleased with the idea, preferring to remain in his home but unable to justify to himself any reason for staying there alone. They had moved in 2 weeks ago, and he had felt an immediate lessening in his grief reaction to his wife's death.

A week ago his son had received an unexpected offer of a better job in another state. Mr. P. related that he felt very proud of the offer to his son, strongly urging him to accept it. The decision had to be made within the month. Since he had previously begun plans to live alone, he had not felt too concerned for himself if his son and daughter-in-law did decide to leave.

That same night he had suddenly awakened, feeling nauseous, tense, anxious, and very depressed, and sleep had become increasingly difficult as these symptoms had increased in the past few days. Although he no longer experienced nausea, there was a loss of appetite, insomnia, and a feeling of total exhaustion. He summed up his feelings by saying that he guess "maybe I'm not as happy about my son leaving as I told him I was."

The therapist thought that Mr. P.'s recovery from the grief at the loss of his wife had evolved through the stage of shock and disbelief. He had anticipated her death realistically and had accepted it as inevitable. He had begun to overcome his feelings of guilt and sense of failure, as well as his persistent longing for a lost object (his wife). Mr. P. was probably in the last phase of mourning, that of emancipation from the image of the lost object and the initial formation of new object relationships. At this stage, before final resolution of his grief, he was unexpectedly threatened with loss of another highly cathected object, his son.

Planning of therapeutic intervention

Mr. P. had few social contacts because of his total involvement with the care of his wife during the past few years. His son and daughter-in-law had been providing situational support before and during his period of mourning, and this support was now in jeopardy. He had unrecognized ambivalence with regard to the job offer made to his son. Although intellectualizing plans to move into an apartment by himself, he lacked skills that would be necessary to repeople his social world. The anxiety generated by his unresolved grief and his ambivalence about his personal future was then compounded by the unexpected threat of a new loss.

When asked how he had coped with stress in the past, he said that he had always been able to keep busy caring for his wife and the housework. He had also been able to talk things over with his son. He now felt unable to talk to his son about his present feelings "for fear he might think he'd have to give up the job offer and stay here with me."

The goal of intervention was to help Mr. P. in gaining an intellectual understanding of his crisis in order to recognize the relationship between the threatened loss of his son and his present severe discomfort. His unrecognized ambivalence between his needs for independence as opposed to dependency would be explored.

Intervention

During the next 2 weeks it became possible for him to see the present crisis and its accompanying symptoms in relation to his reactions to the loss of his wife and the threatened loss of his son.

During Mrs. P.'s illness he had narrowed his own life-style to conform to hers. In failing to acknowledge his lack of the interpersonal skills necessary to maintain a social life of his own, he justified his action as "what would be expected of any husband in a similar situation." Mrs. P. had been the dominant member of the marriage. Even when bedridden, she had guided the decision making that he thought was independent on his part. The additional support and assistance by his son and daughter-in-law only served to increase his dependency on others for decision making.

At times during the past few years he had thoughts of "all the things we could have done if I'd retired when my wife had not been so ill." He had deflected these thoughts into overt sympathy for her rather than for himself and what he was missing. As her death became imminent and inevitable, his wife began to make plans with him for his future. She told him to sell the home and to move into an apartment, even selecting which furniture he should keep and which he should give away.

When she died, he was finally faced with the reality of his inability to cope with the changes. Crisis at this time was circumvented by the offer of his son to move into his home. He was able to continue in much the same life pattern that had previously existed for him, with the son and daughter-in-law assuming the leadership role. With their strong situational support the work of grief had not become overwhelming.

The sudden threat of their loss had precipitated the crisis. Unrecognized feelings of inadequacy and dependency had come into painful focus. He feared both the physical loss of his son and the loss of his son's love if the job were turned down "because he'd think I couldn't take care of myself if he left me here alone."

By the third session, through discussion and clarification with the therapist, Mr. P. was able to recognize his ambivalent feelings and relate them to his own needs for dependency. He saw the disparity between his concept of what he thought others expected of him and what he could actually achieve alone. His acceptance of this enabled him to reestablish meaningful communication with his son and to gain his support in making more realistic plans.

Anticipatory planning

Mr. P.'s exploration of his feelings related to his loss and subsequent grief helped him to gain an intellectual understanding of the process of working through the period of mourning. His recognition of his symptoms as part of the process helped to reduce his anxiety and enabled him to better perceive the reality of the situation and to utilize his existing coping skills. Realization was gained that he himself was withdrawing from available situational support because of his concept that his role was to be "an independent person." He was able to accept the fact that this might not be true and, as a result, felt better about communicating his fears to his son and enlisting his assistance in planning.

By the third week his son had made the decision to accept the position and move out of the state in another month. Through joint efforts they located an apartment-hotel for Mr. P., where he would have the independence to "come and go as I'd always planned for in my retirement." Since the hotel preferred its guests to be in the retirement-age group, there were programs established for the guests' interests and social needs.

Mr. P. moved into the hotel 3 weeks before his son left town. The period of transition was facilitated with minimal rise in his anxiety. There was a gradual removal of his son's situational support, which was being replaced by the support gained in new social contacts. Although he felt grief when his son and daughter-in-law left town, Mr. P. could recognize and relate his symptoms to the event and so was able to cope with them.

In discussion and review of his future plans Mr. P. was optimistic about his ability to live independently within the framework of his new environment. He was slowly entering new activities and making new friends, although he admitted "being a bit rusty about how to do it."

Before termination Mr. P. and the therapist reviewed the adjustments that he had made, as well as his new insights into his own feelings. He thought that the crisis situation, although being very painful to him at the time, had provided him with a "good idea of how to face up to things in the future." His future plans were also reviewed, and he was reassured by the therapist that he could always return for future help should the occasion arise.

Summation of the paradigm

Mr. P. had failed to recognize any relationship between his feelings of increased anxiety and the death of his wife. His inexperience with independent decision making made him inadequate to cope with the stressful event alone. Intervention with strong situational support by his son and daughter-in-law assisted him to begin to work through the grief process and averted a crisis.

The unexpected threat of his son's and daughter-in-law's departure and his inability to communicate his fears resulted in their loss to him as situational supports. These factors were compounded by uncompleted grief work and a failure to see any connection between his recurrence of severe anxiety and his reaction to a second loss.

In the assessment phase the therapist kept focus on the areas of stress to determine the adequacy of his past coping skills with bereavement. Intervention was directed toward assisting him to explore and ventilate his feelings of dependency. Anticipatory planning was directed toward providing him with situational supports when his son moved from town.

REFERENCES

Aguilera, D. C.: Review of psychiatric nursing, St. Louis, 1977, The C. V. Mosby Co.

Allport, G. W.: Pattern and growth in personality, New York, 1961, Holt, Rinehart & Winston.

Amir, M.: Patterns in forcible rape, Chicago, 1971, University of Chicago Press.

Bernstein, R.: Are we still stereotyping the unmarried mother? Soc. Work **5:**22, 1960.

Bowlby, J.: Separation anxiety, Int. J. Psychoanal. **41:**89, 1960.

Brown, H. F., Burditt, Vera B., and Lidell, W. W.: The crisis of relocation. In Parad, H. J., editor: Crisis intervention, New York, 1965, Family Service Association of America.

Burgess, A. W., and Holmstrom, L. L.: "The rape victim in the emergency ward," **73**(10): 1741, 1973.

Burgess, A. W., and Holmstrom, L. L.: "Rape trauma syndrome," Am. J. Psychiatry **131:**982, Sept. 1974.

Caplan, G.: An approach to community mental health. New York, 1961, Grune & Stratton, Inc.

Caplan, G.: Principles of preventive psychiatry, New York, 1964, Basic Books, Inc., Publishers.

Chown, S. M., editor: Human aging, New York, 1972, Penguin Books.

Claridge, G.: Drugs and human behavior, Middlesex, Engl., 1972, Penguin Books, Ltd.

Comstock, B. S., and McDermott, M.: Group

therapy for patients who attempt suicide, Int. J. Group Psychother. 25(1):44, 1975.

Croog, S. H., Levine, S., and Lurie, Z.: The heart patient and the recovery process, Soc. Sci. Med. 2:111, 1968.

Engel, G. L.: Grief and grieving, Am. J. Nurs. 64: 93, Sept. 1964.

Faberow, N., and Shneidman, E., editors: The cry for help, New York, 1961, McGraw-Hill Book Co.

Frederick, C. J.: Organizing and funding suicide prevention and crisis services, Hosp. Community Psychiatry 23(11):346, 1972.

Glass, A. T.: Observations upon the epidemiology of mental illness in troops during warfare, Symposium on Preventive and Social Psychiatry sponsored by Walter Reed Army Institute of Research, Walter Reed Medical Center, and National Research Council, April 15-17, Washington, D.C., 1957, U.S. Government Printing Office.

Gouirand, Y., and Soubrier, J. P.: Possibilities of psychotherapeutic intervention in suicide attempters and those who are suicidal, Perspect. Psychiatriques 3(47):153, 1974.

Greene, B. L.: Sequential marriage; repetition or change. In Rosenbaum, S., and Alger, I., editors: The marriage relationship, New York, 1968, Basic Books, Inc. Publishers.

Hankoff, L. D., Mischore, M. T., Tomlinson, K. E., and Joyce, S. A.: Crisis intervention in the emergency room. Am. J. Psychiatry 131:47, 1974.

Hellerstein, H., and Goldstone, E.: Rehabilitation of patients with heart disease, Postgrad. Med. 15:265, 1954.

Hinkle, L. E., Jr.: Social factors and coronary heart disease, Soc. Sci. Med. 2:107, 1968.

Hollender, M. H.: The psychology of medical practice, Philadelphia, 1958, W. B. Saunders Co.

Holmstrom, L. L., and Burgess, A. W.: Assessing trauma in the rape victim, Am. J. Nurs. 75(8):1288, 1975.

Kaplan, D. M., and Mason, E. A.: Maternal reactions to premature birth viewed as an acute emotional disorder. In Parad, H. J., editor: Crisis intervention, New York, 1965, Family Service Association of America.

King, S. H.: Perceptions of illness and medical practice, New York, 1962, Russell Sage Foundation.

Kubie, L. S., cited by Kaufman, J. G., and Becker, M. D.: Rehabilitation of the patient with myocardial infarction, Geriatrics 10:355, 1955.

Kübler-Ross, E.: On death and dying, New York, 1969, MacMillan, Inc.

Kübler-Ross, E.: Questions and answers on death and dying, New York, 1974, Collier Books.

Laurie, P.: Drugs; medical, psychological, and social facts, ed. 2, Middlesex, Engl., 1971, Pelican, C. Nicholls & Co. Ltd.

Lee, P. R., and Bryner, S.: Introduction to a symposium on rehabilitation in cardiovascular disease, Am. J. Cardiol 7:315, 1961.

Lindemann, E.: Symptomatology and management of acute grief, Am. J. Psychiatry 101:141, Sept. 1944.

Linton, R.: Culture and mental disorders, Springfield, Ill., 1956, Charles C Thomas, Publisher.

Long, L. H., editor: The world almanac and book of facts, New York, 1968, Newspaper Enterprise Association, Inc.

Mason, E. A.: Method of predicting crisis outcome for mothers of premature babies, Public Health Rep. 78:1031, Dec. 1963.

McDonald, J. M.: Rape; offenders and their victims, Springfield, Ill., 1971, Charles C Thomas, Publisher.

McGee, R K. Berg., D., Brockopp, G. W., Harris. J. R., Haughton, A. B., Rachlis, D., Tomes, H. and Hoff, L. A.: The delivery of suicide and crisis intervention services. In Resnik, H.: Suicide prevention the 70's, Rockville, Md., 1973, National Institute of Mental Health.

McIver, J.: Psychiatric aspects of cardiovascular diseases in industry. In Warshaw, L. J., editor: The heart in industry, New York, 1960, Harper & Row, Publishers.

Milbauer, B.: Drug abuse and addiction, New York, 1970, The New American Library, Inc.

Moore, H. E.: Tornadoes over Texas; a study of Waco and San Angelo in disaster, Austin, Tex., 1958, University of Texas Press.

Morley, W. E., Messick, J. M., and Aguilera, D. C.: Crisis; paradigms of intervention, J. Psychiatr. Nurs. 5:540, Nov.-Dec. 1967.

Parsons, F.: The social system, New York, 1951, The Free Press.

Rapoport, L.: The state of crisis; some theoretical considerations, Soc. Service Rev. 36:211, 1962.

Rapoport, R.: Normal crises, family structure, and mental health, Family Process 2:68, 1963.

Rehabilitation of patients with cardiovascular diseases, technical report series, Geneva, 1966, World Health Organization.

Reiser, M. F.: Emotional aspects of cardiac disease, Am. J. Psychiatry 107:781, 1951.

Resnik, H. L. P., and Hathorne, B. C.: Summary of recommendations of the task force on suicide prevention. In Resnik, H.: Suicide prevention in the 70's, Rockville, Md., 1973, National Institute of Mental Health.

Selkin, J.: Rape, Psychol. Today, Jan. 1975, pp. 71-76.

Singh, A. N.; Brown, J. H.: Suicide prevention; review and evaluation, Can. Psychiatr. Assoc. J. 18(2):117, 1973.

Storaska, F.: How to say no to a rapist and survive, New York, 1976, Warner Books, Inc.

Vernick, J.: The use of the life space interview on a medical ward, Soc. Casework 44:465, 1963.

Zinberg, N. E., and Robertson, J. A.: Drugs and the public, New York, 1972, Simon & Schuster, Inc.

7 □ Maturational crises

An individual's life-style is continually subject to change by the ongoing processes of maturational development, shifting situations within his environment, or a combination of both. Potential crisis areas occur during the periods of great social, physical, and psychological change experienced by all human beings in the normal growth process. These changes could occur during concomitant biological and social role transitions such as birth, puberty, young adulthood, marriage, illness or death of a family member, the climacteric, and old age.

Maturational crises have been described as normal processes of growth and development. They usually evolve over an extended period of time, such as the transition into adolescence, and they frequently require that the individual make many characterological changes. There may be an awareness of increased feelings of disequilibrium, but intellectual understanding of any correlation with normal developmental change may be inadequate.

The hazardous situations that occur in daily life may serve to compound normal maturational crises. When an individual requests help at these times, it is necessary to determine what part of the presenting symptomatology is due to transitional maturational stages and what, in turn, is due to a stressful event in his current social orbit.

The theoretical concepts used in this chapter are derived primarily from Erikson's (1950, 1959, 1963) psychosocial maturational tasks (trust, autonomy, initiative, industry, identity, intimacy, generativity, and integrity); Piaget's (1963) ontogenetic development of intellectual abilities (sensorimotor—birth to 2 years; preoperational thought—2 to 7 years; concrete operations—7 to 11 years; and formal operations—11 to 14 years); and Cameron's (1963) personality development, which is based on a synthesis of recent theories of general psychology and dynamic psychopathology.

For the sake of clarity the maturational crises discussed in this chapter are presented in the more generally familiar phases: infancy and early childhood, preschool, prepuberty, adolescence, young adulthood, adulthood, late adulthood, and old age.

The case studies and paradigms presented here illustrate some common maturational crises. It must be emphasized that seldom are hazardous events and maturational crises this clearly defined.

INFANCY AND EARLY CHILDHOOD
Theoretical concepts

The first year of life is one of almost total helplessness and dependency. The infant must learn to trust the maternal figure and become able to allow her out of his sight without fear or rage. He must also be able to develop confidence in the sameness and continuity of his environment and to internalize it through his developing tactile, auditory, olfactory, and visual senses. Deprivation in any one or a combination of these senses could lead to maladaptive response patterns affecting his biopsychosocial development.

During this stage, the symbiotic relationship that develops between the infant and the maternal figure forms a foundation for the behavioral patterns of later personality development. This relationship goes beyond the symbiosis of mutual dependency for biological survival; in the psychosocial development of the infant it implies that the mother is willing and ready to assume responsibility for the infant, who in turn accepts her care passively without reciprocating.

During infancy the mouth is the primary organ of gratification and exploration; feeding becomes an important aspect of meeting needs. This is controlled by someone else, usually the mother, and her consistency in meeting her infant's needs for oral gratification is the beginning of his development of trust in his environment.

As a result of the varied experiences that he and his mother share, the infant develops confidence that his needs will be met. Through her own dependability, the mother structures these situations so that there is a basis for a mutual sense of confidence. For example, if the infant is fed regularly at times when he has come to expect a feeding, his sense of trust is encouraged. But, should the feedings become sporadic, he will become uncertain and anxious about his environment, and a sense of mistrust will begin to appear. His resulting fretful, anxious behavior may inspire further inadequate mothering. Another essential component of the healthy symbiotic relationship is the comfort brought by the mother; if discomfort is inflicted, any continued trust can be destroyed.

Environmental consistency and stimulation are important for cognitive and effective growth. The infant usually becomes aware of his mother as a person by 9 months; however, absence of *mothering* can provoke symptoms of insecurity by the age of 4 weeks, such as crying and rocking, followed by withdrawal, depression, and even death.

Piaget (1963) describes the infant's development of intelligent behavior in this stage as *sensorimotor*. During the first year the reflex patterns he was born with are repeated and strengthened with practice. As a newborn, he is capable of grasping, sucking, auditory and visual pursuit, and other stereotyped behavior patterns. These can be activated by nonspecific stimuli in the environment; after being activated a number of times the response becomes spontaneous without further external stimulation. For example, at birth the infant is able to suck at the breast; continued practice improves his coordination and facility until this ability becomes well adapted to the goal of taking nourishment.

These primary reflex actions become coordinated into new actions. For example, the hand accidentally comes in contact with the mouth and initiates sucking movements that may lead to more coordinated actions and to thumbsucking as an established form of behavior. Later actions become oriented toward objects in the environment that stimulate his seeing and hearing, and intentional behavior emerges as he seeks to repeat these actions. He learns to begin meaningful actions in sequence and to explore new objects within his reach, thus developing goal-oriented activity. In this way physical activity patterns develop into mental activity patterns of response.

By the end of the first year the stage of purposeful behavior is reached, and exploration of further boundaries of the environment is begun. Motor actions have gradually become internalized as thought patterns. During this period the trend is toward a higher level of sensory experiences and related mental activities. By the end of the second year there is a functional understanding of play, imitation, causality, objects, space, and time. By the age of 2 years a child can truly imitate such behavior as eating, sleeping, washing himself, and walking.

If the child does not develop the beginnings of trust, in later life there may be a sense of chronic mistrust, dependency, depressive trends, withdrawal, and shallow interpersonal relationships.

During the second year the child begins a struggle for autonomy. He shifts from dependency on others toward independent actions of his own. As his musculature matures, it is necessary for him to develop the ability of coordination such as "holding on" and "letting go." Since these are highly opposing patterns, conflict may occur; one example is the conflict arising over bowel and bladder control. A power struggle may develop between the child and his parents, since elimination is completely under his control, and approval or disapproval become strong influences because of his parents' attitudes toward eliminative habits. The child is expected to abandon his needs for self-gratification and substitute ones that meet the demands of his parents, representing the later demands of society.

Cognitive development in this stage includes the first symbolic substitutions, words and gross speech. The child begins to manipulate objects and will look for hidden items. He recognizes differences between "I" and "me," "mine" and "you" and "yours." He also begins to manipulate others by words such as "no," and the origins of concrete literal thinking are developed; this is the period of *preoperational thought* that continues to the age of 7 years (Piaget, 1963). One of its characteristics is egocentrism, in which the child is unable to take the viewpoint of another person; at the end of this period, egocentrism is replaced by social interaction. The child has now formed concepts in primitive images, thing to thing. He cannot cope intellectually with problems concerning time, causality, space, or other abstract concepts, although he understands what each is by itself in concrete situations. His perceptions dominate his judgments, and he operates on what can be seen directly.

The psychosocial task during this stage is to develop self-esteem through limited self-control. The achievement of bowel and bladder control within the prescribed cultural expectations allows also for self-control without loss of self-esteem.

This is an important time for establishing a ratio between love and hate, cooperation and willfulness, and freedom of self-expression and its suppression. Failure during this stage is manifested in childhood by feelings of shame and doubt, fear of exposure, and ritualized activity; in later adulthood the failure to achieve "autonomy" is seen in the individual who is a "compulsive character," with an irrational need for conformity and a concomitant irrational need for approval.

PRESCHOOL
Theoretical concepts

Erikson (1950, 1959, 1963) believes that in the preschool stage the child has the task of developing *initiative.* He will discover what kind of person he is going to be, he learns to move around freely and has an unlimited radius of goals, his language skills broaden, and he will ask many questions. His skill in using words is not matched by his skill in understanding them, and he is thus faced with the dangers of misinterpretation and misunderstanding. Language and locomotion allow him to expand his imagination over such a broad spectrum that he can easily frighten himself with dreams and thoughts.

The prerequisites for masculine and feminine initiative are developed. Infantile sexual curiosity and preoccupation with sexual matters arise. Oedipal wishes can occur as a result of increased imagination, and terrifying fantasies and a sense of guilt over these fantasies may develop.

Initiative becomes governed by a firmly established conscience. The child feels shame not only when he is found out but also when he fears being found out; guilt is felt for thoughts as well as deeds, and in this stage anxiety is controlled by play, by fantasy, and by pride in the attainment of new skills.

He is ready to learn quickly and to share and to work with others toward a given goal; he begins to identify with people other than his parents and will develop a feeling of equality of worth with others despite differences in functions and age.

At 4½ to 5 years of age the shift from infantile to juvenile body build is rapid, and the beginning of hand-eye coordination as well as an intellectual growth spurt occurs. The social base of gender role is firmly laid down by the end of the fifth year. If this stage is successfully accomplished, the child develops the fantasy of "I who can become"; but if the child is excessively guilt-ridden, his fantasy is "I who shouldn't dream of it." The desired self-concept at the end of this stage is "I have the worth to try even if I am small."

Failure or trauma at this time leads to confusion of psychosexual role, rigidity and guilt in interpersonal relations, and loss of initiative in the exploration of new skills.

PREPUBERTY
Theoretical concepts

Prepuberty years are characterized as the learning stage; that is, "I am what I learn" (Erikson, 1959:82). The child wants to be shown how to do things both alone and with others; he develops a sense of industry in which he becomes dissatisfied if he does not have the feeling of being useful or a sense of his ability to make things and make them well, even perfectly. He now learns to win recognition by *producing things*. He feels pleasure when his attention and diligence produce a completed work.

There is a slow but steady growth as maturation of the central nervous system continues. In terms of psychosexual development there is reduced pressure in the exploration of sensuality and the gender role while other skills are developed and exploited.

The cognitive phase of development includes the mastery of skills in manipulating objects and the concepts of his culture. Thinking enters the period of *concrete operations* (Piaget, 1963), and the ability to solve concrete problems with this ability increases, so that toward the end of this period the child is able to abstract problems. The solution of real problems is accomplished with mental operations that the child was previously unable to perform. By puberty the child exhibits simple deductive reasoning ability and has learned the rules and the basic technology of his culture, thus reinforcing his sense of belonging in his environment.

Self-esteem is derived from the sense of adequacy and the beginning of "best" friendships and sharing with peers. This also marks the beginning of the individual's friendships and loves outside of his family, as he begins to learn the complexities, pleasures, and difficulties of adjusting himself and his drives, aggressive and erotic, to those of his peers. By learning and adjusting he begins to take his place as a member of their group and social life. In making this adjustment he seeks the company of his own sex and forms groups and secret societies. The gangs and groups, especially the boys, fight each other in games, baseball, and cops and robbers, working off much hostility and aggression in a socially approved manner.

Feelings of inadequacy and inferiority may begin if the child does not develop a sense of adequacy. Family life may not have prepared him for school, or the school itself may fail to help him in developing the necessary skills for competency. As a result, he may feel that he will never be good at anything he attempts.

The following case study is of a 9-year-old boy whose maturational development had been delayed by physical illness and the actions of an overprotective mother. His biopsychosocial skills were inadequate to meet the competition required by his peer group and made him unable to gain their acceptance.

Case study: Prepuberty
Assessment of the individual and the problem

Michael F., a 9-year-old boy, was referred with his parents to a crisis center by his school counselor. He had missed 5½ weeks of school, the first week because of a cold and the rest of his absences because of headaches and vomiting in the morning as he was getting ready to leave for school.

Mrs. F. stated that Michael had always been a sickly child. He had a hernia repaired at 3 months of age and was also subject to colds and allergies. Only the week before she had taken Michael to a hospital for a thorough physical exam, which included an EEG, lumbar puncture, and blood tests. The physician told her that there was nothing physically wrong with Michael and suggested that his illness was "probably psychosomatic"; it was he who had referred them to the therapist.

Michael was average in height and slightly overweight, his mannerisms were awkward and his coordination was poor, he was pale but looked healthy, and he seemed embarrassed by the whole situation. Michael was seen initially by the therapist without his parents present. His speech was hesitant, immature, and more like that of a 5-year-old. When asked why he was out of school, he said he "didn't know." He said he was an A and B student in school and that he disliked the recess period (during which the boys engaged in sports) because he was never picked for a team. He thought that he had no friends because of his dislike for sports and because the other boys said he "talked like a baby."

After seeing Michael alone the therapist talked to his parents to verify the information she had received from him and to assess their feelings about his problems and their ability to cope with them. Mrs. F. was a small, nervous, alert woman who had been in psychotherapy herself for the past few years. Her sister had died of nephritis a few months earlier, and she was concerned that Michael was exhibiting the same symptoms. Mr. F. was a rugged, handsome man, interested in

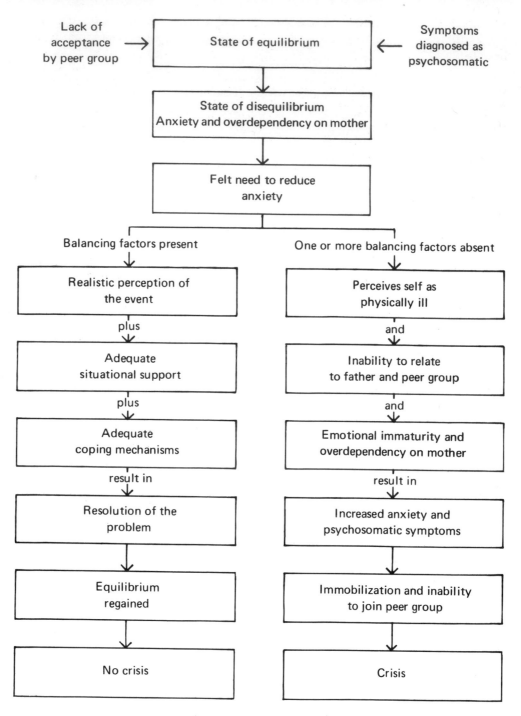

Fig. 10. □ Case study: Michael.

sports and the business world. He said his relationship with Michael had been good until the present illness, but recently he had been unable to relate to Michael because of all the restrictions his wife had placed on their activities.

Michael had a history of frequent illness and had become extremely dependent on his mother, who encouraged this dependency. The school situation was forcing Michael to relate to his peer group, whose interests were in sports and cooperative activities; but Michael's dependency on his mother left him unprepared to enter his peer group, and he had no coping mechanisms in his repertoire with which to handle his anxieties.

Planning of therapeutic intervention

It was thought that Michael's mother and father needed assistance in gaining a realistic, intellectual understanding of the situation. The mother's imagined fears of Michael's serious illness were based on a recent and traumatic experience with her sister. She received little situational support from her husband because he was impatient with her for giving in to Michael's attempts to avoid school and its athletic activities through his morning illnesses. Michael needed to explore his feelings of rejection by the boys at school and to express the fears instilled in him by his mother. Mr. F. needed to take a more active role in his relationship with Michael and to help his wife to allay her fears about Michael's imagined illnesses.

Intervention

Because Mrs. F. continued to imagine new illnesses for her son and to seek additional diagnostic procedures, the first goal of intervention determined by the therapist was to reassure her, by reinforcement of the doctor's statement, that there was nothing physically wrong with Michael. Another goal was to help her to realize that Michael's overdependency on her had impaired his ability to function effectively in school and with those in his own age group. Mr. F. needed to become more actively involved with his son. Michael would require support to allow him to express his feelings of inadequacy about relations with his peer group and in dealing with school activities.

The therapist worked with Michael during the first part of each session, exploring his experiences at school during the previous week. The therapist would ask if Michael had attended school all week and ask for explanations of any absences. Michael's feelings about himself in relation to his peer group were dealt with at this time; the remainder of the hour was spent with his parents. Mrs. F. was continually reassured that Michael was physically well and could engage in activities normal for boys of his age. She was encouraged to retire into the background and to allow the father to take over some of the planning for Michael; Mr. F., in turn, was encouraged to insist that Michael attend school despite morning vomiting episodes. On those mornings when his father was unable to drive him to school, Michael was to ride his bike.

Although Mrs. F. agreed to this with reluctance, her agreement was seen by the therapist as an effort by her to allow him more independence. Mr. F. tried to become more involved with Michael by taking him to his place of work during school vacation periods and letting the boy help him. These events helped Michael to gain self-confidence, and this new independence permitted him to interact more with his peers.

Anticipatory planning

Anticipatory planning revolved around showing the parents that their new behavior was a beginning step in allowing their son to be an independent individual, and the importance of continuing to make him feel that he had capabilities and that they had confidence in him was stressed. The parents were prepared for the next step for freedom because his need for independence would grow, and Mrs. F., particularly, needed to anticipate this so that she would be prepared to allow him more opportunity for growth and independence.

Mr. F. had stayed in the background because he believed that the major responsibility for child rearing belonged to the mother. He wished to be with his son more but had hesitated to overrule his wife when they differed regarding Michael's activities. It was pointed out to him that Michael's conception of masculine behavior would develop largely as a result of interaction with his father and that he should become more involved with Michael in the future.

Summation of the paradigm

Mrs. F.'s overprotection and fears of fatal illnesses served to reinforce Michael's feelings of inadequacy, and her anxiety about his physical well-being impelled her to curtail his activities and limit his involvement with his peer group, thus inducing and reinforcing feelings of inferiority.

When Michael's symptoms were diagnosed as psychosomatic, and Mrs. F. was still reluctant to give him independence, Michael became convinced that "mother was right" and that he was physically ill. As a result, his anxiety and resultant psychosomatic involvement increased, and he avoided school where participation in physical activities with his peers was necessary. His overdependence on his mother and emotional immaturity alienated his father, and Michael was unable to turn to him for support; his symptoms increased, he was unable to attend school, and a crisis was precipitated.

Intervention focused on letting Michael explore his feelings of anxiety and inadequacy, and time was spent in working with his parents to help them understand how much he needed reassurance with regard to his adequacy and abilities. Mr. F. was encouraged to become more involved with Michael to counterbalance Mrs. F.'s overprotectiveness.

ADOLESCENCE
Theoretical concepts

The adolescent has a strong need to find and confirm his identity. There is rapid body growth equaling that of early childhood but compounded by the addition of physical-genital maturity. Faced with the physiological revolution within himself, the adolescent is also concerned with consolidating his social roles. He is preoccupied with the difference between what he appears to be in the eyes of others and what he feels himself to be; in searching for a new sense of continuity, some adolescents must refight crises left unresolved in previous years.

Changes that occur as secondary sex characteristics emerge, making the adolescent self-conscious and uncomfortable with himself and with his friends. Body image changes, and he constantly seeks validation that these physiological changes are "normal" because he feels different and is dissatisfied with how he thinks he looks. If sudden spurts of growth occur, he concludes he will be too tall; conversely, if growth does not occur as expected, he thinks he will be too short, or too thin, or too fat. In this period of fluctuation, half-child and half-adult, the adolescent reacts with childish rebellion one day and with adult maturity the next.

The adolescent is as unpredictable to himself as he is to parents and other adults. On the one hand he seeks freedom and rebels against authority, on the other he does not trust his own sense of emerging maturity and covertly seeks guidelines from adults. In his struggle for an identity he turns to his peers and adopts their mode of dress, mannerisms, vocabulary, and code of behavior, often to the distress of adult society. There is a desperate need to belong, to feel accepted, loved, and wanted.

This is the age for cliques and gangs. The "in group" can be extremely clannish and intolerant of those who do not belong. Banding together against the adult world, its members seek to internalize their identity, but because of different and often rebellious behavior they are frequently incorrectly labeled as "delinquent."

Having achieved a sense of security and acceptance from his peers, the adolescent begins to seek heterosexual involvement. This occurs first at group-oriented social events, such as dances, parties, and football games. As comfort and confidence increase, the adolescent progresses to more meaningful and deeper emotional involvements in one-to-one heterosexual relationships. Because of conflict between sexual drives, desires, and the established norms of his society, this stage can be extremely stressful, and again he is faced with indecision and confusion.

Occupational identity also becomes a concern at this time. There are continual queries by parents and school authorities about career plans for the future. Uncertainties are compounded when a definite choice cannot be made because of an inability to fully identify with the adult world of work. Having only observed or participated in fragments of work situations, the adolescent finds it difficult to commit himself to the reality of full-time employment and its inherent responsibilities. It is easier and more realistic to state what is *not* wanted rather than what is wanted as a career.

Piaget (1963) refers to the cognitive development at this stage as *formal operations,* the period in which the capacity for abstract thinking and complex deductive reasoning becomes possible. At this time the goal is "independence," and in midadolescence acceptance of the idea that it is possible to love and at the same time to be angry with someone is one problem that should be solved. If this stage is successfully negotiated, the individual develops a capacity for self-responsibility; failure may lead to a sense of inadequacy in controlling and competing.

Because of the number and wide variety of stimuli and rapid changes to which he is exposed, the adolescent is in a hazardous situation. A crisis situation may be compounded by the normal amount of flux characteristic of adolescent development (Cameron, 1963; Erikson, 1950, 1959, 1963; Piaget, 1963; Zachry, 1940).

The following case study illustrates some of the conflicts that adolescents face while trying to find their identify, to strive for independence, and to win acceptance from their peer group. It also points out the need for understanding and patience on the part of parents as their adolescents grow up.

Case study: Adolescence
Assessment of the individual and the problem

Mary V., a 14-year-old high school sophomore, was referred to a crisis center with her parents by a school nurse. During the past few weeks she had shown signs of increased anxiety, cried easily, and had lost interest in school activities. That morning for no apparent reason she had suddenly left the classroom in tears. The teacher followed and found her crouched in a nearby utility closet, crying uncontrollably. Mary seemed unable to give a reason for her loss of control and was very anxious. When her mother came in response to a call from the school nurse, they agreed to follow her advice and seek family therapy.

During the first session the therapist saw Mary and her parents together in order to assess their interaction and communication patterns and to determine Mary's problems.

Mrs. V. was quiet and left most of the conversation up to her husband and Mary. When she attempted to add anything to what was being said, she was quickly silenced by Mr. V.'s hard, cold stare or by Mary exclaiming in an exasperated tone, "Oh, Mother!" Mr. V. spoke in a controlled, stilted manner, saying that he had no idea what was wrong with Mary, and Mrs. V. responded hesitantly that it must be something at school.

Mary was particularly well developed for her age, a fact that was apparent despite the rather shapeless shift she was wearing. She might have been very attractive if she had paid more attention to her posture and general appearance.

When questioned, Mary said that she had not been sleeping well for weeks,

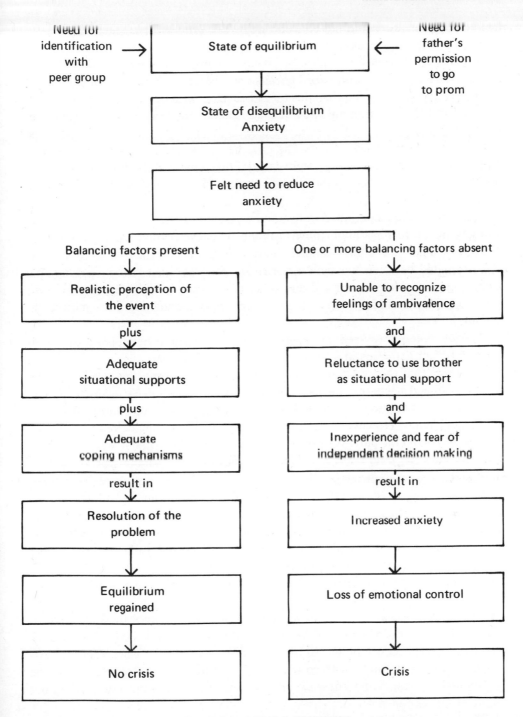

Fig. 11. □ Case study: Mary.

had no appetite, and could not concentrate on her schoolwork. She did not know why she felt this way, and her uncontrolled outburst of tears frightened and embarrassed her. She was also afraid of what she might do next, adding that her crying that morning was probably because she had not slept well for the past 2 nights. At first she tried to brush this off as final exam jitters.

She evaded answering repeated questions about sudden changes in her life in the past few days. When the therapist asked if she would be more comfortable talking alone, without her parents, she gave her father a quick glance and replied that she would. Mr. and Mrs. V. were asked if they objected to Mary talking to the therapist alone. Both agreed that it might be a good idea and went to the waiting room.

For a time Mary continued to respond evasively. It was obvious that she had strongly mixed feelings about how to relate to the male therapist: Should it be "man to woman" or "child to adult?" Throughout this and the following sessions she alternated between her child-adult roles. The therapist recognized the role ambivalence of adolescence and adjusted his role relationship, using whichever was most effective in focusing on the problem areas and making Mary more comfortable.

Mary eventually relaxed and began to talk freely about her relationship with her family, her activities at school, and some of the feelings that were troubling her. She said that she had two older brothers. The younger of the two, Kirk, was 16 years old and a senior in high school. She felt closer to him because "he understands and I can talk to him." Mary said that she had "as good a childhood" as the rest of her friends. However, she did think that her father kept a closer eye on her activities than did the parents of most of her friends. He still called her his "baby" and "my little girl" and lately had begun to place more restrictions on her friendships and activities than usual.

She admitted that during the past year she had gone through a sudden spurt of body growth and development. She was keenly aware of these differences in her appearance and sensed the changing attitudes of her father and her friends. She felt her father was worried about her growing "up and out so fast." He was the one who insisted that she wear the almost shapeless shifts. She said she knew "It wasn't really because I outgrow things so fast right now—he thinks I look too sexy for my age!"

About 3 weeks ago she had been invited to the junior-senior prom by a friend of her brother Kirk. She liked the boy and wanted to go but was not sure Kirk would approve, because he would be at the prom too. Another problem was getting her parents' permission to go and to buy the necessary formal clothes. She had looked at dresses and knew exactly the one she wanted but knew her father would not let her have it.

Mary was asked if she felt able to tell her parents these things that were bothering her if the therapist were present to give her support. She thought that she could if he would "sort of prepare them first" and explain how important it was for her to go dressed like the rest of her girl friends. He suggested that Mary discuss the situation with Kirk to see how he felt about her going to the prom with his friend, and she agreed to do this before the next session. The therapist assured her that he would spend the first part of the next session with her parents to discuss and explore their feelings about this.

Planning of therapeutic intervention

It was thought that Mary needed support to assist her in convincing her parents that she be allowed to grow up. Mr. and Mrs. V. needed to gain an intellectual understanding of some of the problems that adolescent girls face as they search for an identity, seek independence, and feel the need to be like their peers. Mrs. V. would have to be encouraged to give support and guidance to Mary and help to resist Mr. V.'s attempts to keep Mary as the baby of the family.

Intervention

At the next session the therapist went to the waiting room to get Mr. and Mrs. V. and saw that Mary had brought her brother Kirk with her. She asked if he could come in with them at the last half of the session when the family would be together. The therapist agreed, realizing that Mary had brought additional support and that apparently Kirk had approved of her going to the prom.

The first part of the session was spent in discussing with the parents the general problems of most adolescents, as well as the reasons behind their often erratic and unusual behavior. Both parents seemed willing to accept this new knowledge, although Mr. V. said that he had not noticed any of this with the boys. Mrs. V. said, "No . . . but you treated them differently, you were glad they were becoming men." The therapist supported Mrs. V. and said that this was one of Mary's specific problems. He then repeated to the parents what Mary had said about the things that were bothering her. Both parents seemed slightly embarrassed, and Mr. V.'s voice and manner became quite angry as he tried to explain why he wanted to "protect" Mary: "She's so young, so innocent . . . someone may take advantage of her," and so on.

Discussion then focused on Mary's anxiety and the tension she was feeling because her father had made her feel different from her friends. Compromise between Mr. and Mrs. V. and Mary was explored when Mary and Kirk joined their parents in the last half of the session. Mary was more verbal with Kirk present to support her, and Kirk told his father, "You are too old fashioned, Mary's a good kid; you don't have to worry about her; you make her dress like a 10-year-old," and so on. Mr. V. was silent for a while and then said, "You may be right, Kirk, I don't know." He then asked him, "Do you think I should let her go to the prom?"

Kirk answered, "Yes, Dad, I'll be there; she can even double with me and my girl." Her father agreed, adding that Mrs. V. should go with her to pick out a "fairly decent dress." Mary began to cry, and Mr. V. in great consternation asked, "What's wrong now?" She replied, "Daddy, I'm so happy, don't you know women cry when they are happy too!"

Anticipatory planning

The next few sessions were spent in supporting the family members in their changing attitudes toward each other. Anticipatory planning was directed toward establishing open communication between the parents and Mary to avoid another buildup of tensions and misunderstandings. Mary was encouraged to use Kirk as a situational support in the future, since he and his father were not in conflict.

The family was told that they could return for help with future crises if necessary and were assured that they had really accomplished a great deal toward mutual understanding.

Summation of the paradigm

Mary suffered acute symptoms of anxiety because she had to ask her father for permission to go to a dance. She wanted to be a member of her peer group but felt uncomfortable because she was not allowed to dress as they did. She wanted independence but was inexperienced and afraid to make a decision that would oppose her father. Because the situation involved possible conflict with her brother, she did not feel comfortable in talking with him about her problem.

Intervention was based on exploring areas of difficulty with the family and assisting them to recognize, understand, and support Mary's adolescent behavior, her bid for independence, and her need to become a member of her peer group.

YOUNG ADULTHOOD
Theoretical concepts

Young adulthood is the time in which childhood and youth come to an end and adulthood begins. It involves studying for a specific career or seeking employment, as well as sociability with the opposite sex and heterosexual behavior. According to Cameron (1963), socioeconomic developments make it difficult to determine the transition from adolescence to adulthood. Originally this was determined by the young adult maintaining an independent job, having the capacity for marrying, and forming a new family unit. The young unemployed tend to live at home with their families in a dependent relationship that has some of the characteristics of adolescence and some of the independence of adulthood. The young adult can no longer look forward confidently to gainful employment; without technical or professional education he may have to be satisfied with unskilled temporary jobs. The more time he spends in technological or professional training, the longer he remains financially dependent on his family, and changes and uncertainties in modern socioeconomic situations may extend the period of dependence into the middle or late twenties. If the preceding stages of maturation have been successfully negotiated, the young adult will have confidence in himself and his ability for decision making and, as a result, will be able to establish and maintain a real intimacy with the opposite sex.

Adult society demands that he will not deviate from the established norm: the male is expected to remain in school if studying for a career or be consistent and productive in a job while maintaining an active social life. The female is also expected to be in school or working productively and establishing social contacts in order to meet and select her future mate.

There is an exploration and exploitation, or the denial of cultural and familial heritage, and a clarification of self-identity and the social role. The psychosexual task is one of differentiating self from family without complete withdrawal from the family. Cognitive development should be at the level of deductive and inductive logic, with expansion and exploration of cognitive capacities and the beginning of creativity.

Unsuccessful transition at this stage or lack of inner resources may lead to confusion when decisions are made regarding future goals. There is an inability to establish a true and mutual psychological intimacy with another person; there is also a tendency toward self-isolation and the maintenance of only highly stereotyped and formal interpersonal relationships, characterized by a lack of spontaneity, warmth, and an honest exchange of emotional involvement.

In the next case study a young adult is faced with the problem of making a choice between conforming to society's norms for choosing a vocation and marriage or remaining self-absorbed in his own immature interests.

Case study: Young adulthood
Assessment of the individual and the problem

Bob M., 18 years old, came for help at a crisis center stating he was "feeling bad." When the therapist asked him to be more specific, he said he was not sleeping, was nervous, and things seemed unreal to him. When asked who referred him to the center, he replied a friend who had been there when he had been in trouble.

Bob was small in stature, slim, with longer than average black hair, neatly dressed in Levis, sport shirt, and motorcycle boots. During the initial session Bob appeared overtly nervous and depressed. He sometimes spoke in short, rapid bursts, usually after a period of silence but, more often, in a slow, hesitant manner. He would neither establish nor maintain eye contact with the therapist, continually looking down at the floor.

When asked about events occurring before the onset of his symptoms, Bob said that "during the past 10 days so many things have happened it's difficult to remember what happened first." He began to recite events. After working on his car for 6 months "it blew up" the first time he drove it. This was also the first time he had been able to drive in 6 months because his driver's licence had been revoked for speeding. This precipitated a quarrel with his girlfriend, Lauri, because he had promised to take her out when his driver's license was reinstated and his car was fixed. He had recently received a promotion to foreman at work, but he was ambivalent — pleased with the promotion although uncertain of his readiness to accept the responsibility of a permanent job. Last, his best friend, a member of his motorcycle club, was out of town, and he felt that he had no one with whom to talk about his problems.

Further exploration with Bob revealed that his usual pattern of coping with stress was to ride his motorcycle with his friend "as fast and as far as we can go." They would stop someplace and "talk it out." He felt that this relieved his tension; things became clearer, and he could usually solve the problem.

Bob also expressed ambivalence in his relationship with Lauri. He loved her and wanted to marry her but was concerned because he thought that they had conflicting values; she was from a middle-class family with values that emphasized the importance of a steady job, conformity, and so forth, whereas he felt he belonged in the motorcycle club and liked their philosophy, or as he stated it, "to be free, take what you want, don't work." He was afraid that marriage to Lauri would inhibit his freedom and that to please her family he feared he would have to give up riding with his friends and working on his car, and would have to cut his hair.

Planning of therapeutic intervention

Because of the many problems presented it was necessary for the therapist to sift through extraneous data and concentrate on major areas of difficulty. She decided, at this time, to assume the role of available situational support until other support could be found. This would give Bob the opportunity to use his prior successful coping device of "talking it out." As tension decreased, other support would be provided for his attempts to solve his problems.

Intervention

The goal of intervention was established by the therapist to assist Bob to recognize and cope with his feelings of ambivalance toward his job and Lauri and with the implications of making a choice. The areas of difficulty were determined to be a conflict of values and Bob's need to feel that he belonged to something or someone.

In the next two sessions, while the therapist acted as a situational support, Bob's symptoms diminished. He was able to discuss and explore his feelings about Lauri and his job; he also began discussing his fears of "giving up so much"

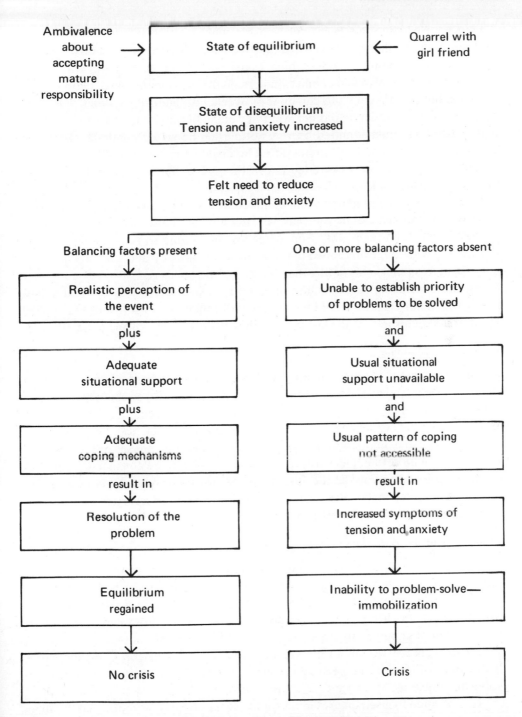

Fig. 12. □ Case study: Bob M.

if they married. Because Bob's relationship with Lauri appeared to be a major problem area, the therapist suggested that she be included in the sessions.

In the subsequent sessions, which Lauri did attend, they began discussing areas of mutual concern and conflict. Lauri said that she did not expect him to give up riding his motorcycle. "He can do it on weekends, and I'll go along." Bob became angry, saying that he did not want her along because she "was too nice for that crowd." He then admitted he was not certain he would continue with them anyway, *but* he wanted it understood that he could go riding with his friend occasionally if he wanted to. Bob added that if they were married, he might not need them because he would have her (his need to belong).

When Bob spoke of her parents' comments about his hairstyle, Lauri said that she liked his hair and that he was marrying her not her family.

She insisted, however, that Bob spent too much time working on his car and not enough with her. Bob replied that the car was his hobby and said that he probably spent less time on his hobby than her father did on his golf.

In the concluding sessions Bob apparently resolved his conflicts and stated firmly that he thought he would be gaining more than he might lose if he married Lauri and kept his job. At the last session they made tentative plans to be married.

Anticipatory planning

The most important phase in anticipatory planning occurred when Bob agreed that Lauri be included in the therapy sessions. The necessity of choosing between present modes of behavior and gratifications and future expectations in his life led Bob to weigh the consequences involved. His decision to include Lauri in future planning indicated an orientation toward reality. In certain phases of life it is necessary to give up certain pleasures of youth that appear to be consistent with freedom. An orientation toward the future, where maturity of decisions reflects not only an inner freedom but also a sense of self-fulfillment and a recognition of one's own strength, is consistent with a strong ego-identity.

Summation of the paradigm

Bob M. was forced to seek help because of increased symptoms of tension and anxiety. So many stressful events occurring in rapid succession had made it impossible for him to decide which problem should be solved first. His usual situational support, the friend from the motorcycle club, was out of town, and his normal method of coping with stress was unavailable.

Ambivalent feelings about his job situation and his girlfriend Lauri increased his feelings of tension; he became immobile and unable to make decisions or to solve his problems.

Intervention focused on providing Bob with the situational support of the therapist, and Lauri was included as an active participant in the later sessions. When

Bob was encouraged to ventilate his feelings, his anxiety decreased and he was able to perceive relationships between the stressful events and his crisis situation more realistically. Previous successful coping skills were reintroduced and proved adequate in assisting him to solve his problem. Major focus of the last sessions was anticipatory planning to help him cope with future areas of stress as he made the transition to increased maturity.

ADULTHOOD
Theoretical concepts

Adulthood is the usual period in life when the responsibilities of parenthood are assumed, involving the abilities of a man and woman to accept the strengths and weaknesses of one another and to combine their energies toward mutual goals. It is a crucial time for reconciliation with practical reality.

Maturity is always relative and is usually considered to develop in adulthood. Many adults who marry and have children never do achieve psychological maturity whereas others who choose not to marry may show a greater degree of mature responsibility than many of their married peers.

Adult normality, like maturity, is also relative. Normality requires that a person achieve and maintain a reasonably effective balance, both psychodynamically and interpersonally. The normal adult must be able to control and channel his emotional drives without losing his initiative and vigor. He should be able to cope with ordinary personal upheavals and the frustrations and disappointments in life with only temporary disequilibrium and be able to participate enthusiastically in adult work and adult play, as well as have the capacity to give and to experience adequate heterosexual gratifications in a stable relationship. He should be able to express a reasonable amount of aggression, anger, joy, and affection without undue effort or unnecessary guilt.

In actuality it is unreasonable to expect to find perfect normalcy in any adult. Absolute perfection of physique and physiology are rare rather than normal, and an adult with a perfect emotional equilibrium is equally as exceptional.

This case study concerns a young woman whose lack of psychosocial maturity created problems when she was faced with the responsibility of motherhood. Her husband's competence and pleasure in caring for their baby increased her feelings of inadequacy and rejection.

Case study: Adulthood
Assessment of the individual and the problem

Myra and John, a young married couple, were referred by Myra's obstetrician to a crisis center because of her symptoms of depression. Myra said she was experiencing difficulty in sleeping, was constantly tired, and would begin to cry for no apparent reason.

recent events Myra was an attractive but fragile blonde of 22 years whose looks and manners gave her the appearance of a 16-year-old. John, 28 years old, had a calm and mature demeanor. They had been married a year and a half and were the parents of a 3-month-old son, John, Jr.

notes John was an engineer with a large corporation. Myra had been a liberal arts major when they met and married. John was the oldest of four children and was from a stable family of modest circumstances; Myra, on the other hand, was an only child who had been indulged by wealthy parents.

When questioned by the therapist specifically about the onset of her symptoms, Myra stated that they had really begun after the baby was born, with crying spells and repeated assertions that she "wasn't a good mother" and that taking care of the baby made her nervous. She said she felt inadequate and that even John was better with the baby than she. John attempted to reassure her by telling her she was an excellent mother and that he realized she was nervous about caring for the baby. He suggested that he get someone to help her. Myra said she did not want anyone, because it was her baby, and she could not understand why she felt as she did.

When questioned about her pregnancy and the birth of the child, she said there had been no complications and had added hesitantly that it had not been a planned pregnancy. When asked to explain further, she replied that she and John had decided to wait until they had been married about 3 years before starting a family. She went on to explain that she did not think she and John had enough time to enjoy their life together before the baby was born.

After she had recovered from the shock of knowing that she was pregnant, she became really thrilled at the thought of having a baby and enjoyed her pregnancy and shopping for the nursery. Toward the end of her pregnancy she had difficulty sleeping and was troubled by nightmares. She began to feel uncertain of her ability to be a good mother and was frightened because she had not been around babies before.

When she and John brought the baby home, they engaged a nurse for 2 weeks to take care of the child and to teach Myra baby care. She thought that basically she knew how, but it upset her if the baby did not stop crying when she had picked him up. When he was at home, John usually took care of the baby, and his competency made her feel more inadequate. The precipitating event was thought to have occurred the week before when John had arrived home from work to find Myra walking the floor with the baby, who was crying loudly. Myra told him she had taken the baby to the pediatrician for an immunization shot that morning. After they returned home he had become irritable, crying continuously, and repeatedly refusing his bottle. When Myra said she did not know what to do, John told her the baby felt feverish. After they took the baby's temperature and discovered that it was 102° F., John called the pediatrician, who recommended a medication

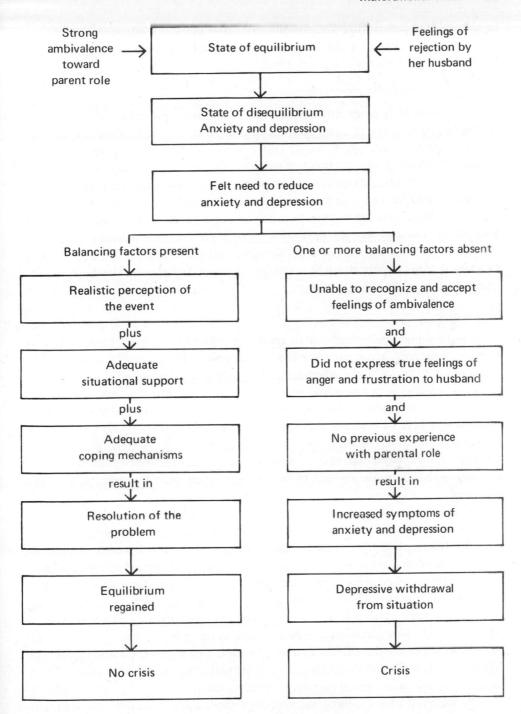

Fig. 13. □ Case study: Myra.

to reduce the temperature and discomfort; John got the medication and gave it to the baby; he also gave the baby his bottle. The baby went to sleep, but Myra went to their bedroom crying and upset.

Planning of therapeutic intervention

Myra's mixed feelings toward the baby would be explored in addition to her feelings of inadequacy in caring for him. She apparently resented the responsibility of the parental role, which she was not ready to assume. Unable to express her hostility and feelings of rejection toward the baby, she turned them inward on herself, with the resulting overt symptoms of depression. Bringing these feelings into the open would be a necessary goal. Myra also needed reassurance that her feelings of inadequacy were normal because of her lack of contact and experience with infants and also because most new parents felt this same inadequacy in varying degrees. John obviously was comfortable and knowledgeable in the situation as a result of his experience with a younger brother and sisters; he should be utilized as a strong situational support.

Intervention

The therapist, believing that a mild antidepressant would help to relieve Myra's symptoms, arranged a medical consultation. It was not thought that she was a threat to herself or to others, and intervention was instituted.

Myra's mention in the initial session that she and John had not had enough time to enjoy each other before the baby was born was considered to be an initial reference to Myra's negative feelings regarding her pregnancy and the baby. In subsequent sessions, using direct questioning and the reflection of verbal and nonverbal clues, Myra was able to express some of her feelings about their life as a family with a baby in contrast to her feelings when there had been just herself and John.

Their previous life pattern revealed much social activity before the birth of the baby and almost none afterward. Myra said that although this had not really bothered her too much at first, recently she had felt as if the walls were closing in on her. John appeared surprised to hear this and asked why she had not mentioned it to him. Myra replied with some anger that it apparently did not seem to bother him, because it was obvious that he enjoyed playing with the baby after he came home from work. The possibility of reinstating some manner of social life for Myra and John was considered to be essential at this point. John told her that his mother would enjoy the chance to babysit with her new grandson and that he and Myra should plan some evenings out alone or with friends. Myra brightened considerably at this and seemed pleased at John's concern.

The therapist also explored their feelings about the responsibilities of parenthood and Myra's feelings of inadequacy in caring for the baby. Myra could communicate to John and the therapist her feelings that the baby received more of John's attention than she and that she resented "playing second fiddle." John explained that he had originally assumed care of the baby so that she could get some rest and that he enjoyed being with her more than the baby. He told her that he loved her and that she would always come first with him.

Myra was eventually able to see that she was being childish in resenting the baby and was competing for John's attention; as her social life expanded, her negative feelings toward the baby lessened and she said she was feeling more comfortable in caring for him. After the fourth session the medication was discontinued, and Myra's symptoms continued to decrease.

Anticipatory planning

Because of John's maturity it was thought important that he be aware of the possibility that Myra could occasionally have a recurrence of feelings of rejection. If the original symptoms returned, he would recognize them by the pattern they would take and would be able to intercede by exploring what was happening, discussing this openly with Myra. When the progress and adjustments they had made in learning to cope with the situation were reviewed with them, both expressed satisfaction with the changes that had occurred. They were told that they could return for further help if another crisis situation developed.

Summation of the paradigm

Myra was an only child and rarely had to accept responsibility for others before her marriage. Because she had planned to wait 3 years before having a child, she experienced strong mixed feelings about the responsibilities of motherhood before that time and felt unprepared. Her husband's adequacy in caring for the baby when she failed reinforced her mixed feelings. Loss of the social life shared with her husband, combined with the diversion of his attention from her to the baby, reinforced her strong feelings of rejection.

Because she was unable to recognize and accept her feelings of ambivalence and was also unable to tell her husband of her anger and frustration, she turned them inward. Lack of previous experience in caring for infants made her unable to cope with the situation, increased her frustration and anger, and resulted in overt symptoms of depression and anxiety.

LATE ADULTHOOD
Theoretical concepts

Late adulthood is the final stage of development discussed in Erikson's (1950, 1959, 1963) theory of maturation. If an individual has successfully negotiated the preceding stages, he should be mature enough to accept responsibility for his lifestyle without regrets.

To the average person, reaching late adulthood implies that life patterns have been fairly well set and no longer are open to choices for change. Anxiety results if a man or woman has not demonstrated some capacity for success in either family or career roles. Symptoms of this are frequently noted in such forms as excessive use of alcohol, psychosomatic symptoms, feelings of persecution, and depression (English and Pearson, 1955:43).

Our culture seems unable to place any firm boundary lines on phases of the aging process. The general tendency is to view life as uphill from infancy and over the hill and decline after reaching the peak of middle years. With cultural emphasis on youthfulness it is not unusual for a person of 50 years to view his future with regret for things left unaccomplished. Hahn* refers to this stage as "heads against the ceiling," a time when "The realization strikes home that the probability for appreciable advancement is remote . . . The ceiling is encountered relatively early by some and at an amazing late time by others, but for all of us the ladder eventually ends at a ceiling." He further describes this as a period when "Younger men and women are beginning to crowd into the competitive economic, political and social arenas."† With the rapid technological changes affecting businesses and professions, younger persons are often better prepared to supply the necessary knowledge and skills.

Family life changes as children grow up and become involved with school, careers, and marriage. For parents it is a time when specific tasks of parenthood are over, and they must return to the family unit of two, making rciprocal changes in role status in relation to their children and to the community. New values and goals must be developed in the marriage to replace those values no longer realistic in the present; failure to recognize this need can open the way to frustration and despair. The wife and mother now has freedom from parental responsibility, but if her entire life-style was centered around the parental role, she may lack interests, skills, and abilities with which to make the role change.

Menopausal changes occur in women at this time. Usually around the age of 45 years there is a relatively rapid decrease in activity of the sexual glands occurring over a period of 2 to 3 years. Sometimes this is accompanied by a syndrome of psychophysiological symptoms, such as hot flashes, dizziness, cold shivers, and anxiety attacks. According to English and Pearson (1955:43), it is thought that personality plays a larger part of the symptomatology than the cessation of glandular activity. Many women go through this phase without any stressful symptoms; others become panicky and afraid of a loss of sexual identity.

There appears to be no definite evidence that sexual gland activity in the male

---

*Hahn, M. E.: Psychoevaluation; adaption, distribution, adjustment, New York, 1963, McGraw-Hill Book Co., pp. 92-93. Used with permission of McGraw-Hill Book Co.
†*Ibid.*, p. 70.

undergoes similar rapid decline and cessation; however, men can experience symptoms similar to those of women at the same age period. English and Pearson (1955:43) consider these syndromes to be neuroses rather than a result of any changes in the sexual gland activity.

The unmarried individual with thoughts of eventual marriage and a family is now faced with the reality of advancing years. This is a particularly critical time for the woman. If her reliance for social status and emotional security has been strongly dependent on physical attractiveness, she faces the inevitability of physical decline. Like the man, she can continue her career interests; but she, too, may be confronted with limitations for further career advancements.

The following case study concerns a 40-year-old wife and mother whose planned changes in her family role after the marriage of her daughter seem to be threatened by the onset of early menopause.

Case study: Late adulthood
Assessment of the individual and the problem

Mrs. C., a 40-year-old, youthful-appearing mother of three daughters (ages 17, 20, and 22 years) was referred to a crisis center by her physician because of severe anxiety and depression, as evidenced by recent anorexia, weight loss, insomnia, crying spells, and preoccupation, which had begun after a visit to her physician 3 weeks earlier. At that time she had been told that she was entering early menopause. Her youngest daughter was to be married in a month; the two older ones were already married and living out of the state.

She described herself to the therapist as having always been socially active both in community affairs and in her husband's business and social life. Mr. C. was employed as a senior salesman for a nationwide firm selling women's clothing. His work required frequent trips out of town and much business entertaining while at home. She seldom traveled with him (because of the children) but was deeply involved with planning and hostessing his in-town social engagements. She said that she enjoyed this and had always been confident of her ability to do it well. Part of her wife role was to wear the clothes of her husband's company as an unofficial model, and her husband had always expressed his pride in her attractiveness.

In recent weeks she had begun to feel inadequate in this role, and strong feelings of doubt regarding her ability had begun to plague her. At the same time she sensed that her husband was becoming indifferent to her efforts to keep herself and their home attractive to him. Her symptoms had overtly increased in the 2 days just past, until now she feared a complete loss of emotional control.

Mr. C. was 2 years older than she. He was socially adept, and her women friends frequently told her they thought he was "such a youthful, good-looking, and considerate person." She herself felt fortunate to have him for a husband. He

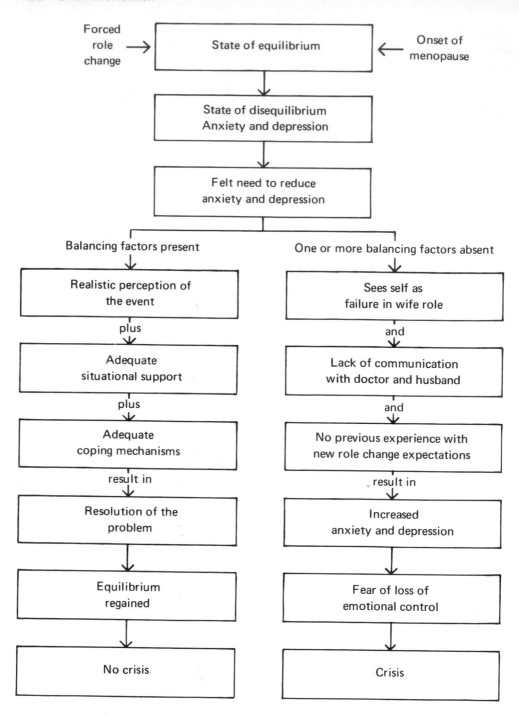

Fig. 14. □ Case study: Mrs. C.

Was aggressive in business and could be sure of advancement. She said they had always been sexually compatible and shared interests and mutual esteem for one another.

When asked about what had occurred in the past 2 days to increase her symptoms, she said that her husband had come home 2 nights ago and found her disheveled and crying and not ready to go to a scheduled business dinner for the second time in a week. He angrily told her that he did not know what to do and to "pull yourself together and find someone to help you because I've tried and I can't!" Then he left for the dinner alone. The next day he left town on a business trip after securing her promise to see a physician.

Mrs. C. said that she had seen several physicians during the past few months because of various physical complaints. None had found any organic cause, but all had advised her to get more rest—one even told her to find a hobby. The last physician, whom she saw 3 weeks ago, told her she was entering early menopause.

Mrs. C. had not told her husband of this, because she feared his reaction in view of her own negative feelings; her initial reaction had been disbelief. This was followed by fear of "change of life," as she had heard of so many unfortunate things that could happen to a woman during this time. In common with all women, she did not want to become old and unattractive and was angry that it could be happening to her so soon! She thought that she would no longer be an asset to her husband in his work because his clothes were not designed for middle-aged women.

Mrs. C. had looked forward to traveling with her husband after their youngest daughter's marriage. They had planned such a future together enthusiastically, and she felt proud to have contributed to his success but was now afraid that he would not need her anymore and that all her plans were ruined.

It was thought that the crisis-precipitating events were her expressed feelings of guilt and a fear of the loss of her feminine role. She was not seen as a suicidal risk or as a threat to others, although she was depressed and expressed feelings of worthlessness. She was highly anxious but could maintain control over her actions.

Planning of therapeutic intervention

Mrs. C. had withdrawn from her previous pattern of social and family activities. Her husband was frequently out of town, and the last of the daughters living at home had transferred many of her dependency needs to her fiancé. Mrs. C. in the past 3 months had felt physically ill and had narrowed her social activities to infrequent luncheons "when I felt up to it." Her peer group was in the 35- to 40-year age level and were all actively involved in community affairs, family activities, and so on. Conversation with women friends still centered around problems of raising young children, and she believed that because her children were grown she no longer had much to offer to the conversation.

Her goals for a role change from busy parenthood to active participation with her husband in his business-social world were threatened, and she had no coping experiences in this particular situation. Previous methods of coping with stress were discussed. She related that she had always kept busy with their children and either forgot the problems or talked them out with close friends or her husband. She could not recall a close woman friend who had reached the menopausal stage and with whom she could discuss her feelings, and she was too fearful of the reaction she imagined her husband would have to discuss it with him. Her inability to communicate her feelings and the loss of busy work with her children eliminated any situational supports in her home environment, obviating the use of previously successful coping mechanisms. The goal of intervention was established by the therapist to assist Mrs. C. to an intellectual understanding of her crisis.

Intervention

It was obvious to the therapist that Mrs. C. had little knowledge of the physiological and psychological changes that occur in menopause. There was no insight to her feelings of guilt and fear of the threatening loss of her feminine role. Unrecognized feelings about her relationship with her husband would be explored.

During the next 5 weeks, through the use of direct questioning and reflection of verbal and nonverbal clues with Mrs. C., it became possible for her to relate the present crisis and its effect to past separations from her husband (business trips) and her previous successful coping mechanisms.

Mrs. C. had married when she was 17 years old. She described herself as having been attractive and popular in school, busy at all sorts of school activities. Mr. C. had been what everyone considered quite a catch. He came from a prosperous family, had been a high school football captain and class president, and was sought after by many of her girlfriends. At the time of their marriage he was a freshman in college.

She always had a high regard for her physical attractiveness and her ability to fulfill the social role Mr. C. expected of her. Throughout the years when he traveled alone, she felt left out of a part of his life and had looked forward with great expectations to being able to be with him all of the time. Knowing that his business brought him in frequent contact with attractive women buyers and models, she regarded her own physical attractiveness as a prime requirement to "meet the competition." With Mr. C.'s frequent trips away from home she had magnified her role in the husband-wife relationship to be more on the physical-social level than in the shared role of parental responsibilities.

Anticipatory planning

Mrs. C. never questioned her physician after he informed her of his diagnosis of early onset of menopause, and obviously her knowledge was inadequate and based almost entirely on hearsay and myth rather than on fact. The physiological basis of the process of aging was discussed, and much of her fear was allayed. This was an important phase of anticipatory planning.

She was given situational support in which to talk out her feelings of insecurity in her marriage and to view it in much more realistic terms. Relationships between the precipitating events and the crisis symptoms were explored.

By the third week Mrs. C. had made significant progress toward reestablishing her coping skills. She no longer feared "getting old overnight" and was able to tell her husband that she was entering early menopause.

His response was, "What the hell! Is that why you have been acting so peculiar lately? You might have told me; the way you've been carrying on anyone would have thought you had just been told you had 6 months to live!" Although her first impulse was to interpret this as evidence of his indifference to her as a women, she later saw it as positive proof of her own unrealistic fears. She returned to her medical doctor as advised for continuing care and planning for any physical problems that might arise in the future.

By the fifth week she expressed confidence in her ability to meet the goals that she and her husband had set for their future. Their daughter was married, and Mrs. C. was ready to leave town with her husband on a business trip. Before termination the adjustments she had made in coping with the crisis were reviewed and discussed with her.

Summation of the paradigm

Mrs. C. had been unable to cope with the combined stresses of early menopausal symptoms and the need to change her family role. She avoided communicating her fears to anyone who might have given her situational support for fear they would confirm her own negative reactions. Increasing feelings of inadequacy, resulting in anxiety and depression, led to a crisis level of disequilibrium.

Initial intervention focused on the exploration of Mrs. C.'s knowledge of the physical and psychological changes that could occur in menopause. As she was encouraged to explore and ventilate her feelings about her relationship with her husband, her perception of the stressful situation became more realistic and her coping skills were reintroduced successfully.

OLD AGE
Theoretical concepts

Erikson's formulation of the stages of man's development stops with late adulthood. Unfortunately, he has not extended his analysis to crisis stages encountered by the retrenching organism.

In man the aging process must not be viewed only in terms of chronological years but with regard for the complex interrelationships of biological, psychological, and sociological changes that occur during these years. There is no exact age of onset.

Generally, psychologists look on aging as a period of decline. The pace of physical decline is highly individual, occurring throughout life, yet it is most commonly attributed to the period loosely called old age. "Old age with respect to what?" is a most significant question. It could be one of many things — organic, sensory, or structural changes — and the significance of each is not fully understood.

Personality changes have been substantially investigated, but problems of interpretation have arisen because studies have been directed toward the segmentalized personality traits rather than the total organization or adaptiveness. Individual studies have found the aged to be "more set" in problem solving and to be "more stable" in their habits and tendencies than are younger subjects.

Abnormal behavior in the aged is difficult to diagnose due to the increase of organic damage with longevity. These abnormal patterns of experience and behavior develop along new lines with age and raise questions as to the exact nature of endogenous psychosis and what part is played by reactive ill humor or somatically based psychosis. Abnormal mental attitudes may develop as reactions to loss of influence, destruction of or unfulfilled life goals, onset of human isolation, and threats to economic security.

Considerable research has been done in social attitudes and forces creating the role of the aged in our culture. Goffman's (1961:4) denotative grouping of total institutions defines those for the aged as being established to care for people thought to be helpless and insecure — the blind, orphaned, indigent, and aged. In essence this might define the negative attitudes of our society for the aged.

Our culture values mutual independence of the aged and their married children. Feelings of obligation on the part of adult children to support and care for their aging parents have declined with the establishment of social insurances of medical and other community forces. An exaggerated premium is placed on the physical and psychological attributes of youth. When a culture assigns a role to the individual, his acceptance and performance of it depend greatly on his conception of the role as it relates to his own self-concept.

Sullivan (1953:19) refers to the "self" as the reflected appraisal of others that comes into being as a dynamism to preserve the feelings of security. As new evaluations are reflected, the individual is obliged to reconcile these new concepts of self with those preexisting. Increasing conflictual appraisals may result in increased tension and anxiety, leading to a state tantamount to the acceptance of, or resignation to, old-age status.

As in the first years of adolescence, these later years of life are characterized by physical, emotional, and social crises. The onset of physical infirmities may require that the aged person turn to his milieu for a measure of care and security.

The presence or absence of environmental resources, as well as the degree to which help from others is required for survival, becomes of prime importance. The elderly who are economically secure, alert, and outgoing may be able to rise above social attitudes and be in the position of continuing to influence the lives of others, whereas those who are not in this position may be forced to play the roles designated by society's attitudes. Reisman's (1954:484) three ideal-typical outcomes of the aging process are as follows: (1) the autonomous people with creative resources who use them to advantage in old age, (2) those who are adjusted and remain so, and (3) those who are neither and so decay.

A study of centenarians by Dunbar and Dunbar, as quoted by Solomon (1954: 237), found a high correlation between longevity and a particular type of ego structure, and most of the subjects had chosen independence from their children as a way of life. In many cases they contribute to the support of their dependents, many have an active sex life into the very late years, and few were found who retired to do nothing. They were not susceptible to feelings of uselessness and had maintained involvement in activities in which they took pride.

An apparent correlation between the degree of ego organization in early life and the degree maintained in the senescent years has been found. Those with strong ego organizations seem better able to withstand the increased stresses and conflicts of later years. According to Palmore (1973), it is highly probable that much of the functional mental illness among the aged is due chiefly to stresses caused by loss of income, loss of role and status, bereavement, isolation through disability, and loss of cognitive functioning.

Fear of death is not unique to the aged; its proximity is undeniably closer to some. This is verified as groups of contemporaries become smaller because of attrition by death. The old *are* living longer. Various studies and observations have noted that feelings of anxiety about death are most commonly coped with by the mechanism of denial, but it is not unusual to hear the very aged speak of "welcoming death" or saying that they "have lived a full life and have no fear of death." The social taboos that our culture places on frank discussion about death may lead to suppression of fear, to increased anxiety, and to resulting disequilibrium.

The aged are also faced with the fear of invalidism or chronic debilitating illness that might lead to dependency on society for survival. This may lead to a regression to earlier childlike levels of ego organization as a means of adjusting. According to Slater (1963), the increased powerlessness and loss of authority status of the aged weakens the respect of youth. This may be followed by anger at the reversal in dependency roles, the ultimate destruction of the child role, and the anticipation of desertion by death. As a means of handling guilt that may arise due to ambivalence, young people project their feelings. It is the aged who become malevolent, isolated, and alienated and who are denied participation in society for all of the evils for which they are blamed.

Cumming and Henry (1961) have noted two critical events that take place during this period of life: the loss of a spouse and retirement. Both represent conclusions of central tasks of the adult life.

The loss of a spouse is particularly traumatic for the aging person. For both the widow and widower this represents the loss of a highly cathected object, one that has been a primary source of need satisfaction. There is a loss of emotional security and a feeling of intense loneliness at a time in life when only the most resourceful may be able to find means to redistribute the cathexis. The surviving spouse loses those aspects of social identity that were solely dependent on a marital partner role. Both the widow and the widower must develop social identities of their own, based on their own interests, economic status, and social skills as old social systems become closed to them and they are faced with finding and integrating into new ones.

Retirement is a highly critical time in a person's life. It is one thing if this occurs of one's own volition and planning; it becomes more complex when mandated by another. Losses include status identity based on identification with a productive and functional role in society. The retiree is also faced with the loss of a peer group.

Some people do not move easily into the role of pure sociability. Their focus of sociability has been directed toward their occupational peer groups, and loss of these groups through retirement leaves a void with few purely social skills to fill it.

Role reversal necessitated by a debilitating illness of a spouse is also a fertile area for the development of a crisis. Rarely is either spouse prepared socially, psychologically, or physically to assume all of the responsibilities of such a role change; the adjustments involved may be beyond the older individual's ability to cope and adapt.

It is evident that a continuation of maturational stages of development would be more difficult to define for the aged than for younger groups, since the processes of decline and growth occur concomitantly but not in equal balance. The process is highly individualized in all cases, and the variability of physiological, psychological, and sociological factors makes definite chronological relationships highly improbable.

When an elderly individual seeks help, his symptomatology requires particularly close scrutiny before an interpretation for intervention is undertaken. The therapist must first be aware of his own tendencies to stereotype the client's appearance and symptoms as a normal aging syndrome. Determining which of the crisis symptoms may be due to organicity is particularly important, since rapid onset of behavioral changes is not infrequently due to cerebrovascular or other organic changes associated with longevity. A professional review of the current medical history of the individual must be a recognized part of the initial assessment phase.

Too often the individual, because of organic changes, cannot gain an intellectual understanding of the crisis or recognize his present feelings. It may also be that those who directed him to the therapist are themselves in crisis; if this is true, the therapist may first have to resolve the feelings of the referrer that have been projected toward the aged individual who seems to be in need of help.

In the aging process there is need for the ego organization to withstand increasing biopsychosocial threats to its integrity, and unfortunately the individual's coping abilities may fail to adapt to meet the threats. The ability to accept new value systems and adapt to necessary changes in the achieved maturational development of earlier years without loss of achieved integrity may indeed be a developmental task for the aged.

Case study: Old age
Assessment of the individual and his problem

Sarah was accompanied to the crisis center by her husband, John, a former client who, about 10 years ago, had come there for help when in crisis following the death of their only son.

Sarah was 69 years of age, 3 years younger than John. She was neatly dressed, appeared to be slightly apprehensive, and walked with obvious difficulty, supported by a Canadian crutch and her husband's arm. After being assisted into a chair in the therapist's office, she quickly asked that John be allowed to remain with her during the interview. She stated that it "had really been John's idea that we both come here today. I'm sure that he can explain the problem better than I."

After a slight pause and several hesitations John began to speak. Sarah sat tensely forward on her chair, never taking her eyes from his face as he spoke.

According to John, their problem "probably first began" about 3 months ago when Sarah had fallen in the house and fractured her hip. After a month in the hospital she had been sent home in his care. The plan was for her to continue physiotherapy as an outpatient. Despite all of the therapy and exercises at home she was apparently not making the progress they had expected. "Look at her . . . she still can't walk alone! She still needs someone to help her about or she might fall again — and God knows what would happen to us then! It's been a worry for both of us."

As John continued to speak, it became quite obvious that he was avoiding any direct references to himself. He described Sarah as having recent symptoms of insomnia, anxiety, and depression and expressed the fear that she might be going into the same crisis symptoms that he had been treated for at the center 10 years ago. "It was sheer hell to feel the way I did then . . . she doesn't deserve to go through what I did then if she can be helped now."

As he spoke he was becoming obviously more agitated. He avoided eye contact with Sarah, kept moving about restlessly in his chair, was increasingly tense and tremulous, and chain smoked. His eye frequently became tearful, and his voice broke on several occasions. In almost direct contrast to his behavior, Sarah had assumed a very supportive role, reaching out several times to pat his arm in a calming gesture and, finally, holding his hand tightly.

At the point when it seemed he might begin to cry openly, he abruptly stood up and said, "O.K., Sarah, I've told her all about the problem. Now I'm going to go take a walk for a while and let you do some of the talking, too." With that, he said he'd be back in about 20 minutes and left the office.

As soon as John had left, Sarah began to cry quietly. Then she gave several deep sighs and, for the first time, relaxed back into her chair. "Please," she asked the therapist, "can you help him again like you did the last time?" She stated that for the past week he had not slept more than an hour at a time during the night, paced constantly, cried easily and often for no apparent reason, and had reached the point where he now seemed too anxious and too preoccupied to make even the simplest of decisions.

According to Sarah, she and John had been married for 42 years. They had had only one son, who had died, unmarried, 10 years ago. While Sarah had never held a salaried job, she had always been very actively involved in both civic and church organizations in their community. After John's retirement from a federal service, she had withdrawn from several of these organizations in order to devote more time to acitivtes that they could participate in together. They had developed many new social interests in common and maintained a fairly active social life. Sarah felt that the past 10 years had included some of the best times in their life together. They had always seemed to be planning something "for the future" and had acquired many new friends. Their home was completely paid for; they had planned wisely for financial security "in their old age"; and, until her accident, had had few health problems to worry about.

Even after her hip fracture they had apparently been able to provide each other with the situational support needed to cope adequately with the many new changes arising in their daily lives. "After all," Sarah said, "it wasn't as though our world was going to come to an end because of this . . . only that it might have to slow down a bit until we could catch up again."

After a month in the hospital Sarah went home and arranged to continue therapy as an outpatient. Despite regular visits to physiotherapy and John's rigidly imposed schedule of exercising at home, her recovery had been much slower than they had anticipated. Last week her physician, also not satisfied with the rate of her progress, recommended that she seriously consider admission as a full-time inpatient to a well-known rehabilitation center in a nearby city. He was unable to guarantee how long she might have to remain, estimating only that it would be a minimum of 1 month.

She stated that at the time John seemed to be as much in agreement as she with the idea, although, she recollected, he had seemed a bit preoccupied on the drive home. He took her out to dinner that night to celebrate her improved chances for a full recovery.

That same night she was awakened several times by John getting out of bed and pacing about the house. When she mentioned it to him in the morning, he quickly apologized for disturbing her and blamed it on "too much coffee and food" the night before. She noticed, however, that he seemed very preoccupied that day, even to the point of having to be reminded by her when it was time for her exercises. Several times he asked if she felt confident that they were making the right decision, or if they should try to find another physician for her who might suggest "better treatments."

His tension and anxiety continued to increase over the next few days. He seemed unusually concerned with how she felt about the decision, and no amount of reassurance from her could convince him that she really wanted to go into the hospital for treatment. Several times yesterday she found him looking at her sadly with tears running down his face. His only explanation was that he felt "so sorry for you . . . having to go to a strange place . . . and I might not be there when you need me!" Last night he had not gone to bed at all but had sat chain smoking in the living room. She had not dared go to sleep for fear he would drop a cigarette and start a fire.

Several times during the past few days she had suggested he contact the crisis center to speak to his former therapist. At first he ignored her, then finally yesterday he had countered with the proposal that they go together. "I'm sure," he told her, "that you must be feeling just as anxious as I am about all of this." She said that she agreed to this because she could think of no other way to convince him to come alone. "Of course I'm upset about having to go back to a hospital," she told the therapist. "Anyone in my condition would like to have some sort of a guarantee that they are going to improve . . . but my greatest concern is what this all has done to John." After discussing her feelings a bit longer with her, the therapist determined that Sarah appeared to be coping adequately with the recent events in her life and, although anxious and concerned about them, was indeed not in crisis.

Finding that John had returned from his walk, the therapist arranged to have Sarah wait outside and called him back into the office. He still appeared very tense, yet when confronted with his evident symptoms of depression and anxiety, he at first denied their severity. Then, after several evasive responses, he began to openly describe just how frightened and overwhelmed he had been feeling for the past week. "I just don't know what's going to happen to us next . . . I don't think I'll be able to handle much more. I was so sure she'd be back walking by this time. We did everything that the doctors told us to do . . . I worked so hard with her to keep up with the exercises and all of the appointments . . . and they haven't helped. Now she has to go back to the hospital. I feel that some of this is all my fault . . . maybe I didn't work hard enough with her . . . or maybe I was doing the exercises the wrong way. She hates being crippled like this. Sometimes I think she must hate me because she has to be so dependent on me for doing everything."

After Sarah had come home from the hospital 2 months ago, John had been kept very busy and involved in driving her to appointments, arranging the household schedules, and helping her exercise at home. He found many rewards in this role, feeling that he was contributing greatly toward her eventual recovery. However, as the weeks and months passed without too much apparent improvement in her condition, he was disturbed to find himself angry toward her, even at times blaming her for not trying harder. Lately he had been finding it increasingly difficult to hide these feelings from her and found himself wishing that he could just get away from the situation for awhile, to take a trip like they used to — even if it meant going off without her!

Now, because of her decision to go into the rehabilitation center for treatment, he was being given the opportunity to "get away from it all" for a while, to turn the responsibility for her daily exercises and care completely over to others, and he felt very guilty. Perhaps he had not really tried hard enough to help her walk; maybe he should have found ways to encourage her more? The more he ruminated on these thoughts, the more he convinced himself that her lack of progress was entirely his fault. Therefore it was his fault that she had to go back to a hospital, and it would be completely his fault if she were never able to return home again!

Planning the intervention

The goals of intervention were to help John obtain a realistic perception of the situation, to assist him to ventilate his feelings about the effects on his life of Sarah's disability, and to provide him with situational support to help him cope with the pending loss of Sarah, albeit temporary at this point in time. Before the next session and with his consent, his personal physician was contacted to determine if there were any organic bases for his behavioral changes. The physician's report was negative.

Intervention

During the next two session through questioning and reflection, John was helped to ventilate his feelings about his fears that Sarah might never recover beyond her present level of functioning. With situational support supplied by the therapist, he was able to begin to openly discuss the anger that he had felt toward Sarah for "threatening the security of their future" by her accident. All of the careful planning they had made for their "old age" seemed to be falling apart more each day. "It wasn't just the financial security," he said, "we have enough insurance to take care of our illnesses. Our plans were all made for the *two* of us, together . . . not for just one of us, *alone!*" His fears of losing her had been displaced into anger against her for being the cause of his very unpleasant feelings.

It became quite apparent during the first session that John really did not have any clear idea as to the nature of Sarah's injury. To him, a broken bone was just that, regardless of which one. It broke; therefore, it should heal! He had never sat down with her orthopedic surgeon to ask questions, leaving it to her to keep him informed. He was advised to make an immediate appointment with this physician in order to get direct information about Sarah's expected progress rather than to continue to rely on his own uneducated conclusions. By the next session he reported that he had followed through, kept the appointment, and was relieved to learn that while Sarah's progress was a bit slower than expected, the physician expected her to return to a fairly normal level of functioning. But, he was advised, it would take time, and he would be expected to help Sarah have patience. The recommendation that she enter the rehabilitation center in the next city was made in an effort to speed up her progress and was not to be construed by him as a sign that she might never recover.

As John's anxiety and depression decreased, he began to perceive the events leading up to his crisis in a more realistic manner. He realized that his anger was a normal response to his situation with Sarah but that what he *did* with that anger was not normal. Rather than openly discussing his feelings with Sarah as he would have at any other time in their lives, he found himself "protecting" her from them, yet blaming her for all of the misery it was causing him. Lacking any other available situational support, his anxiety and depression had increased, even further distorting his perceptions of the event.

When the suggestion was made that Sarah enter a rehabilitation center for further therapy, John's anxiety level interfered with his ability to perceive this as anything other than the beginning of a final loss of Sarah from his life. As he later described it to the therapist, "I guess this is always in the back of a person's mind once they get around my age. When you're young you go to a hospital and the odds are good that you come home again . . . but when you get to be Sarah's and my age, the odds *aren't* so good that you come home again! And she was asking me to help her make the decision to go to that hospital . . . *me,* who was already mixed up in my feelings about having to take care of her like this the rest of my life!"

By the end of the third session John's symptoms had lessened greatly, and he was now able to help Sarah pack and move into the rehabilitation center without any increase in anxiety. He realized now that in overprotecting her from his true feelings, he had only created anxiety for her as well as a crisis for himself. He planned to visit her three times a week. They agreed that this would give her full time to concentrate on "being able to walk home," and he would begin to reestablish ties with their old friends so that he would not feel so lonely while she was away.

Anticipatory planning

Exploration with John about his feelings concerning the possibility that Sarah might not improve beyond her current level of functioning helped prepare him for this eventuality. He was able to begin to consider alternative modes of life for the two of them. For example, he decided that they should seriously consider selling their two-story home. "After all," he said, "if it isn't her broken hip, sure enough it's going to be my arthritis in the next few years that is going to make those stairs seem like Mount Whitney!" Furthermore, John found himself faced with the realities of what he would have to be able to do for himself if Sarah ever left him forever. While she was in the rehabilitation center, he knew that he would have to begin learning how to plan a life for himself. Granted that she might outlive him, he recognized that this time without her was a sample, for him, of what life "might be for him . . . and only a complete idiot would not recognize that I had better learn what to do and learn pretty damned fast!"

Summation of the paradigm

Unprepared to assume his new role in caring for Sarah, John's increased anxiety distorted his perceptions of their stressful situation. When Sarah failed to make the progress that he had expected, he became frustrated and angry and perceived himself as a failure in his new role. Unable to communicate these feelings appropriately, he displaced his anger on Sarah. When asked to help her decide about reentering a hospital, he felt threatened by a permanent role reversal and the eventuality of her loss. He lacked adequate coping mechanisms to deal with the increasing stresses of the situation; he became immobile and unable to make any decisions for their future.

Intervention focused on helping John to ventilate his feelings and to obtain a realistic perception of the event. As his anxiety and depression decreased, he became able to anticipate and plan for their future. The major focus of the last session was to help him recognize and accept that with increasing age there could be future threats to his biopsychosocial integrity and that he should learn to seek help as they arose and not try to assume all of the responsibility himself.

Addendum

Two months later the therapist received a telephone call from John. Sarah had come home from the rehabilitation center about 2 weeks before. Her progress, unfortunately, was not what they had expected. However, according to John, she was at least able to stand there in the kitchen and make the "best damned dinner I have eaten in a month" and that was "good enough for me!" They had already put their home up for sale and were looking for a large mobile home into which they could move and begin traveling around the country to begin living the retirement they had planned.

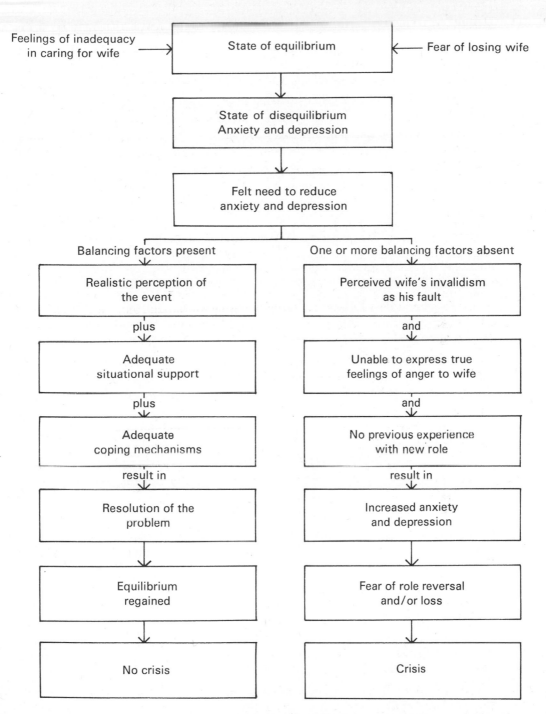

Fig. 15. □ Case study: John.

REFERENCES

Cameron, N.: Personality development and psychopathology, Boston, 1963, Houghton Mifflin Co.

Cumming, E., and Henry, W. E.: Growing old, New York, 1961, Basic Books, Inc., Publishers.

Dunbar, F., and Dunbar, F.: A study of centenarians. Quoted in Solomon, J. C.: A synthesis of human behavior, New York, 1954, Grune & Stratton, Inc.

English, O. S., and Pearson, G. H. J.: Emotional problems of living, New York, 1955, W. W. Norton & Co., Inc.

Erikson, E. H.: Growth and crises of the health personality. In Senn, M. J. E., editor: Symposium on the healthy personality, New York, 1950, Josiah Macy, Jr., Foundation.

Erikson, E. H.: Growth and crises of the healthy personality. In Identity and the life cycle. Psychological issues, vol. 1, No. 1, monograph I, New York, 1959, International Universities Press.

Erikson, E. H.: Identity and the life cycle. Psychological issues, vol. 1, No. 1, monograph I, New York, 1959, International Universities Press.

Erikson, E. H.: Childhood and society, ed. 2, New York, 1963, W. W. Norton & Co., Inc.

Goffman, E.: Asylums, New York, 1961, Doubleday & Co., Inc.

Goldman, G. D., and Milman, D. S., editors: Modern woman; her psychology and sexuality, Springfield, Ill., 1969, Charles C Thomas, Publisher.

Palmore, E. B.: Social factors in mental illness of the aged. In Busse, E. W., and Pfeiffer, E., editors: Mental illness in later life, Washington, D.C., 1973, American Psychiatric Association.

Piaget, J.: The child's conception of the world, Totowa, N.J., 1963, Littlefield, Adams & Co.

Reisman, D.: Individualism reconsidered, New York, 1954, The Free Press.

Slater, P.: Cultural attitudes toward the aged, Geriatrics 18:308, 1963.

Sullivan, H. S.: Conceptions of modern psychiatry, New York, 1953, W. W. Norton & Co., Inc.

Zachry, C. B.: Emotion and conduct in adolescence, New York, 1940, Appleton-Century-Crofts.

ADDITIONAL READINGS

Bach, G. R., and Deutsch, R. M.: Pairing, New York, 1970, Avon Books.

Bach, G. R., and Wyden, P.: The intimate enemy, New York, 1968, Avon Books.

Busse, E. W., and Pfeiffer, E., editors: Mental illness in later life, Washington, D.C., 1973, American Psychiatric Association.

Chandler, H. H.: Family crisis intervention; point and counterpoint in the psychosocial revolution, J. Natl. Med. Assoc. 64:211, May 1972.

Chown, S. M.: Human aging, Baltimore, Md., 1972, Penguin Books.

Donner, G. J.: Parenthood as a crisis, Perspect. Psychiatr. Care 10:(2):84, 1972.

Foreman, N. J., and Zerwekh, J. V.: Drug crisis intervention, Am. J. Nurs. 71:1736, July 1971.

Friedman, J. H., and Bowes, N.: Experience of a geriatric crisis-intervention screening team, J. Psychiatr. Nurs. 9(5):11, 1971.

Hinton, J.: Dying, Baltimore, Md., 1971, Penguin Books.

Howells, J. G., editor: Modern perspectives in the psychiatry of old age, New York, 1975, Brunner/Mazel, Inc.

Kübler-Ross, E.: Questions and answers on death and dying, New York, 1974, Collier Books.

Laing, R. D., and Esterson, A.: Sanity, madness, and the family, Baltimore, Md., 1964, Penguin Books.

Langsley, D. G., and Kaplan, D.: The treatment of families in crisis, New York, 1968, Grune & Stratton, Inc.

Rubenstein, D.: Rehospitalization versus family crisis intervention, Am. J. Psychiatry 129:715, Dec. 1972.

Strickler, M., and La Sor, B.: The concept of loss in crisis intervention, Met. Hyg. 54:301, April 1970.

Thompson, C. M.: On women, New York, 1971, The New American Library, Inc.

Williams, F.: Intervention in maturational crises, Perspect. Psychiatr. Care 9:240, 1971.

8 □ Crisis intervention with the chronic psychiatric patient

Theoretical concepts

Crisis intervention has gained recognition as a viable therapy modality to assist individuals through acute traumatic life situations. As large psychiatric facilities, slowly or rapidly according to individual state laws, are beginning to shorten the length of hospitalization, the chronic psychiatric patient is returning to his community where continuity of care must be maintained. The questions to be asked and answered are: (1) Does crisis intervention work successfully with chronic psychiatric patients, and (2) if not, what other methods must be employed to keep this patient functioning in his community?

With a chronic psychiatric patient, as with any patient, identification of the precipitating event, the symptoms the patient is exhibiting, his perception of the event, his available situational supports, and his usual coping mechanisms are crucial factors in resolving his crisis.

Situational supports are those persons in the environment whom the therapist can find to lend support to the individual. A patient may be living with his family or friends; are they concerned enough—and do they care enough—to give him help? The patient's situational supports can serve as "assistants" to the therapist and the patient. They are with him daily and are encouraged to have frequent communication with the therapist. Usually situational supports are included in some part of the therapy sessions. This provides them with the knowledge and information they need to help the identified patient.

If the patient is living in a board-and-care facility, one must determine if any of its members are concerned and willing to work with the therapist to help the individual through the stressful period. This involves visits to the facility and conducting collateral or group therapy with the patient and other members to get and keep them involved in helping to resolve the crisis.

Occasionally the patient has *no* situational supports. He may be a social isolate; he may have no family, and may have acquaintances but no real friends with whom he can talk about his problems. Usually an individual such as this has many difficulties in interpersonal relationships at work and school and socially. It is then the therapist's role to provide situational support while the patient is in therapy.

Our experiences have verified for us that crisis intervention can be an effective therapy modality with chronic psychiatric patients. If a psychiatric patient with a history of repeated hospitalizations returns to the community and his family, his reentry creates many stresses. While much has been accomplished to remove the stigma of mental illness, people are still wary and hypervigilant when they learn that a "former mental patient" has returned home to his community.

In his absence the family and community have, consciously or unconsciously, eliminated him from their usual life patterns and activities. They then have to readjust to his presence and include him in activities and decision making. If for any reason he does not conform to their expectations, they want him removed so that they can continue their lives without his possible disruptive behavior.

The first area to explore is to determine who is in crisis: the patient or his family. In many cases the family is overreacting because of its anxiety and are seeking some means of getting the "identified" patient back into the hospital. The patient is usually brought to the center by a family member because his original maladaptive symptoms have begun to reemerge. Questioning the patient or his family about medication he received from the hospital and determining if he is taking it as prescribed are essential. If the patient is unable to communicate with the therapist about what has happened or what has changed in his life, the family is questioned as to what might have precipitated his return to his former psychotic behavior.

There is usually a cause-and-effect relationship between a change, or anticipated change, in the routine patterns of life-style or family constellation and the beginnings of abnormal overt behavior in the identified patient. Often families forget or ignore telling a former psychiatric patient when they are contemplating a change because "he wouldn't understand." Such changes could include moving or changing jobs. This is perceived by the patient as exclusion or rejection by the family and creates stress that he is unable to cope with; thus he retreats to his previous psychotic behavior. Such cases are frequent and can be dealt with through the theoretical framework of crisis intervention methodology.

Rubinstein (1972) stated that family-focused crisis intervention usually brings about the resolution of the patient's crisis without resorting to hospitalization. In a later article in 1974, he advocated that family crisis intervention can also be a viable alternative to rehospitalization. Here the emphasis is placed on the period immediately after the patient's release from the hospital. He suggested that conjoint family therapy begin in the hospital before the patient's release and then continue in an outpatient clinic after his release. His approach has also served to develop the concept that a family can and should share responsibility for the patient's treatment.

In Decker's 1972 study, two groups of young adults were followed for 2½ years after their first psychiatric hospitalization. The first group was immediately hospitalized and received traditional modes of treatment, and the second group was hospitalized after the institution of a crisis-intervention program. The results of the study indicated that crisis intervention reduced long-term hospital dependency without producing alternate forms of psychological or social dependency and also reduced the number of rehospitalizations.

The following brief case study illustrates how one can work with a chronic psychiatric patient in a community mental health center using the crisis model.

Case study: Chronic patient in the community
Assessment of the individual and his problem

Jim, a man in his late thirties, was brought to a crisis center by his sister because, as she stated, "he was beginning to act crazy again." Jim had many prior hospitalizations, with a diagnosis of paranoid schizophrenia. The only thing Jim would say was, "I *don't* want to go back to the hospital." He was told that our role was to help him stay out of the hospital if we possibly could. A medical consultation was arranged to determine if he needed to have his medication increased or possibly changed.

Information was then obtained from his sister to determine what had happened (the precipitating event) when his symptoms had started and, specifically, what she meant by his "acting crazy again." His sister stated that he was "talking to the television set . . . muttering things that made no sense . . . staring into space . . . prowling around the apartment at night," and that "this behavior started about 3 days ago." When questioned about anything that was different in their lives before the start of his disruptive behavior, she denied any change. When asked about any changes that were contemplated in the near future, she replied that she was planning to be married in 2 months but that Jim did not know about it because she had not told him yet. When asked why she had not told him, she reluctantly answered that she wanted to wait until all of the arrangements had been made. She was asked if there was any way Jim could have found out about her plans. She remembered that she had discussed them on the telephone with a girl friend the week before.

She was asked what her plans for Jim were after she married. She said that her boyfriend had agreed, rather reluctantly, to let Jim live with them.

Since her boyfriend was reluctant about having Jim live with them, other alternatives were explored. She said that they had cousins living in a nearby suburb but that she did not know if they would want Jim to live with them.

Planning the intervention

It was suggested that Jim's sister call her cousins, tell them of her plans to get married and her concerns about Jim, and in general find out their feelings about him living with them. The call was placed, and she told them her plans and concerns. Fortunately their response was a positive one. They had recently bought a fairly large apartment building and were having difficulty getting reliable help to take care of the yard work and minor repairs. They felt that Jim would be able to manage this, and they would let him live in a small apartment above the garage.

Intervention

Jim was asked to come back into the office so that his sister could tell him of her plans to marry and the arrangements she had made for him with their cousins. He listened but had difficulty comprehending the information. He just kept saying, "I *don't* want to go back to the hospital."

He was asked if he had heard his sister talking about her wedding plans. He admitted that he had and that he knew her boyfriend would not want him around—"they would probably put him back in the hospital." As the session ended he still had not internalized the information he had heard. He was asked to continue in therapy for 5 more weeks and to take his medication as prescribed. He agreed to do so.

By the end of the sixth week he had visited his cousins, seen the apartment where he would be living, and had discussed his new "job." His disruptive behavior had ceased, and he was again functioning at his precrisis level.

Anticipatory planning

Since Jim had had many previous hospitalizations and did not want to be rehospitalized, time was spent in discussing how this could be avoided in the future. He was given the name, address, and telephone number of a crisis center in his new community and told to visit them when he moved. He was assured that the center could supervise his medication and be available if he needed someone to talk to if he felt he again needed help.

Summation of paradigm

Jim's sister neglected to tell him about her impending marriage, which he perceived as rejection. Because of his numerous hospitalizations, he feared that his sister would have him rehospitalized "to get rid of him." He was unable to verbalize his fears, retreated from reality, and experienced an exacerbation of his psychotic symptoms.

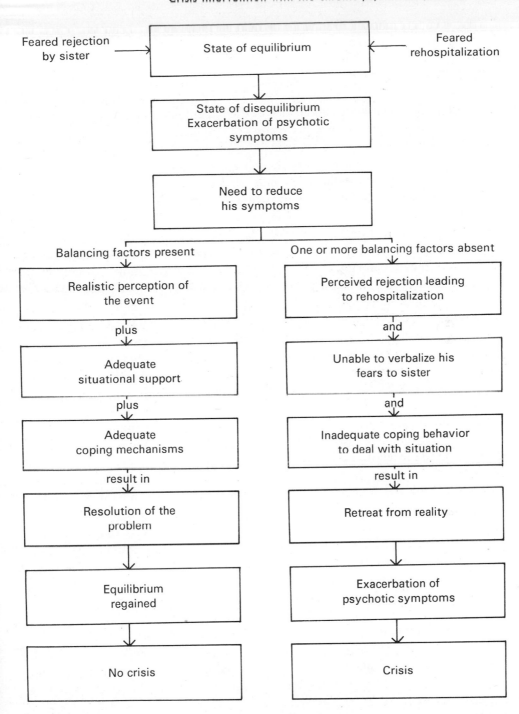

Fig. 16. □ Case study: Jim.

The therapist adhered to the crisis model by focusing the therapy sessions on the patient's immediate problems, *not* on his chronic psychopathology.

Conclusion

Since community mental health centers have become so well known with their philosophy on prevention, maintenance of the patient in his community, and hospitalization only as a last resort, more chronic psychiatric patients and their families are seeking help from crisis centers.

As a result of the demand from the community, an expansion of services is needed as an attempt to meet this demand, and this is not always easy.

To accommodate the influx of new patients, community mental health centers may have to decrease the number of sessions from six to four. Some have established a day treatment center, where the patients may spend the day in a structured environment and return home in the evenings. Others have established a small emergency inpatient unit that is staffed 24 hours to care for patients for a maximum of 48 hours while the patients are being assessed for possible hospitalization or are medicated and, hopefully, stabilized. Many maintain a 24-hour, 7-days-a-week medication station where medications can be obtained as needed for the patients. Many also have instituted an emergency hot line to handle calls from patients or their families and have ongoing, long-term group therapy sessions for the chronic psychiatric patient.

Smitson (1972) states that an effective mental health delivery system must include three levels of intervention: a crisis intervention unit, a maintenance walk-in service, and a time-limited individual and group therapy program. Such a system, he feels, can maintain individuals outside the hospital and can in many cases minimize the need for rehospitalization.

De Smit (1972) writes that interest in crisis theory and intervention is intense among the public in the Netherlands, indicating dissatisfaction with the present structure of mental health care. Long waiting lists and complicated and prolonged admission procedures of institutionalized care are contrasted with easy accessibility, low threshold, and absence of waiting lists in crisis intervention centers. Another aspect is the absence of a psychiatric label. De Smit states that a well-functioning mental health center can greatly reduce hospitalization and rehospitalization of the chronic psychiatric patient.

Wales (1972) stated that placement of trainees in clinical psychology in crisis intervention centers has produced many positive results for the trainees. Some of these are: (1) the development of a sense of responsibility for patients, (2) the development of self-confidence on the part of the trainee, and (3) the more rapid development of professional maturity than is possible at the slow pace that most clinical placements allow.

When a supervisor of trainees receives a telephone call at 1:30 A.M. from a new trainee with a high anxiety level because he has just had a call from a patient, the supervisor must determine again who is in crisis: the patient or the trainee. It is usually the trainee, needing support and validation that he did indeed say the *right* thing to the patient.

An interesting and unanswered question is the extent to which a hospital-based program sees patients with greater pathological conditions than does the typical community-based crisis intervention program. The percentage of individuals with previous hsopitalizations seen at the Benjamin Rush Center in Los Angeles is 12.2%. This percentage is almost identical with that reported for a hospital-based program, Kings County of New York, where it was 12.5%. At the same time the Rush Center diagnosed only 16.7% of the patients in the same series as being psychotic, whereas the Kings County program diagnosed 46% of their admissions as psychotic (Jacobson, 1974).

What may appear to be a greater pathological condition in a hospital-based program may, at least in part, be due to different diagnostic conventions and a greater staff orientation to seeing pathological conditions rather than life problems, with a reverse orientation in community-based crisis intervention programs.

In summary, crisis intervention can be used successfully with chronic psychiatric patients. However, the approach may have to be modified and the therapist flexible. An extension of emergency services should be maintained on a 24-hour basis to meet the needs of the patient and his family.

In essence, one must determine: Can the patient be helped using crisis intervention techniques only? Does he need longer-term outpatient care? Or does he in fact need to be rehospitalized?

If, as stated earlier, the family is concerned and caring, the task is one of reeducating the family and giving them support. If, on the other hand, the family members are uncaring and simply want the patient out of their lives and back into the hospital, then the task is more difficult. Somehow, they will manage to find a private hospital to accept the patient, and the patient and family will never return to the center.

Thus, working in a community mental center with chronic psychiatric patients can be extremely rewarding or extremely frustrating. To us, crisis intervention is not a "band-aid" or a second-class citizen in the realm of therapy modalities. Those of us who select to use crisis intervention techniques do so because we sincerely believe that it *is* effective, and it is *our* treatment of choice.

REFERENCES

Decker, J. B., and Stubblebine, J. M.: Crisis intervention and prevention of psychiatric disability; a follow-up study, Am. J. Psychiatry **129**(6):725, 1972.

De Smit, N. W.: Crisis intervention and crisis centers; their possible relevance for community psychiatry and mental health care, Psychiatria, Neurologia, Neurochirugia **75**(4):299, 1972.

Jacobson, G. F.: Emergency services in community mental health; problems and promise, Am. J. Public Health **64**(2):124, 1974.

Rubenstein, D.: Rehospitalization versus family

crisis intervention, Am. J. Psychiatry **129**(6): 715, 1972.

Rubenstein, D.: Family crisis intervention as an alternative to rehospitalization, Current Psychiatric Therapies **14**:191, 1974.

Smitson, W.: Focus on service, Men. Hyg. **56**(4): 22, 1972.

Wales, E.: Crisis intervention in clinical training, Professional Psychology **3**(4):357, 1972.

ADDITIONAL READINGS

Arnhoff, F. N.: Manpower needs, resources, and innovation. In Barten, H. H., and Bellak, L., editors: Progress in community mental health, vol. 2, New York, 1972, Grune & Stratton, Inc., pp. 35-61.

Bard, M.: The role of law enforcement in the helping system, Community Ment. Health J. **7**(2):151, 1971.

Barten, H. H., and Bellak, L., editors: Progress in community mental health, vol. 2, New York, 1972, Grune & Stratton, Inc.

Barthal, H. S.: Resistances to community psychiatry, Psychiatr. Q. **45**(3):333, 1971.

Board, M.: The role of law enforcement in the helping systems, Community Ment. Health J. **7**(2):151, 1971.

Brandon, S.: Crisis theory and possibilities of therapeutic intervention, Br. J. Psychiatry **117**: 541, Dec. 1970.

Bruder, E. E.: The clergyman's contribution to community mental health, Hosp. Commun. Psychiatry **22**:207, July 1971.

Cassell, W. A., and others: Comparing costs of hospital and community care, Hosp. Commun. Psychiatry **23**:197, July 1972.

Chandler, H. M.: Family crisis intervention, point and counterpoint in the psychosocial revolution, J. Natl. Med. Assoc. 64:211, May 1972.

Cobb, C. W.: Community mental health services and the lower socioeconomic classes; a summary of research literature on outpatient treatment (1963-1969), Am. J. Orthopsychiatry **42**: 404, April 1972.

Daniels, R. S.: Community psychiatry; a new profession, a developing subspecialty, or effective clinical psychiatry? Community Ment. Health J. **2**:47, 1966.

Decker, J. B., and Stubblebine, J. M.: Crisis intervention and the prevention of disability; a followup study, Am. J. Psychiatry **129**:725, Dec. 1972.

De Smit, N. W.: The crisis center in community psychiatry; an Amsterdam experiment. In Masserman, J. H., editor: Current psychiatric therapies, vol. 2, New York, 1971, Grune & Stratton, Inc.

De Smit, N. W.: Crisis intervention and crisis centers; their possible relevance for community psychiatry and mental health care, Psychiatr. Neurol. Neruochir. **75**:299, 1973.

Donovan, James M., and others: Psychiatric crisis; a comparison of schizophrenic and non-schizophrenic patients, J. Nervous and Mental Disease **161**:172, 1975.

Edgerton, J. W.: Evaluation in community mental health. In Rosenblum, G., editor: Issues in community psychology and preventive mental health, Task Force on Community Mental Health, Division 27 of the American Psychological Association, New York, 1971, Behavioral Publications, Inc.

Ewalt, J. R., and Farnsworth, D. L.: Psychiatry and religion. In Ewalt, J. R., and Farnsworth, D. L., editors: Textbook of psychiatry, New

Feirstein, A., Weisman, G., and Thomas, C.: A crisis intervention model for inpatient hospitalization. In Masserman, J. H., editor: Current psychiatric therapies, vol. 11, New York, 1971, Grune & Stratton, Inc.

Flomenhaft, K., and others: After the crisis, Ment. Hyg. **55**:473, Oct. 1971.

Huessy, H. R.: Rural models. In Barten, H. H., and Bellak, L., editors: Progress in community mental health, vol. 2, New York, 1972, Grune & Stratton, Inc.

Kretz, H.: Structure and function of a psychiatric polyclinic; possibilities, limitations, and practical perspectives of work at the Polyclinic of the Heideberg University Psychiatric Clinic, Nervenarzt. **45**(4):215, 1974.

Mackenzie, M., and others: Family crisis unit, Lancet **1**:642, March 1972.

McClellan, M. S.: Crisis groups in special care areas, Nurs. Clin. North Am. **7**:363, June 1972.

Morehead, M. A.: Evaluating quality of care of the neighborhood health center program of O.E.O., Med. Care **8**:118, 1970.

Naylor, H.: New trends in volunteer services for the mentally handicapped, Hosp. Commun. Psychiatry **22**:109, April 1971.

Polak, P.: Techniques of social system intervention, Curr. Psychiatr. Ther. **12**:185, 1972.

Polak, P., and others: Prevention in mental health; a controlled study, Am. J. Psychiatry **132**(2):146, 1975.

Raphael, B.: Crisis intervention; theoretical and methodological considerations, Aust. N.Z.J. Psychiatry 5:183, 1971.

Rosenbaum, C. P., and Beebe, J. E.: Psychiatric treatment; crisis/clinic/consultation, New York, 1975, McGraw-Hill Book Co.

Schneider, B.: Preparing general practitioners for community mental health work, Hosp. Commun. Psychiatry 22:346, Nov. 1971.

Schwartz, D. A.: Community mental health in 1972; an assessment. In Barten, H. H., and Bellak, L., editors: Progress in community mental health, vol. 2, New York, 1972, Grune & Stratton, Inc.

Schwartz, J. L.: First national survey of free medical clinics, 1967-1969, HSMHA Health Report 86:775, Sept. 1971.

Schwartz, S. L.: A review of crisis intervention programs, Psychiatr. Q. 45:498, 1971.

Weinstein, R. M., and Brill, N. Q.: Social class and patients' perceptions of mental illness, Psychiatr. Q. 45(1):35, 1971.

Wellisch, D. K., and Gay, G. R.: The walking wounded; emergency psychiatric intervention in a heroin addict population, Drug Forum 1: 137, Jan. 1972.

Wilson, S. E., Courtney, C. G., Ota, K. Y., and Radauskas, B.: Evaluating mental health associates, Hosp. Commun. Psychiatry 22:371, Dec. 1971.

Wolberg, L. R.: Psychiatric technics in crisis therapy, N.Y. State J. Med. 72:1266, 1972.

Zelbach, J. Z.: Crisis in chronic problem families; psychiatric care of the underprivileged, Int. Psychiatry Clin. 8(2):101, 1971.

INDEX

A

Abnormal, definition of, 47
Abreaction, 18, 19
Adaptation, 3-4, 47
  of infant, 133-134
Adaptational psychodynamics, 4
Adaptational psychotherapy, 4
Adolescence, 4-5
  anxiety in, 116
  case study regarding, 40-44, 142-146
  crisis group therapy for, 40
  father-child relationship and, 142-146
  formal operations period in, 142
  growth in, 141
  identity in, 141-142
  independence in, 142
    case study regarding, 142-146
  responsibility in, 141-142
  roles in, 141-142
  theoretical concepts regarding, 141-142
Adulthood; *see also* Late adulthood; Old age;
    Young adulthood
  case study regarding, 151-155
  theoretical concepts regarding, 151
Age, old; *see* Old age
Aging, 156, 161-163
  attractiveness and, case study regarding,
    157-161
  behavior and, 162
  culture and, 162
  personality changes with, 162

Alcoholic as suicidal risk, 115
Anticipatory planning
  in case study of chronic psychiatric patient,
    176
  in crisis intervention, 66
  in maturational crises from case studies,
    140, 146, 150, 155, 160-161, 170
  in situational crises from case studies, 77,
    79, 85, 90-92, 94, 105, 110, 121, 128-129
Anxiety, 73, 115
  in adolescence, 116
  death and, 123
  in heart disease, 98, 100, 103
  in late adulthood, 156, 167, 169, 170
  management of, 71-72
  in prepuberty, 139
  problem solving and, 62, 63
Assessment
  in case study of chronic psychiatric patient,
    175-176
  in crisis intervention, 64-66
  in maturational crises from case studies,
    137-139, 142, 144-145, 147-148, 151-152,
    154, 157, 159, 165-168
  in situational crises from case studies, 76,
    81, 83-84, 102-103, 107-108, 117-119,
    124, 125-127
Attitudes
  sociocultural factors in, 46
  toward marriage, 107
  toward mental illness, 55-56

Attractiveness, aging and, case study
  regarding, 157-161
Authority figures, 30

B

Behavior, 3, 4, 6
  abnormal, in aged, 162
  aging and, 162
  automatization of, 4
  cultural values and, 47
  group forces and, 29-30, 44
  infant, 133-134
  normal, 3
  psychotic, 115, 174
  schizophrenic, 124
  stress and, 73-74
  suicidal
    acute, 115-116
    chronic, 116
Benjamin Rush Center for Problems of
Living, 8, 179
  crisis group study at, 38
Bereavement, 5, 22, 25
Brief psychotherapy, 19-21
  diagnostic evaluation in, 20
  duration of, 21, 26
  focus of treatment in, 20, 26
  free association in, 19, 20
  goals of, 19, 20, 26
  indications for, 21, 26
  interpretation in, 19
  personnel in, 19
  procedures for, 20-21
  therapist's role in, 20, 26
  transference in, 20
  treatment in, termination of, 21
Bronx Mental Health Center, 8-9

C

California Community Mental Health Act
  (1958), 8
Caplan, G., 5-6
Cardiac disease; see Heart disease; Physical
  illness
Career choice, 141-142, 146-147
  case study regarding, 147-151
Careers in mental health, 10
Cathartic hypnosis, 16, 17
Child; see also Adolescence; Infancy; Infant
  concrete operations period of, 136
  conscience in, 135
  guilt in, 135, 136
  prepuberty of
    case study regarding, 136-137
    theoretical concepts regarding, 136-137
  preschool
    initiative development in, 135
    theoretical concepts regarding, 135-136

Child—cont'd
  psychosomatic illness in, 137, 139, 140
  self-esteem in, 136
  skill mastery in, 136
Child abuse, case study regarding, 57-59
Childbirth, 74-76; see also Prematurity
Childhood, early, theoretical concepts
  regarding, 133-135
Chronic psychiatric patient
  case study of, 175-178
    anticipatory planning in, 176
    assessment in, 175-176
    intervention in, 176
    planning intervention in, 176
  crisis intervention with, 173-179
  hospitalization of, 173, 174, 175, 176, 178
  medication of, 174, 176, 178
  stresses of, 174
  theoretical concepts regarding, 173-175
  therapist's role with, 174, 179
Churches, crisis intervention services in, 9
Class; see Middle class; Social class
Climacteric, 156-157
Cliques, 141
Cognitive development, 132-133, 135
  concrete operations as, 136
  formal operations as, 142
  preoperational, 135
  sensorimotor, 134
  in young adulthood, 147
Collateral therapy, 35
Communication, 46, 49, 50, 54
  nonverval, 37
  and suicide, 111-112, 116
Community caretakers in mental health
  programs, 10-11, 12
Community mental health programs,
  volunteers in, 11, 12
Community mental health service, 54, 55
  178, 179
  emergency inpatient unit as, 178
  personnel in, 9-13
  referrals to, 55
Community psychiatry, 5, 178
  evolution of, 6-9
  general hospital and, 8
  as multidisciplinary, 7
  specialist training in, 8
  versus hospital psychiatry, 179
Compulsiveness, 135
Concrete operations period, 136
Conjoint therapy, 35
Conscience in child, 135
Coping mechanisms, 1, 2, 6, 25, 173, 174
  in crisis groups, 39, 40
  in crisis intervention, 71-72
  group psychotherapy and, 34
  in problem solving, 62